Native American

ALSO BY EDWARD J. RIELLY
AND FROM MCFARLAND

*The Sister Fidelma Mysteries: Essays on the Historical
Novels of Peter Tremayne* (2012)

*Murder 101: Essays on the Teaching
of Detective Fiction* (2009)

*Baseball in the Classroom: Essays on Teaching
the National Pastime* (2006)

Native American Women Leaders

Fourteen Profiles

Edward J. Rielly

McFarland & Company, Inc., Publishers
Jefferson, North Carolina

Library of Congress Cataloguing-in-Publication Data

Names: Rielly, Edward J., 1943– author.
Title: Native American women leaders : fourteen profiles / Edward J. Rielly.
Description: Jefferson, North Carolina : McFarland & Company, Inc., Publishers, 2022 |
Includes bibliographical references and index.
Identifiers: LCCN 2022001666 | ISBN 9781476686684 (paperback : acid free paper) ∞
ISBN 9781476645759 (ebook)
Subjects: LCSH: Indian women—United States—Biography. | Indian activists—United
States—Biography. | Indian civic leaders—United States—Biography. | Women in public
life—United States—Biography. | BISAC: SOCIAL SCIENCE / Ethnic Studies /
American / Native American Studies | SOCIAL SCIENCE / Women's Studies
Classification: LCC E98.W8 .R54 2022 | DDC 305.48/89700922 [B]—dc23/eng/20220126
LC record available at https://lccn.loc.gov/2022001666

British Library cataloguing data are available

ISBN (print) 978-1-4766-8668-4
ISBN (ebook) 978-1-4766-4575-9

Front cover: *clockwise from top left,* LaDonna Harris, president of Americans for Indian Opportunity (courtesy of Americans for Indian Opportunity, photograph by Wakeah Vigil); Debra Haaland, one of the first two Native American women elected to Congress, became, as Secretary of the Interior, the first Native American to be named to a Presidential Cabinet position (courtesy of then–Representative Haaland's Congressional Office); Janine Pease, educator, advocate for Crow language studies, and former president of Little Big Horn College (courtesy of Dr. Janine Pease, photograph by Adam Singsintimber); Kathryn Harrison acknowledges receiving a "History Makers" Award at the Oregon Historical Society on September 27, 2012 (courtesy of *Smoke Signals* Michelle Alaimo photo); Joy Harjo at her induction as Poet Laureate of the United States (courtesy of Joy Harjo, photograph by Shawn Miller)

Printed in the United States of America

*McFarland & Company, Inc., Publishers
Box 611, Jefferson, North Carolina 28640
www.mcfarlandpub.com*

To my wife, Jeanne, whose support helps
make all things possible.

Table of Contents

Acknowledgments

I am grateful to many individuals and organizations that responded generously, courteously, and efficiently to my request for help. Locating photographs would have been even more difficult, if not impossible, without the assistance provided by wonderful individuals at the LBJ Presidential Library, Richard Nixon Presidential Library and Museum, William J. Clinton Presidential Library and Museum, University of Georgia Libraries, Museums of the Bethel Historical Society, Nevada Historical Society, History Nebraska (Nebraska State Historical Society), Center for Western Studies at Augustana University, and *Smoke Signals* (newspaper of the Confederated Tribes of Grand Ronde). I also deeply appreciate the help of Janine Pease and Laura Harris, and the staffs of Secretary (then–Representative) Debra Haaland, Representative Sharice Davids, and Poet Laureate Joy Harjo. I also am grateful for helpful information provided by Janine Pease, Lisa Watson, and Michael Cherry either through email communications or phone conversations. Throughout this enterprise, my editor at McFarland, Layla Milholen, has been a consistent support, providing prompt, courteous, and informative answers to my questions and providing invaluable advice. This is my fourth book published by McFarland, and I feel very much a part of the McFarland family. Finally, and most importantly, I thank my wife, Jeanne, for putting up with my countless hours at my computer.

Preface

The idea for this book, *Native American Women Leaders: Fourteen Profiles*, came to me as I was researching a book on Native Americans who led the resistance to Euro-American dominance. It became clear to me that most Indigenous history focused on male leaders, the result at least in part of the historical emphasis on warfare and political leadership. Some books, of course, have been written about Native American women, but the library of such works is seriously deficient, an opinion shared by many, including Joy Harjo, the current Poet Laureate of the United States and the subject of one of the chapters in this book, who stated in an interview with *Triplopia* in 2005 and since included in *Soul Talk, Song Language: Conversations with Joy Harjo*, "Historically, there are no female voices, and especially no female Native voices." She adds that the only two who have been widely presented are Pocahontas and Sacajawea. Neither is within this book, but Joy Harjo is.

Similarly, Janine Pease, lifelong educator and former president of Little Big Horn College, writes in the Introduction to *The Spirit of Indian Women* that "American Indian women are virtually ignored by the historians." Chelsey Luger writes in "5 Indigenous Women Asserting the Modern Matriarchy," "One of the least visible groups in historical narratives is Native American and First Nations women." The story of Dr. Pease's accomplishments also appears in this book, as does an account of Chelsey Luger's efforts to promote Native American wellness.

My hope is that *Native American Women Leaders* helps to rectify the shortage of attention given to Native American women, so many of whom have made enormous contributions in a variety of ways over the centuries. This book narrates and analyzes the contributions of fourteen Native American women who have excelled in their respective professions and/ or self-chosen missions. All have been leaders, some explicitly so, others by example and accomplishment although they were not likely to think of themselves in those terms.

The fourteen women who are the subjects of this book are

1

representative of the countless women who have contributed much to their respective tribal nations and to the broader United States of America. In making my choices, I decided to include individuals from across the centuries and from a range of tribal nations. The selections also represent a wide range of societal areas, including politics, the arts, health care, business, education, fitness, feminism, environmentalism, and social activism. Most of the women about whom I write actually made their mark in more than one area. Some are reasonably well known; others are not. None are as known and as appreciated as they deserve to be.

In short, I tell the stories of fourteen exceptional women. And I feel honored to do so.

Structurally, *Native American Women Leaders* includes a preface followed by fourteen narratives (each telling the life story of a particular woman). Each chapter includes biographical information as well as information regarding that person's public life. Each chapter concludes with a list of suggested readings, which includes but is not limited to crucial sources that I used. In researching the lives of these remarkable women, I made use of primary and secondary sources. Some of the individuals have given us much in writing, including memoirs, while others have left behind little or nothing in the way of written materials. Even in the absence of their own words, though, their actions still speak eloquently to us. I hope that this book helps them speak a bit more loudly as well, and with more people listening.

1

Mary Musgrove
(ca. 1700–ca. 1764)

Mary Musgrove, also known as Coosaponakeesa, as well as by her later married names of Mary Mathewes and Mary Bosomworth, was born in Coweta in present-day central Georgia. According to Mary, she was the niece of Brims, the leading chief of the Lower Creeks. She was born to a Creek mother and an English father, Edward Griffin, a trader from Charles Town (Charleston) in colonial South Carolina around 1700. The identity of her mother is unknown.

Griffin took Mary and her brother, also named Edward, to the Indian village of Pon Pon, South Carolina (located where Jacksonboro now stands), when she was about seven years of age. In Pon Pon, she apparently lived with her father's English family, mastering English, becoming a baptized Christian, and learning the ways of her father's people.

From this immersion into a second culture, Mary absorbed a dual cultural identity that would prepare her for a life lived in two cultures, an existence marked by the ability to serve both Creek and English as an interpreter, diplomat, liaison, military recruiter, trader, and entrepreneur. This ability to bridge two cultural worlds without ever abandoning her Creek heritage helped to make her perhaps the most irreplaceable person in the early years of colonial Georgia. It also presented her with a vision of how very different peoples could live together in harmony, a vision that unfortunately did not come to pass.

The Early Years

During Mary's childhood in South Carolina with her father, Edward Griffin, Mary's mother seems to have been absent. According to Steven C. Hahn, in *The Life and Times of Mary Musgrove*, the mother most likely had died, as a Creek mother and her extended family would be unwilling to

3

give a child over entirely to the father, especially a non–Creek father (36). Unlike most girls of her time, who were illiterate, Mary learned to read and write within an educational context that would have wedded academic learning with religious instruction. Not only was she baptized as a Christian, but she developed a lasting interest in theology that later would be manifested in extensive religious discussions with the founder of Methodism, John Wesley, during his stay in America (Hahn 103–07).

Griffin continued as a trader within the very substantial English deerskin trade that brought guns, English cloth, and many manufactured household items to the Creeks and Yamasees with whom Griffin and other English traders dealt. Helen Todd, in her biography of Tomochichi, who became a good friend of Mary Musgrove's, points out that on the whole Native Americans in the South Carolina-Georgia area preferred to trade with the English rather than the French or Spanish because the market for deerskins in England was more robust than in the other European countries, which would translate into a better return for the Native suppliers (18–19).

The close, even intimate, relationship among English, Creek, and Yamasee (like the Creek, a Muskogean linguistic tribe) was split apart by what is referred to as the Yamasee War, which began with a surprise attack on Good Friday, April 30, 1715. Traders and Indian agents were the first victims in a predawn attack in the Yamasee town of Pocatalico. Raids on colonial settlements followed. Yamasees were joined in the conflict by Creeks and members of several other Native American groups. The colonists probably should have been less surprised than they were, as complaints regarding such matters as physical abuse of Creeks and Yamasees and business disagreements had largely been ignored by the colonists or viewed as less serious than they were (Ramsey).

Mary and others living near her were warned of an impending attack and succeeded in fleeing to Charles Town. Her father was not with her at the time, and Mary, according to Hahn, must have waited anxiously for his return, which did not happen, as he apparently died during the war (54). At some point during the conflict, a relationship developed between Mary and a man who shared a similar cultural background.

John Musgrove, like Mary, was the product of two cultures. His mother also was Creek, while his father, named John as well, was English. The senior Musgrove was a trader and planter, had served as a captain and later would become a colonel in the Carolina militia, and was a member of both the Commons House of Assembly and the Carolina Commission of Indian Trade. John senior, an influential colonist, had significant marital difficulties. Hahn describes the breakup of the marriage as having included an individual referred to as the "Tuckesaw Indian King," who somehow took Musgrove's wife away from him, the two eventually compromising on a payment to Musgrove of three Native American slaves (58), slavery being regularly practiced by both the English and Native Americans in the region. As was the case with Mary, young John lived with his father, also in South Carolina.

Details regarding any courtship that may have occurred are quite sparse, and even the marriage remains somewhat unclear and may have been related to the conclusion of the Yamasee War. The date of the wedding is unknown and has been posited as occurring as late as the 1720s but more likely occurred much closer to the date of the treaty itself. Captain Musgrove was named to lead a peace delegation to Coweta in the spring of 1717. The younger John and Mary may have accompanied him. Michael Green (31), following Helen Todd (80), states that the marriage between Captain Musgrove's son and the Coweta leader Brims' niece was a way of sealing the peace. Both also place the agreement in 1716. Hahn, however, argues convincingly that the marriage occurred before February 1717, and in South Carolina, quoting a neighbor who also was Mary's midwife and certainly knew her well that the two were newlyweds when John purchased land in Colleton County in February (62). Hahn does not discount the possibility, though, that the couple may have undergone a second marriage at Coweta "in accordance with Creek customs, as a way of validating their [earlier] Christian ceremony" (63).

The fact that young John was himself the son of an English father and a Creek mother probably made the arrangement seem quite natural to his father. That Mary's husband spoke her language would not only make the marital relationship easier but also enable him to play an important role in partnership with Mary as the couple interacted with both Creeks and the English settlers. As Michele Gillespie posits in "The Sexual Politics of Race and Gender: Mary Musgrove and the Georgia Trustees," racial intermarriage "aided the exchange of cultures that hastened both English colonization and Native American acculturation in southeastern North America in the eighteenth century" and therefore was generally encouraged as a means of conquest by the English (188).

Mary and John apparently lived among the Creeks with John working as a trader. At some point, perhaps around 1725, they moved to Pon Pon in South Carolina, where Mary had spent part of her youth (Green 31; Hahn 69). By the early 1730s, Mary had given birth to three sons, although Todd states four (80), none of whom lived to adulthood, and the couple had become landowners in Colleton County in Carolina, working as cattle ranchers while John continued his career of trading and also served the government in various roles, including leading a war party against the Yamasees (Hahn 71).

In 1732, the Musgroves, at the invitation of the Yamacraws—a group closely allied with the Creeks and consisting of Creeks and Yamasees and including Tomochichi—moved to Yamacraw Bluff near the Savannah River. The governor of Carolina, Robert Johnson, also encouraged the move (Hahn 78–79). There they constructed a house and trading post. They sold such goods as hoes, knives, copper pots, guns, and blankets to the Yamacraws in exchange for animal skins, honey, and bear oil. The Musgroves also raised cattle and crops, including peas, corn, and potatoes. The entire complex was known as the Cowpen. The trading post, as Gillespie points out, involved more than bartering products. It was the point at which an "exchange of cultures" took place and also served "diplomatic and military purposes" (190–91). The location would soon become Savannah, the primary market center for the new colony of Georgia. Hahn asserts that given "the benefit of hindsight, it is clear that the Musgroves' move to Yamacraw Bluff in June 1732 was one of the seminal events in Georgia history" (74). It might not have been such a "seminal" event, however, were it not for the arrival in the region of a particular Englishman on January 11, 1733.

By this time, Mary Musgrove was well on her way to becoming, according to Michael Green, the richest woman in Georgia (33). Land ownership and her financial condition would remain vital interests for her, and much of the latter part of her life was taken up with attempting to consolidate and maintain her properties, receive compensation for money that she had fronted for gifts that helped to solidify peaceful relations between Creeks and the English, and persuade the English to make good on what she believed were financial commitments made to her. In fact, much that has been written about Mary Musgrove has focused heavily on her financial interests. As important as economic issues were to her, they are not the primary reasons for her historical importance in colonial Georgia. Her greatest accomplishments derived from her ability to be a cultural broker between her own people and the English, at ease within each culture and able to move easily between both. Her role as a cultural intermediary receives perceptive analysis throughout Michelle Gillespie's essay on "The Sexual Politics of Race and Gender."

Mary's dual cultural identifications and her career as a businesswoman, however, did intersect in significant ways. As a trader, she did much more than merely exchange one set of products for another. In addition to the trading post as a center for cultural exchange in which people from diverse backgrounds could learn about each other's ideas, customs, and beliefs, Mary gained vital intelligence about Creek and English goals, plans, fears, and potential for violent actions, which served her well in her efforts on behalf of both Georgia and Creeks. Throughout her work as a trader, she served two masters—the Creek and the English—in ways that benefited both and helped to keep the peace. It is also true, of course, that she had her own personal interests in mind, as almost anyone would, as she sought to achieve financial success. While she was something of a double agent, and her heart certainly was securely tucked inside her Creek heritage, she knew that peace and justice could be achieved for her own people only if she could serve as a fair broker. That balance she maintained throughout most of her life. When her role as a broker faltered later, it did so largely through injustices committed against her.

James Edward Oglethorpe and the Creation of Georgia

James Oglethorpe would prove to be the catalyst for Mary Musgrove's very public and historic life in which her dual cultural background would bear much fruit. Oglethorpe was born in Surrey, England, in 1696. A participant in the Austro-Turkish War of 1716–18, member of the British Parliament, and humanitarian committed to prison reform, he arrived in South Carolina on January 11, 1733 (the colony of Carolina having been divided into North Carolina and South Carolina in 1729). In England, Oglethorpe had chaired a committee of Parliament that examined problems in prisons. Finding that many debtors were ultimately released without any means of support, Oglethorpe and some of his associates decided to establish a colony in the Americas to which individuals could go in order to establish a new and productive life for themselves. Accordingly, they formed the Trustees for the Establishment of the Colony of Georgia. Land ownership would be limited to fifty acres—including a town lot, garden, and forty-five-acre farm—in order to keep parcels of land small enough to be worked by a single family and to prevent rich landowners from establishing huge estates and land speculators from buying up large tracts and reselling them. The petition to establish the colony was approved in 1732, and Oglethorpe embarked for the Americas in November aboard the *Anne* with approximately 120 men, women, and children (see Spalding's *Oglethorpe in America* for these and the following details of Oglethorpe's actions in colonial America).

Ultimately, few debtors managed to join the effort to establish the new colony of Georgia, but significant numbers of English tradesmen and craftsmen, Scots pioneers, and religious refugees from other western European countries joined the effort. All religions were accepted except for Roman Catholicism, which the English associated with their Spanish adversaries that controlled Florida and were a constant threat to the colonies to their north.

Oglethorpe understood that he faced a number of challenges, including the Spanish threat and possible hostility from area Native Americans who held the balance of power within any English-Spanish conflict. He needed an intermediary who knew these peoples, especially the Creeks, and was trusted by them—someone that he also could trust and rely on to furnish him with accurate information. This individual could prove indispensable if he (or she) were able to facilitate a strong political and military alliance between English and Creek while also recruiting Creek warriors to fight alongside the English against the Spanish.

That was where Mary Musgrove came in.

Interpreter, Diplomat, Recruiter

Oglethorpe quickly came to rely on Mary and her husband, John. By August 1733, Oglethorpe was writing to fellow Trustees that Mary and John were "the only interpreters we have" (quoted in Hahn 92). Mary was instrumental in forging an agreement between Oglethorpe and Tomochichi, the Yamacraw chief, to establish Savannah at Yamacraw Bluff in 1733. She had also demonstrated her willingness to cooperate with Oglethorpe by agreeing in 1733 to move the Cowpen further upstream in exchange for a new plot of land as well as a town lot in the infant Savannah. The Yamacraws also moved their village to a site about one mile from the Cowpen (Hahn 84). Given the various roles that a trading post played, and increasingly confident of the value of Mary's services, Oglethorpe by 1738 had asked her to establish another post on the Altamaha River. Known as Mount Venture, the site became, in Michael D. Green's words, "part trading post, part supply depot, part listening post, part recruiting station, and part diplomatic mission," while it also served therefore to assist Oglethorpe in planning a raid on Florida (32).

John died in 1735, his health having declined during his journey to England with a party that included Oglethorpe and Tomochichi during the second half of 1734, with John serving as interpreter, leaving substantial land holdings in South Carolina and Georgia, including the trading post, house, and ranching area collectively known as the "Cowpen" on Yamacraw Bluff. Because Mary was a Creek, her right of inheritance and ownership was not recognized by the English authorities, although the Georgia Trustees did permit her to hold the land until one of her children reached adulthood and to sell a portion of the land to pay creditors, as Mary had to buy the goods with which she stocked her trading post. Her remaining two sons, James and Edward, however, died not long after their father's passing (Hahn 82), and the restrictive land ownership regulations that the Trustees had established in order to limit the amount of private ownership, along with the special problems that Mary encountered as a Creek who could not claim in her own name any land that she had not been given by her tribe (and therefore could not gain title to lands that her husband and she had acquired, thus preventing her from selling portions of the land), led to her continuing financial conflict with English authorities for much of the rest of her life. These legal issues surely played a role in her decision to marry one of her indentured servants, Jacob Mathewes, in 1737, for he, as an English male, possessed land rights that she lacked. The issue of land ownership and the freedom to do with it what one wished was heightened when Tomochichi granted Mary the Yamacraw Bluff land on December 13, 1737. While he had the right to transfer the land to another Creek, she could not legally possess the land under English law, land titles, as Michael Green points out, having to come from the Crown (35–36).

Meanwhile, Mary's value to James Oglethorpe increased as war between the English and Spanish approached. After John Musgrove's death, Mary was the only remaining translator that Oglethorpe could count on. As Helen Todd states, "Oglethorpe would not hold a conference or council with the Indians without having Mary present as an interpreter" (88). Her linguistic knowledge was substantial, demonstrated by, among other evidence, her instructing of John Wesley and his assistant, Benjamin Ingham, in the Muskogee language, and her collaboration with Ingham and the Moravian missionaries Andrew Dober and David Nitschmann in creating a vocabulary of Muskogee, English, and German words (Hahn 104–06). Her value to Oglethorpe, though, extended far beyond interpreting.

The War of Jenkins' Ear

As a result of the Treaty of Utrecht in 1713 ending the War of the Spanish Succession, Britain gained the *asiento*, that is, the exclusive right to supply slaves to the Spanish colonies in America, and also the right to engage in trade with Spanish America by importing goods up to a limit of five hundred tons per year (*The Assiento*). As the eighteenth century progressed, England and Spain engaged not only in economic competition but also periodically in military conflict, including the Anglo-Spanish War (1727–29). This conflict ended with the Treaty of Seville in 1729, which allowed Spanish warships to stop and search English vessels in order to determine whether the English were obeying the limits on the amount of goods shipped to Spanish America under the terms of the Treaty of Utrecht.

The incident that supplied the name for the war that broke out between England and Spain in 1739 occurred eight years earlier when the Spanish boarded the English ship *Rebecca* and charged that the ship's captain, Robert Jenkins, was smuggling goods into America in order to contravene the weight limit mandated by the Treaty of Utrecht. Julio León Fandiño, captain of the Spanish *La Isabela*, cut off Jenkins' left ear and reportedly told Jenkins to inform his king that Fandiño would treat any other smugglers the same way. Jenkins testified before Parliament on the incident in 1738, causing considerable outrage against the Spanish. England formally declared war against Spain on October 23, 1739. Given the historical mistrust and competition between England and Spain, the mistreatment of Jenkins was far from the only, or even primary, reason for the subsequent outbreak of hostilities, and Jenkins undoubtedly has received more attention historically than he deserves, thanks to Thomas Carlyle's assigning of the now well-known appellation to the conflict in the mid-nineteenth century in his *History of Friedrich II of Prussia*. The war actually lasted until 1748, although most of the conflict occurred by 1742 (Harding).

With war looming, James Oglethorpe worked assiduously to prepare. An important piece of that preparation involved Mary Musgrove. Oglethorpe, realizing the necessity of solidifying the support of the Native Americans in the Southeast and preventing what would be catastrophic to English interests—an alliance between them and the Spanish—accepted an invitation previously extended by Creeks to visit them. Although Mary apparently was at Mount Venture when Oglethorpe journeyed to Creek villages in August 1739 and negotiated the Anglo-Creek Treaty in which the Creeks pledged their loyalty to the British king, without her previous involvement as interpreter and liaison in his relations with the Creeks, concluding the alliance would at the very least have been more challenging.

As Hahn points out (120–27), Oglethorpe relied on Mary heavily during his construction of war plans, especially as a recruiter. In November 1739, Spanish troops beheaded two English guards stationed on Amelia Island. Then at Fort Frederica, a fort and town complex on St. Simons Island off the Georgia coast, Oglethorpe turned to Tomochichi's nephew, Tooanohui, along with Hillispilli, the war chief of the Lower Creeks, to lead a Yamacraw party to St. Augustine in a retaliatory attack. However, a second Spanish attack on Amelia Island occurred with the Yamacraws having made it no farther than the island and resulted in their retreat to Fort Frederica.

At Oglethorpe's request, Mary traveled to Fort Frederica to consult with him. There she recruited thirty Creeks and Yamacraws to join her husband, Jacob Mathewes, a relative named Thomas Jones, and William Grey, a trader, to fight the Spanish. Mary also apparently supplied names of acquaintances from South Carolina to join the anti–Spanish effort. Victories in attacks on the Spanish forts Picolata and Pupo on the St. John's River boosted morale, and Oglethorpe readied for a military excursion into Florida.

Mary, according to Hahn, probably was at Mount Venture during the assault on St. Augustine. There she was close to the Creeks and could continue relaying to both Oglethorpe and the Creeks valuable intelligence regarding attitudes and actions that either should know about. Her efforts especially were beneficial when she accompanied Malatchi, a relative and close friend who had reportedly been tabbed by Brims as his successor, to Fort Frederica to meet with Oglethorpe. Malatchi reported that his uncle, Chigelly, was promoting neutrality for the Creeks, a position with which Malatchi strongly disagreed. The relationship between Mary and her kinsman thus proved instrumental in retaining the Creeks as English allies.

Oglethorpe's invasion of Florida began in May 1740. Victories at Fort Diego and Fort Mose quickly followed. Governor Manuel de Montiano of Florida then ordered a counterattack to try to reclaim Fort Mose. Among the Creeks at the fort were Thomas Jones and Mary's brother, Edward Griffin. The battle resulted in a disastrous defeat for the English and their allies with one hundred men either killed by the Spanish or taken prisoner. Among the dead were Edward Griffin and several other Creeks who were close to Mary. Hahn writes that "Mary seems never to have gotten over the battle of Fort Mose and referred to her losses on several occasions in memorials and petitions she later submitted in defense of her land claims" (125), although Mary may have gained some consolation from Oglethorpe's high praise of Griffin's bravery. Mary's brother had been wounded in both legs yet on his knees repeatedly kept loading and firing until being killed.

The defeat at Fort Mose forced Oglethorpe to abandon hope of capturing St. Augustine, and the Georgian forces turned to a more defensive military posture. Mary, despite her deeply felt losses at Fort Mose, shuttled back and forth between the Cowpen and Fort Frederica. While remaining busy recruiting warriors, translating, and consulting with Oglethorpe, Mary also was caring for her husband, who back at the Cowpen was seriously ill and suffering from periods of paralysis. Jacob died on June 6, 1742, and shortly thereafter hostilities between Georgia and Spanish forces picked up. On July 5, a convoy of Spanish ships and some two thousand soldiers arrived at St. Simons Island, quickly taking the southern portion of the island. Oglethorpe's forces, however, counterattacked successfully in a series of encounters, most notably at Gulley Hole Creek and Bloody Marsh, leading the Spanish, who feared a possible arrival of a British fleet, to withdraw into Florida by the middle of July.

Oglethorpe wrote to Mary, who had remained at the Cowpen after Jacob's death to handle business there, telling her of the victory and suggesting that they had some satisfaction for the earlier defeat at Fort Mose. Mary responded by continuing to recruit Native allies and direct them to Frederica, for while the Spanish had withdrawn from St. Simons Island, they remained a threat. In November, aided by Yamasees, the Spanish attacked Mount Venture. The dead included Mrs. William Francis, whom Mary and Jacob had befriended and taken into their home. Also killed was Francis's baby daughter. The destruction of Mary's trading post at Mount Venture proved counterproductive for the Spanish, as it further galvanized Creek loyalty to Mary and therefore also to the English (Hahn 139).

Mary visited Fort Frederica in April 1743, again serving as an interpreter and advisor to Oglethorpe. The relationship between the two was professional but also had developed into one of friendship. Oglethorpe, having fallen out of favor with the Georgia Trustees, especially for his perceived financial mismanagement, left for England in July 1743, but before doing so gave Mary 200 pounds (or, as Mary later claimed, 180 pounds) and a diamond ring that he had personally worn, along with, according to Mary, a promise to assist her in resolving her land claims and gaining the financial compensation that she believed was due her (Gillespie 191–92; Green 36).

Mary's role in Georgia would change dramatically after Oglethorpe's departure. Never again would any of Georgia's leaders exhibit the deep and consistent respect for Mary and appreciation for her contributions that Oglethorpe demonstrated.

Declining Influence

For a short period of time, however, Mary retained her role as recruiter, diplomat, and intermediary. Oglethorpe's successor at Fort Frederica, William Horton, relied on Mary to recruit more Native allies for an invasion of Florida that Horton expected to occur in March 1744. Mary visited Frederica to consult with the Native American allies and perhaps assisted with the planning that went into a number of forays into Florida starting in December 1743, but major hostilities did not materialize, as by this time the conflict had become absorbed into the War of the Austrian Succession with England and Spain focusing most of their military resources on the widening conflict in Europe. With the Spanish threat diminished, the importance of Fort Frederica also declined. The English regiment there was disbanded in 1749, and much of the fort was destroyed by fire in 1758. Today the Fort Frederica National Monument reminds visitors of the site's historical importance in the survival of Georgia.

On one of her trips to Fort Frederica, Mary met the Rev. Thomas Bosomworth, who would become her third husband in July 1744. Bosomworth, about twenty years younger than Mary, was born in 1719 in England and came to Georgia in 1741. The age and cultural differences surprised many observers, but Bosomworth apparently had various reasons for marrying the much older, half–Creek Mary. He clearly enunciated one reason, stating that the marriage would "'better enable me to carry on the great work of promoting Christian knowledge among the natives of America'" (quoted in Hahn 158). Her status as a devout Christian fit well with this missionary effort. In addition, he came from a very modest financial background, whereas Mary was a substantial property owner. One should not conclude, though, that the reasons were all self-serving, as Bosomworth proved a loyal, deferential, and determined advocate for Mary and stayed with her even when her financial prospects were at their lowest.

Mary Musgrove and the Reverend Thomas Bosomworth, her third husband, confront Georgia officials on behalf of Creeks, who gather behind the couple (courtesy Hargrett Rare Book and Manuscript Library/University of Georgia Libraries).

By 1747, Mary was petitioning the British government for the compensation that she believed was owed to her for lost property and unfulfilled promises of pay for her services in support of the Crown, including compensation for gifts that she had acquired for the English to give their Native allies, the giving of gifts being an essential part of Indigenous culture. As Michael Green states, presents were an important element in Native American diplomacy. "They were symbolic representations of the ideas and agreements discussed, and in their exchange, they signified the peaceful and honorable intent of the parties" (39). In that same year, she and Thomas began their relocation to St. Catherines Island, one of the Golden Isles also off the Georgia coast, located between St. Catherine's Sound and Sapelo Sound where they established a cattle ranch and their primary residence. However, the same legal issues discussed earlier regarding Yamacraw Bluff applied equally here. Her desire for a legal title to the island proved far more difficult to attain; as Green points out, at that time "all land titles derived from the Crown," and while Native Americans could give or receive land among themselves, they could not sell land, or gift it, to Englishmen (36). Mary could receive land from other Creeks and use it but was not free to sell the land because she did not possess an English title to it. Her ambition on St. Catherines Island, according to Green, was not solely to establish a thriving cattle business there but also to sell off parcels of the island to settlers (38). The issue of a title to the land thus became part of Mary's ongoing financial conflict with the English.

The English found themselves with a new adversary in 1744 when war arose between England and France in what became known as King George's War. The French were entrenched in Louisiana and sought to entice Creeks and other Native Americans to their side. Mary's popularity with the English was declining, with William Stephens, secretary and later president of the Georgia government, especially hostile to her and, with Oglethorpe no longer present, openly antagonistic. The dislike apparently came from his antipathy toward all Native Americans but especially focused on Mary, who seemingly did not exhibit, in Stephens' opinion, the proper deference and subservience (Green 38). Yet Lieutenant Colonel Alexander Heron, who followed Horton as commander at Frederica, acknowledged in a letter dated 10 August 1747 to Deputy Secretary of State Andrew Stone, "'It is Impossible for me to establish a Strict Friendship with the Creek Indians without the Friendship of Mrs. Mary Bosomworth'" (quoted in Green 38).

However, peace between England and France was achieved in 1748. Shortly afterward Fort Frederica was closed and Georgia was left with limited military support, making peace potentially more dangerous than war. Mary's help was needed as much as ever, but the English seemed not to see things that way. An important part of her diplomacy consisted, as mentioned earlier, of gift giving, which represented to Creeks and other Native allies not so much a financial matter as an expression of respect and solidarity. Georgia and South Carolina officials were astute enough to continue this practice of rewarding their Native allies with gifts. At the same time, Mary had fronted the money for gifts in the past without being adequately reimbursed. This issue of gift giving would lead to the most humiliating incident in Mary's life, what is referred to as the "Savannah incident," and which Hahn narrates in considerable detail in his biography of Mary (176–83).

Mary met her husband and Malatchi in Savannah on July 21, 1749, in the aftermath of the return from England of her brother-in-law, Abraham Bosomworth, who had seemingly succeeded in representing Mary and Thomas's appeal for funds for presents to be distributed to England's Native allies, with Mary expecting to share in the disbursement as compensation for her previous expenses. In order to pressure Georgia officials to yield to Mary's financial claims, Thomas apparently had solicited the arrival of dozens of Creeks with the promise of gifts.

In what certainly was intended, and received, as an insult, the Georgia magistrates, in preparation for meeting with the Creeks and the Bosomworths, removed Mary as interpreter. When the Georgia magistrates met with the Creeks and the Bosomworths on August 11, Malatchi requested Mary's reinstatement as interpreter, a request that the magistrates denied. Mary responded angrily, rejected allegiance to the English king, and described herself as Queen of the Creeks, a position that the Creeks did not have but one that Mary knew the English would understand. She presented herself, that is, as an ally rather than a subject of the King. That evening, at Stephens' home, Mary again expressed considerable anger and was arrested, although she was quickly released and ordered to return the following day to meet again with Stephens and the Creeks.

Stephens, at the following day's session, managed to drive a temporary wedge between Mary and the Creek attendees by pushing Malatchi into denying that Mary, rather than he, was the leader of the Creeks. Further, Stephens asked them whether they wanted to share their presents with Mary. Taken out of context, the question drew a negative response, as the Creeks apparently were unaware of the degree to which Mary had not been compensated for previous gift purchases.

It was during this meeting of August 12 that one first finds Mary's use of the name "Coosaponakeesa," which Hahn translates as "Coosa language holder/bearer" (180). The renaming, if that is what occurred, supports Mary's increasing identification as a Creek, but it also is consistent with the practice of Creeks and many other Native American peoples who renamed individuals as they grew older and established a particular identity.

The next installment of this "Savannah incident" transpired on August 17, when some seventy Creeks arrived in Savannah to receive their presents. Malatchi appeared to try to undo whatever harm he had done to Mary's cause by reaffirming her land claims and "royal" lineage. Stephens, however, again managed artfully to resurrect his previous issues of Creek leadership and the sharing of presents while adding other insulting accusations, among them his claim that Mary was lowborn, not even a relative of Malatchi's, and actually owned no land. It was an extraordinary performance by Stephens against a woman who had contributed so much to the survival and growth of the Georgia colony.

At a gathering of the magistrates and Creeks at a tavern that evening, Mary appeared, angrily renewing her claims, and was again arrested. This time, she spent the night in jail and was released the next morning only when Thomas promised that she would "behave as a prudent woman ought," according to the *Colonial Records of Georgia* (quoted in Hahn 181).

The reaction to what the English viewed as arrogant, even treasonous, had been to have her arrested. The apology and promise from Thomas Bosomworth managed to secure her release, but what was most damning in Stephens' mind was that despite having been baptized, taken communion, and served as a godmother, Mary still explicitly identified herself, when questioned about her beliefs in the evening of August 11, as an Indian (Coleman and Ready 27:173–74). Gillespie adroitly sees the irony in Stephens' response. Having supposedly accepted Christianity, Mary Musgrove must have renounced her Native identity, the two identities in his mind being incompatible. However, retaining both identities gave her the ability to serve both Native Americans and the English and, along the way, certainly saved many lives (195–96). Hahn points out as well that Mary's refusal to be dutifully deferential violated what the English expected in a woman, and even more so in a Native woman, and that Stephens had managed, in suggesting Mary's claimed dominance over the Creeks, a triggering of a certain level of misogyny in Creek attitudes (182).

Despite this treatment, Mary remained willing to aid the English. In 1752 she agreed to help Governor James Glen of South Carolina in his attempt to keep South Carolina out of the war that had arisen between the Creeks and Cherokees. Glen had hosted a meeting between members of the two warring tribes at Charles Town. As the Cherokees left, they were ambushed by Creeks and several of their party (estimates vary from four to ten) were killed.

Glen, needing to find some way to persuade the Creeks to give the Cherokees satisfaction in order not to enlarge the war and perhaps bring the English into the middle of it, turned to Mary, who might have been expected to refuse his request for help. Instead, she embarked on a complex plan that resulted in the sacrificing of a Creek warrior named Acorn Whistler in what Steven Hahn has called "one of the signature achievements in her eventful life" (189).

Mary used her considerable negotiating skills as well as her closeness to Creek leaders in order to fashion a plan that would satisfy Glen, prevent extensive bloodletting, provide the Cherokees with their revenge, and protect her kinsman Malatchi and the Lower Creeks, who apparently were indeed guilty of the ambush. A sacrificial victim needed to be chosen as an offering that would accomplish these goals. Mary, by this time revered by the Creeks as a "great beloved woman," used her skills and standing to persuade the Lower Creeks to accept the sacrifice, which would prevent retaliation from the Cherokees and possible punishing actions by the English. In addition, it was vital that the plan also prevent retaliation by Acorn Whistler's clan, which would be bound to seek retribution. The solution involved a nephew of Acorn Whistler's committing the act and claiming self-defense, thus keeping the killing within the same clan. The subsequent killing of the nephew safeguarded the plan from being disclosed. The outcome, obviously questionable from a moral standpoint, was more than satisfying to South Carolina's governor as it led to the cessation of hostilities between Creeks and Cherokees, preventing the colonists from being dragged into their war (Hahn 189–202; also Piker throughout). Formal ratification of the peace by the Creeks in May 1753, with Mary in attendance, solidified the peace between Creeks and Cherokees, much to the advantage of the Southeastern colonies.

Having succeeded at these diplomatic efforts, Mary again focused on her lengthy and frustrating battle to receive the land rights and financial compensation that for years she had struggled to gain. Toward this end, she and Thomas set sail for England in the summer of 1754. Thomas had previously traveled to England alone to plead Mary's case, meeting with Oglethorpe in October 1745. At that time, Thomas presented a "memorial" that Mary had composed detailing her services to the Crown and her claims, one of several that she would compose with Thomas. Occupied with the Scottish "Bonnie Prince Charlie" Rebellion, Oglethorpe nonetheless reportedly offered to help once the rebellion had been quelled and did write to both William Horton and the Georgia Trustees on Mary's behalf. In the letter to Horton, he urged Horton's support, referring to the "'friendship she has at all times shewed to me, as well as the interest of the colony'" (quoted in Hahn 162). Unfortunately, Oglethorpe was court-martialed regarding alleged dereliction of duty, a charge for which he was acquitted but that limited his ability to intervene on behalf of Mary.

During the 1754–55 trip, Mary and Thomas petitioned the Board of Trade, the Treasury, and the King's Privy Council (the latter consisting of senior advisors to the monarch, at that time George II). Despite the Board's negative reaction in light of reports from Stephens and others, a response that the Board kept secret, it directed John Reynolds, Georgia's governor, to come to some final arrangement with Mary and her husband. Mary and Thomas returned to St. Catherines Island and continued waiting for a resolution of their issues. (For a detailed discussion of their difficult and frustrating time in England, see Hahn 211–18.)

In early 1757, Henry Ellis arrived as the new governor of Georgia. By this time, another war was underway: the French and Indian War between England and France (known in Europe as the Seven Years' War). Weak militarily, Georgia again relied on Native allies, and that meant that once again Georgia had need of Mary. Governor Ellis's response was to try to increase English immigration and to settle Mary's financial and land claims. Without achieving the latter, he knew that he could not settle the Georgian islands legally. Therefore, Ellis offered a compromise: Mary would give up her claims to Yamacraw Bluff and Sapello and Osabaw islands (the two islands, along with St. Catherines, having been granted to Mary and Thomas by Malatachi in 1748). She also would renounce her claims to back salary and other lands. In return, she would receive 2,100 pounds (from the sale of land on Yamacraw Bluff and the two islands) and title to St. Catherines.

Mary accepted these terms in July 1759 and once again threw herself into shoring up the relationship between Creeks and the English. She also served as Ellis's interpreter. In October, she attended a conference at Savannah as an intermediary with Creek leaders. Perhaps her final effort on behalf of Georgia occurred in June 1760 when she probably interpreted for an individual named Mad Dog, who was reporting on the murder of some English traders (Hahn 229).

Now approaching sixty years of age, Mary returned to St. Catherines Island with Thomas. The specific date of her death is unknown, but it is believed to have occurred around 1764. She left behind a Georgia and a South Carolina that would endure, in no small measure because of her ability to bridge the cultural and political divide between Native American and Englishman, eventually becoming member states of the United States of America. Unfortunately, most people in positions of authority in the Southeast came to share the attitude of a William Stephens rather than that of James Oglethorpe: that Native Americans were to be valued only if they rejected their identity in favor of some sort of imitation white person and pledged themselves to serve white society. Had Mary Musgrove been accepted as a true model for imitation, how different the history of white and Native relations in America might have been.

REFERENCES

The Assiento: or, Contract for Allowing for the Subjects of Great Britain the Liberty of Importing Negroes into the Spanish America. London: Printed by John Baskett, printer to the Queen, 1713.

Chirhart, Ann Short, and Betty Wood, eds. *Georgia Women: Their Lives and Times*. Vol. 1. Athens: U of Georgia P, 2009.

Coleman, Kenneth, and Milton Ready, eds. *Colonial Records of the State of Georgia: Original Papers of Governor John Reynolds, 1754–1756*. Vol. 27. Athens: U of Georgia P, 1978.

Gillespie, Michele. "The Sexual Politics of Race and Gender: Mary Musgrove and the Georgia Trustees." *The Devil's Lane: Sex and Race in the Early South*. Ed. Catherine Clinton and Michele Gillespie. New York: Oxford UP, 1997. 187–201.

Green, Michael D. "Mary Musgrove: Creating a New World." *Sifters: Native American Women's Lives*. Ed. Theda Perdue. New York: Oxford UP, 2001. 29–47.

Hahn, Steven C. *The Life and Times of Mary Musgrove*. Gainesville: UP of Florida, 2012.

Harding, Richard. *The Emergence of Britain's Global Naval Supremacy: The War of 1739–1748*. Rochester: Boydell, 2010.

Piker, Joshua. *The Four Deaths of Acorn Whistler: Telling Stories in Colonial America*. Cambridge: Harvard UP, 2013.

Ramsey, William L. *The Yamasee War: A Study of Culture, Economy, and Conflict in the Colonial South*. Lincoln: U of Nebraska P, 2007.

Spalding, Phinizy. *Oglethorpe in America*. Chicago: U of Chicago P, 1977.

Todd, Helen. *Tomochichi: Indian Friend of the Georgia Colony*. Atlanta: Cherokee Pub. Co., 1977.

2

Molly Ockett (ca. 1740–1816)

In Fryeburg, Maine, boys and girls attend the Molly Ockett Middle School. In Bethel, Maine, the annual Molly Ockett Day is a time for celebration of perhaps Bethel's most famous adopted daughter. A gravestone in Andover, Maine, identifies her as the "Last of the Pequakets." Her name adorns such natural landmarks as "Molly Ockett's Cave" in Fryeburg and "Mollyockett Mountain" in Woodstock, Maine.

Stories, likely fanciful, are still recounted of buried treasure that Molly Ockett had left behind. Molly Ockett Day features a Princess Molly Ockett. Although Molly Ockett is reported to have claimed that her father and grandfather were chiefs (True 68), she hardly considered herself a princess and was not described as one during her lifetime. However, she was viewed with considerable respect and admiration by a great many of the settlers in the Northeast who knew her and counted her a friend and healer.

It is often difficult to discern truth from myth, especially when one must rely on a limited number of first-hand accounts of someone who lived long ago, in the case of Molly Ockett, a woman who died over two hundred years ago. Enough is known with reasonable certainty, however, to know that Molly Ockett was an important individual who led, not through politics or war, but in bridging the growing gap between very different cultures. And she accomplished that bridging, perhaps most of all, by demonstrating concern for the people around her. She deserves being remembered as a woman of many talents and as a woman who put those talents to use in helping others, including many of the early settlers in the Northeast, especially in Maine. She was, in effect, an early and a very effective cultural ambassador to the people who brought into the Northeast a radically different way of life. That she had a positive impact on many of those early settlers is clear given the accounts of Molly Ockett that have survived.

Marie Agathe

Molly Ockett was born sometime around 1740 in the Saco River Valley in southwestern Maine. She was a member of the Pigwacket (also spelled Pequawket). Residing especially at the head of the Saco River in western Maine, the Pigwackets were referred to by that name as early as the 1640s (Winthrop 2:89). The word may mean "at the cleared place," referring to the area that Pigwackets cleared of trees in order to cultivate corn (True, quoted in Barrows 3). A Western Abenaki group within the Wabanaki, they apparently were closely related to other Western Abenakis, making tribal distinctions, according to Gordon M. Day, difficult to determine. Close alliances among the Pigwackets, Penacooks, and Winnipesaukees may reflect cultural relationships as well (268–69). Lack of linguistic data for the Pigwackets and other Western Abenaki groups makes definitive categorizing of tribes extremely difficult. In fact, some of the probable tribes have left behind little linguistic information beyond tribal names and some names of people and places, in many cases untranslated. Day points out that early nineteenth-century documentation conducted at Odanak in Quebec demonstrated the existence of a Western Abenaki group of peoples distinguishable linguistically from Eastern Abenaki, or more broadly, Wabanaki tribes in eastern Maine, although a precise geographical point of separation between the two groups is impossible to ascertain and probably did not actually exist. Regrettably, little is known about the Pigwacket dialect that Molly Ockett learned as a child (Day 104, 173, 202).

Molly's original Abenaki name also has been lost to history, but at baptism she received a French name—Marie Agathe—from the Catholic priest who baptized her. As Catherine Newell explains in a pamphlet published by the Bethel Historical Society, Dr. Nathaniel Tuckerman True (1812–87), who did extensive research on the history of Native Americans in Maine, and whose historical accounts of Bethel, originally published in *The Bethel Courier* (1859–61) and which supplied the basis for his *History of Bethel, Maine*, apparently was the first to discover the etymology of the name by which Marie Agathe has come down to the present: Molly Ockett. Newell states that Christian names were written phonetically as Native Americans pronounced them. Marie Agathe sounded like Mari Agat when given a French pronunciation; with the Wabanaki pronunciation of *r* in Mari added to the mix, her name became Mali Agit. English ears then completed the transition to Molly Ockett (2–3, 22n.2).

When Molly Ockett was about four years old, conflict broke out between the French and English. King George's War (1744–48), named after the British king, George II, who reigned from 1727 to 1760, followed an earlier series of conflicts that put the Pigwackets in a precarious position caught in the middle between the French and the English. Most Abenakis favored the French with whom they shared the Catholic religion, Catholic missionaries having entered Abenaki territory in the 1640s, and with whom they were able to seek refuge in Canada. However, the English were geographically closer and increasing in numbers. The French and English both instituted bounties on enemy scalps, which made the Abenaki position not just politically or economically challenging but a matter of life or death (McBride and Prins 324). So King George's War was not an isolated event but the latest in a serious of conflicts that impacted the Pigwackets.

During Queen Anne's War (1702–13), named after the British queen and also referred to in Europe as the War of the Spanish Succession, fought to decide who would ascend the Spanish throne, Abenakis had faced attacks from the English. Major Hilton led a contingent of about one hundred men to the village of Pigwacket, later to be the approximate site of Fryeburg, Maine, but found the village recently deserted (McBride and Prins 325). The Pigwackets eventually made their way to Saint Francis, a Catholic mission of Saint-Francois-de-Sales at the mission village of Odanak near the St. Lawrence River west of Quebec, arriving about 1705 (Day 50). After the Treaty of Utrecht (1713) concluding the war, they returned to Pigwacket in 1714 (Day 208).

Then came Dummer's War (1722–25), named after William Dummer, the lieutenant governor of Massachusetts, a major leader of the New England forces. The war primarily involved the Western Abenakis and the English. The war, however, did not leave the French unaffected. The prominent French missionary and Wabanaki ally, Father Sébastien Rale, was killed during an attack by the English on Norridgewock in August 1724. Where the Pigwackets were concerned, the most serious and notorious campaign during the war was waged by John Lovewell. John Stuart Barrows in his *Fryeburg Maine: An Historical Sketch* offers a detailed account of the pivotal battle between Pigwackets and Lovewell's men. The account is based ultimately on a sermon given by the Rev. Thomas Symmes on May 16, 1725, eight days after the May 8 battle. The account was enlarged and reprinted in various stages over the years, culminating in Frederick Kidder's *Lovewell's Fight* (1865).

The account from Symmes to Barrows largely reflects the English point of view. According to their description of the action, Pigwackets ambushed Lovewell's force as it was approaching the village of Pigwacket. The fighting was intense, with forty Abenakis and twelve English, including Captain Lovewell, killed during the battle and three more of Lovewell's men succumbing to wounds later. It was estimated that about twenty Pigwackets were still alive when they withdrew, leaving the field to the English. During Fryeburg's centennial celebration of the battle on May 19, 1825, Henry

Wadsworth Longfellow, then a student at Bowdoin College, read an ode honoring the victory. However, a contemporary account of the centennial events does include references by speakers to the Pigwackets as "enterprising, resolute and intelligent," with their spirit "as noble as the mountains around them" (Barrows 6, 13–27).

The Pigwackets, having experienced a great deal of warfare, including the devastating loss of life as a result of Lovewell's raid, were understandably anxious to find a way out of further conflict. When King George's War began, Molly's father and five other Pigwacket men, the Pigwackets having returned to their home area in Maine, where Molly had been born, allied themselves and their families with the English despite their previous interaction and alliances with the French, apparently believing that it would offer them greater safety. The advancement of English settlements had made major inroads into the land that the Pigwackets had used for hunting, fishing, and trapping, and by the early eighteenth century, the number of adult Pigwacket males had been reduced from one hundred to twenty-four, placing their very existence in question (McBride 47).

The English consequently demanded that these Pigwackets, except for the men, who were required to scout for the English army, move to Massachusetts. So Molly moved south, settling near Rochester close to Buzzards Bay in Plymouth County, in the southeastern corner of the state. When hostilities ceased in 1748, most of the Pigwackets returned to Maine. Molly, however, remained in Massachusetts with two other girls, likely as hostages against the Pigwackets' renewed alliance with the French. Precisely how Molly spent her time in Massachusetts is unknown, as is the additional length of her stay, although it seems to have been less than a year (Newell 3–4). She apparently did learn some English at this time, and McBride conjectures that she may have spent time as a servant in a British home (48–50).

As McBride and Prins point out, Molly spent especially impressionable years (approximately ages five to nine) among the English (328). She likely made friends and had at least some enjoyable experiences there. John Wheelwright, Commissary General of the Province of the Massachusetts Bay, a position that put him in charge of managing trade with the Native tribes, wrote that when the girls were finally returned, the Abenakis "'carried them into the Woods, tho much against their Inclinations'" (quoted in McBride and Prins 328).

Molly's childhood continued to be far from easy. Renewed conflict between the French and English developed in 1754, with the prize being control of North America. The contested land especially included Canada, New York, and New England. The fighting precipitated a larger war between the two countries known in American history as the French and Indian War (1754–1763), and, in England, as the Seven Years' War (1756–1763). The English attacked the Abenakis because of their historical association with the French, placing bounties on their scalps. About the same time, a smallpox outbreak spread among the Abenakis with its usual deadly force, leading Molly's family to seek safety in Canada, where they had periodically journeyed, especially to the St. Francis Mission at Odanak along the St. Lawrence River to seek absolution for their sins and pray for deceased family members (Newell 4).

Canada, however, was no safe refuge for Molly and her family. In 1759, the English under Major Robert Rogers and his "Rangers" attacked and burned the Wabanaki village of Odanak, including the church. Rogers' Rangers were trained for fighting behind enemy lines, as they did at Odanak. General Jeffrey Amherst ordered the attack in a manner sufficient "'to disgrace the enemy'"; his orders to Rogers included remembering "'the barbarities that have been committed by the enemy's Indian scoundrels on every occasion.'" "'Take your revenge,'" Amherst stated, but cautioned Rogers "'that no women or children are killed or hurt.'" Rogers, however, failed to follow Amherst's directive to spare women and children, as his Rangers, while not coming close to killing two hundred residents of Odanak as Rogers claimed to have done, did include twenty-two women and children among the thirty-two people they killed while Rogers lost just one of his own men during the attack. The retreat, though, was a disaster. With Rogers' men near starvation even before the attack, they suffered horribly from hunger afterward. With French and Abenaki fighters in pursuit, Rogers split his men into groups but lost forty-three Rangers to starvation or wounds. One of the survivors, Lieutenant George Campbell, wrote in his diary that some of the rangers ate their dead in order to survive (Bruchac 3–6). Yet despite the loss of life, the destruction of the village, along with Rogers exaggerating the success of his raid, turned the attack into a major psychological victory for the English. Rogers' exploits much later would inspire the novel *Northwest Passage* (1936) by Kenneth Roberts.

Molly, then about nineteen years old, survived the attack, perhaps as oral accounts, later printed by Nathaniel True, assert, by hiding behind a bush, but both of her parents were killed (McBride 52–53 143–44). With nothing left for her in Canada, Molly returned to Maine with other surviving Pigwackets. According to Day, the raid on Odanak did not destroy the Pigwackets as a tribe but "did disrupt it so severely that it was not fully reestablished until 1767 or 1768" (267).

Molly Ockett and the Settlers

By the early 1760s, Molly was back at the site of the old Pigwacket village. The area had changed, though, and what she found was a village named Fryeburg. The founder of this village, Joseph Frye, had come from Andover, Massachusetts. A veteran of the French and Indian War, Frye wanted a more peaceful life and found in the valley of the Saco River an attractive area that also offered both farming and lumbering potential. The Pigwackets had already demonstrated that the area was good for growing crops. He petitioned for a grant of land in 1761, and by February 1763 the grant had been approved and confirmed. He received an area six miles square to be divided into sixty-four parts to be distributed among fifty families, with parts also for the minister, a parsonage, a school, and for use by Harvard College. By May 2, 1763, Frye had issued fifty deeds to settlers, and the village was born (Barrows 28–33).

Little is known about Molly Ockett's personal life apart from her interactions with Euro-Americans who moved in increasing numbers into Molly's home area after England's victory in the French and Indian War. She had a daughter, Marie Marguerite (Molly) Susup with her husband, Piol Susup (also referred to in written accounts as Piel Susup, Pierre Joseph, or Peter Joseph), whom she had married by 1764. In the same year, the daughter was baptized at St. Francis, which she and other Abenakis continued to visit for baptisms, marriages, and to confess their sins (McBride and Prins 330). As Bethel came to be a focus for Molly Ockett's life, her daughter went to school there, learned English, and interacted with the children of Bethel's settlers (Lapham 78). The daughter also was reported to be quite athletic and often superior to boys in sports. However, as she became older, failed romantic relationships embarrassed her mother, who thought that the daughter's conduct reflected badly on her (True 67).

After Susup's death, Molly Ockett had a lengthy relationship with Sabbatus, like Molly a Pigwacket, with whom she apparently had three children (Newell 5–6). Little is known about her children, especially those by Sabbatus. Newell relates the conclusion of Molly Ockett's relationship with Sabbatus: His former wife returned, a physical fight between the two women ensued for the right to be with Sabbatus, and Molly lost, subsequently leaving for the Bethel, Maine, area (6). Other accounts have Molly winning (e.g., Barrows 10), but in either case the relationship, which actually may not have been a marriage, ended, as Lapham reports, because "of his intemperate habits and quarrelsome disposition" (78).

It was in relation to the Euro-American settlers that Molly Ockett would achieve her lasting fame. She had many talents that would come into play, foremost among them her ability as a healer. These talents often benefited her non–Native neighbors, leading to the respect and fondness that many of them exhibited toward her. The most famous example of her medical ability concerned a future Vice President of the United States, Hannibal Hamlin (1809–91), who was born in Paris Hill, Maine, and served as governor of Maine, a member of the United States House of Representatives and Senate, and later Vice President of the United States during Abraham Lincoln's first term as President (1861–65). Hamlin was not nominated for a second term as Vice President and later returned to the United States Senate.

During the winter of 1809–10, Molly Ockett was traveling to Paris Hill and sought shelter when the weather turned especially bitter. According to the often-repeated account of the incident, she finally was welcomed at the home of Cyrus and Anna Hamlin, "one of the finest families in the State of Maine." There she learned that the Hamlins' infant, Hannibal, was ill. Molly nursed the baby

Hannibal Hamlin, Vice President of the United States during Abraham Lincoln's first term, was nursed back to health as an infant by Molly Ockett (Collections of the Bethel Historical Society).

back to health and, according to Arthur D. Woodrow's narrative, prophesied that the baby would not only recover but also "become a great man" (69). The latter element in the story may be a later addition, given what the infant Hamlin would ultimately achieve, but that she applied her medical talents successfully to the baby appears genuinely to have happened. Other versions of the event stipulate that the successful remedy consisted of cows' milk (Newell 13), which hardly seems like much of a cure given the herbal remedies, salves, and poultices she elsewhere is credited with using.

That Molly Ockett's doctoring knew no social bounds is demonstrated in her caring for Henry Tufts, a notorious petty criminal, thief, and general con man, who recorded his story in a frank memoir originally titled *A Narrative of the Life, Adventures, Travels and Sufferings of Henry Tufts, Now Residing at Lemington, in the District of Maine. In Substance as Compiled from His Own Mouth* (1807). Publication was followed by the burning of the publisher's establishment and his stock of books, most likely arson perpetrated by the citizens of Dover, New Hampshire, where Sam Bragg had his print shop. Nonetheless, the book was published a second time in 1930, with that edition reprinted in 1993.

Tufts relates the story of a self-inflicted injury that he suffered in 1772 and his subsequent recovery through the ministrations of Molly Ockett. Tufts joined in a contest to see who could open a "half bent jackknife without touching the blade." When Tufts made his attempt, he stuck the knife into his thigh. He recalls losing so much blood that he was incapacitated for three months. Finally, a Captain Josiah Miles suggested that he visit the Indians at Sudbury, referred to in the text as being in Canada, but most likely near Bethel, Maine (Tufts 49, McBride 59).

Tufts does not say how, given the severity of his injury, he was able to make the trip to present-day Bethel, but once there he was welcomed and offered the services of "Molly Occut, at that time the great Indian doctress, to superintend the recovery of my health" (53). According to Tufts, she tended him with "roots, herbs, barks and other materials," visited him daily, and in two months had restored him to as healthy a condition as he had ever experienced: "This happy restoration to pristine ability I attributed principally to the good offices of my doctoress, who during my convalescence, was indefatigable in her care and attention. Her character was, indeed, that of a kind and charitable woman" (54).

Tufts then offers another example of Molly Ockett's kindness and generosity. A Pigwacket resident who had fallen into great poverty and thus was unable to feed his family journeyed to Bethel and applied to Molly for help. She loaned him twenty dollars and told him that he could return the following winter and hunt furs in order to pay her back. Tufts adds that the man returned and fulfilled his obligation (54–55).

So impressed was Tufts with his "doctoress" and her medical skills that he became something of what one might call today an intern, following along with her for three years (McBride 59):

> Since beginning to amend in health under the auspices of madam Molly, I had formed a design of studying the Indian practice of physic, though my intention had hitherto remained a profound secret. Indeed I had paid strict attention to everything of a medical nature, which had fallen within the sphere of my notice. Frequently was I inquisitive with Molly Occut, old Plilps, Sabattus and other professed doctors to learn the names and virtues of their medicines. In general they were explicit in communication, still thought them in possession of secrets they cared not to reveal [56].

Not given to excessive humility, Tufts pronounced himself of "being naturally possessed of a strong retentive memory," and asserted that he "made rapid proficiency" (57).

Other accounts of Molly aiding settlers appear in various references to her. She cured the wife of John Evans, despite his being a former scalp hunter and one of Rogers' Rangers, reportedly by applying pounded roots from the Solomon's seal plant to a hand infection that she suffered from (McBride 55, Newell 10). The settlers consistently overcame whatever reluctance they may have had to accept the medical ministrations of a Native American, probably because of both Molly's reputation and their own lack of doctors and knowledge of herbal treatments, welcoming her into their homes during some of their most difficult moments. Her knowledge of traditional natural remedies was extensive and, as modern science has demonstrated, often effective because of the healing properties of enzymes, penicillin, and allicin, among other ingredients, in the natural products that she used (McBride and Prins 331–33).

Molly became friendly with the Ezekiel Merrill family, who were the first settlers in Andover, Maine, and assisted Mrs. Merrill at the birth of Susan, the Merrills' first child, in 1790. Arthur Woodrow reports that Molly and Mrs. Merrill remained the only women in Andover for three years, a condition that certainly contributed to their friendship (72). New England mothers usually relied on midwives rather than physicians to help them give birth, a practice that continued well into the nineteenth century, so Molly fit well this role as well as that of healer (McBride and Prins 332).

Catherine S-C. Newell relays Samuel Sumner's account, written in 1860, of the Pigwacket healer curing Vermont children of dysentery with a cure made from spruce bark. According to Sumner, Molly, who sometimes was quite secretive about the nature of her cures, shared this one the following year in response to a settler giving her some pork after she had run short on food (11–12). Martha Russell Fifield, a resident of Newry near Bethel, often welcomed Molly as she passed by on her journeys. Molly reciprocated Martha's hospitality, according to Martha Fifield Wilkins, a descendant of Martha Fifield's, by sharing a great deal of medical knowledge with her as well as how to make root beer and dyes from roots and herbs (McBride and Prins 336).

William Lapham, in his *History of the Town of Bethel, Maine* (first published in 1891), notes, "She was well skilled in roots and herbs, and spent the latter portion of her life in going from place to place, and giving advice and medicine to the sick" (79). Later in the *History*, Lapham offers considerable detail as he writes of her visits to Bethel:

> Molly Ockett often came to Bethel. She was acquainted with all the families and was ever ready to prescribe for any who were sick. She carried no remedies along with her in her journeyings to and fro, but when asked to prescribe she would start for the woods where she was sure of finding what she wanted. Her remedies in part consisted of blood-root, Solomon's seal, buck-thorn,

skunk-cabbage, oak, elm, basswood and pine barks, sweet elder, sumach berries, mountain ash bark and a great variety of herbs. She had great skill in collecting them and also in concocting drinks, in making salves and poultices and in applying them. Many had great faith in her remedies and skill, and at some homes she was ever a welcome visitant. She was often present at the births of children, and was sometimes retained in families for weeks that she might be present on such occasions [241–42].

The James Swan residence is an example of those homes where Molly was often "a welcome visitant." Molly befriended Swan and his family in Fryeburg "and visited them so often that she became a kind of adjunct member of their household whenever she camped nearby" (McBride 56). The relationship continued when the Swans moved to Bethel, where Molly often spent considerable time. The services that Molly supplied to the Swans are not recorded, but they likely involved Molly's medical expertise and perhaps other talents that she possessed, such as beadwork, weaving, embroidery, and quillwork, which she employed in creating baskets and bark boxes, as well as moccasins and other leather work, and perhaps even hunting, at which she was quite skilled.

The Bethel Historical Society is home to a birchbark box decorated with porcupine quills that Molly gave to the Israel Kimball family of Bethel. The Maine Historical Society possesses a similar, though larger box, and a pocketbook made for another Bethel resident, Eli Twitchell, that Molly decorated with hemp and moose hair dyed blue, green, red, and yellow. Other items that she made included a pudding dish for a Mrs. Bragg of Andover and a duck feather bed for Mrs. Swan of Bethel, the latter resulting from Molly's skill as a hunter as well as her artistry. Many details about Molly's artistic creations and much other information are to be found in the online text for *Molly Ockett and Her World*, which is based on an exhibition held at the Bethel Historical Society.

An especially strong claim for Molly's hunting prowess is made by Arthur Woodrow, who describes her as "a great huntress, often going into the woods and killing moose and bears, returning to the settlement for aid in bringing in the game" (66), details borrowed from Nathaniel True's earlier account (68). She is reported as having at times gone hunting with settlers. In the spring, she would trade furs from her hunting and, reportedly, even trapping that she did during the winter. There were occasions when she combined her trading with religious objectives in trips to the St. Francis Mission (McBride and Prins 337)

Not inconsequential among Molly Ockett's qualities that led settlers to admire her was her sociability. She liked people and enjoyed talking with them. As Catherine Newell points out, she often dined with her non–Native neighbors and liked to tell stories. Nor was she averse to a glass or two of rum, which typically would lead to some storytelling. Her tales were likely within the framework of her functioning as an "oral historian, transmitting past events she had heard from others" (15–17). Nathaniel True describes her as "loquacious" as well as "pretty" and "genteel." She "possessed a large frame and features, and walked very erect even in old age." Except for a pointed cap, according to True, she dressed in traditional clothes (67, 69). Her appearance obviously was engaging and likely added to the effectiveness of her storytelling.

Among the stories attributed to her was a recounting of the practice of Native Americans who left for Canada burying gold in the Paris, Maine, area. An almost certainly false story of Molly herself burying money, supposedly in a teakettle, took root over the years and was passed down (Newell 15–16, 19). A poem published by Addie Kendall Mason in the *Bethel News* in 1895 ("Moll Lockett's Curse") concludes with the stanza:

> And beneath the stately hemlock
> In the shadows you'll behold
> Molly Lockett's ghostly figure
> Keeping watch o'er buried gold [Woodrow 80].

Colonel Clark

An incident that cemented Molly's positive standing with settlers occurred in August 1781. Tumkin Hagen, referred to in Benjamin Willey's *Incidents of White Mountain History* (1856) and other accounts as Tom Hegan or Tomhegan, led a band of Native Americans on raids in Maine and New Hampshire, invading houses, robbing, and killing several men. As Willey recounts the story, one of Hegan's intended victims was a Colonel Clark from Boston who regularly visited the White Mountains to trade with Native peoples. Fortunately for Clark, a member of Hegan's band drunkenly confided the plan to kill Clark to Molly Ockett (258–59).

The decision to inform on Hegan, apparently also a Pigwacket, may have been a difficult one for Molly, but overriding the tribal connection were several factors. At the outbreak of the Revolutionary War, the Pigwackets generally chose to seek survival by allying with their closest neighbors, the prospective members of the new United States. In addition, Hegan and his men, supporting the British, had attacked, among other villages, Bethel, a town that Molly had come to view as her primary home (McBride and Prins 338–39). As Lapham reports, she considered herself an "original proprietor" of Bethel (178). Also, Colonel Clark was well known in the area. Although from Boston, he had visited the area annually, according to Willey, trading for furs. Willey writes, "He was much esteemed for his honesty, and his visits were looked forward to with much interest." Molly hurried through the woods for several miles to warn Clark, arriving just in time. Two of Clark's companions who had camped within a mile or two of Clark had already been killed by Hegan (259). A group of men from Fryeburg, with Sabattus as scout, went after Hegan but were unsuccessful in locating him (McBride and Prins 339). Eventually, though, according to Willey, Hegan was apprehended and made to pay a horrible price for his actions. He was tied on a horse with spurs arranged so that they constantly inflicted pain, causing the horse to keep running through the woods until "the trees tore him to pieces" (260).

Clark, having escaped to safety, resolved to repay Molly for saving his life. The avenue for expressing his gratitude in a concrete way finally opened when Molly was nearing the end of her life and finding that old age and increasing frailty were making self-subsistence difficult. Clark persuaded her to join his family in Boston. City life, however, was not for Molly. She stayed with the Clarks for about a year, bearing urban life, as Willey states, "with a martyr's endurance," before explaining that she must return to die among the trees that had been her lifelong companions (259).

Consequently, according to Willey, Clark supported her return to Maine and "built her a wigwam on the Falls of the Pennacook [Rumford Falls], and there supported her the remainder of her days. Often did he visit her, bringing the necessary provision for her sustenance" (259–60). That Clark actually provided for Molly until her death seems an overstatement, although there is no reason to doubt his good intentions or efforts.

In 1816, the final year of Molly's life, she was camping with Metallak and his small group of Abenakis about twenty miles from Andover. Metallak was a member of an Abenaki group referred to in the Woodrow narrative as the Cooashaukes. He is reputed to have been the last of the group, at least in Maine. A first-hand account by Peter Smith Bean published in the *Oxford County Advertiser* of January 17, 1890, states that Metallak and the author's grandfather were friends. The grandson recalls sharing many meals with Metallak, sitting on his knee, and very much enjoying his company. According to Bean, Metallak was well liked and decided to stay in New England when his two sons left for Canada. An accident led to his loss of sight in both eyes. The Woodrow account states that he died destitute but was supported by citizens of Stewartstown, New Hampshire, until his death in 1847. He was buried in North Hill Cemetery (44–45); a plaque near the grave site calls him "the last survivor of a band of Abnaki inhabiting the Upper Androscoggin."

When Molly became ill, Metallak brought her to Andover. Knowing that Molly had doctored a number of people in the area, he thought that she would find support there (McBride 66). Perhaps the most accurate account of her death is given by Agnes Blake Poor, niece of Silvanus Poor, an early Andover settler. Agnes interviewed her uncle in 1883 when he was seventy-eight years old for a history of Andover titled *The Andover Memorials*, which was privately printed by the Poor family by mimeograph in the 1880s and reprinted in 1997 by the Andover Educational Fund. According to this account, Molly's Native American companions stayed with her for about two weeks, after which "they represented to the authorities of the town [Andover] that it would be better for the town to take charge of her than to have the whole party on their hands, for if they stayed to take care of her they could not hunt and support themselves." Thomas Bragg of Andover subsequently prepared a small camp for Molly when she declined to stay in his house. Cared for by the citizens of Andover, she died on August 2, 1816, and was laid to rest in the Andover cemetery. Funds to finance erection of a stone to mark her grave were raised by auctioning off her possessions (128–29).

Molly Ockett was not forgotten by the people of Andover. In 1867, ladies of the Andover Congregational Church raised money for a new gravestone. The citizens of Andover dedicated the stone on July 4, 1867, as part of a celebration that included a parade, a poetry reading, a brass band, and a speech by Dr. Nathaniel True. The stone is engraved as follows:

> Molly Ockett
> Baptized Mary Agatha
> Died in the Christian Faith
> August 2, 1816
> The Last of the Pequawkets

It could have included: A great Native American healer and ambassador. McBride and Prins also offer a fitting memorial to Molly Ockett as being "among the very few native women carried through the centuries in the memory of dominant white society" (322).

References

Barrows, John Stuart. *Fryeburg Maine: An Historical Sketch*. 1938. Berwyn Heights, MD, 2015.

Bethel (Maine) Historical Society. *Molly Ockett and Her World*. From an exhibition at the Bethel Historical Society. July 2004–May 2007. bethelhistorical.org/catalog/exhibits/show/mollyockett/introduction.

Bruchac, Margaret. "Reading Abenaki Traditions and European Records of Rogers' Raid." *Vermont Folklife Center*. repository.upenn.edu/anthro_papers/155.

Day, Gordon M. *In Search of New England's Native Past: Selected Essays by Gordon M. Day*. Ed. Michael K. Foster and William Cowan. Amherst: U of Massachusetts P, 1998.

Lapham, William B. *History of the Town of Bethel, Maine*. Somersworth, NH: New England History P in collaboration with the Bethel Historical Society, 1981.

McBride, Bunny. *Women of the Dawn*. Lincoln: U of Nebraska P, 1999.

McBride, Bunny, and Harald E. L. Prins. "Walking the Medicine Line: Molly Ockett, a

Pigwacket Doctor." *Northeastern Indian Lives 1632–1816*. Ed. Robert S. Grumet. Amherst: U of Massachusetts P, 1996. 321–47.

Newell, Catherine S-C. *Molly Ockett*. Bethel, ME: Bethel Historical Society, 1981.

Poor, Agnes Blake. *The Andover Memorials*. ca. 1880s. Andover, ME: Andover Educational Fund, incorporated by the descendants of Silvanus Poor, 1997.

True, Nathaniel Tuckerman. *The History of Bethel, Maine*. Ed. Randall H. Bennett. Bowie, MD: Heritage Books, 1994.

Tufts, Henry. *The Autobiography of a Criminal*. Foreword by Neal Keating. Port Townsend, WA: Loompanics Unlimited, 1993.

Willey, Benjamin G. *Incidents in White Mountain History*. Boston: Nathaniel Noyes, 1856.

Winthrop, John. *The History of New England from 1630 to 1649. From His Original Manuscripts. With Notes by James Savage*. 2 vols. Boston: Little, Brown, 1853.

Woodrow, Arthur D., ed. *Metallak: The Last of the Cooashaukes with the Life of David Robbins, the Story of Molly Ockett, the Adventures of Lieut. Segar and the Killing of the Last Moose*. Rumford, ME: Rumford Publishing Co., 1928.

3

Louisa Keyser (Dat So La Lee)
(ca. 1850–1925)

Louisa Keyser, also known as Dat So La Lee and Dabuda, is one of the most famous—and certainly one of the most accomplished and significant—basket makers in American history. Unable to read or write English, she did not leave a first-hand account of her life and work. What was left behind was a long string of falsified statements about her life conveyed both orally and in writing by Amy and Abe Cohn to aid in their marketing of Louisa Keyser's baskets. Unfortunately, these falsehoods were routinely accepted, reprinted in contemporary accounts of Louisa's basket making, and promulgated as true in subsequent accounts. The result is that little of her life can be described with full certainty of the facts.

The Cultural Importance of Basket Making

Baskets served many purposes for the Washoe and other American Indian peoples. For the Washoe, who historically were hunter-gatherers, baskets were used to gather seeds, acorns, piñon nuts, and other foodstuffs. Lined with pitch, they could be rendered largely waterproof, allowing transportation and storage of water for drinking and cooking. In the absence of metal pans, baskets were used for cooking. Meat (such as deer and rabbits) and vegetables were cooked in the baskets by means of hot rocks dropped into the liquid-food mix. A combination of periodically shaking the baskets to prevent the wooden containers from catching fire and replacing cooling rocks with newly heated ones maintained a temperature suitable for cooking the food without destroying the basket. Baskets even served as cradles for infants (Gigli 3).

The baskets traditionally were functional rather than works of art, designed to meet some of the people's most basic needs. Given their importance to daily life, baskets were, as J.M. Adovasio has stated, "one of the oldest aboriginal crafts in North America" (100). Baskets and basket fragments have survived especially in dry caves in arid and semiarid areas, including the Western Basin Center of the Great Basin of the United States, an area in west central Nevada that was home to the Washoe. Evidence of aboriginal basket making has been discovered dating back ten or eleven thousand years (Orr 50; Adovasio 113).

By the time that Louisa Keyser was born around 1850—birth dates of 1829 and 1834 often assigned to her having been convincingly demonstrated by Marvin Cohodas to be fabrications (122–23)—baskets were receding in importance for the Washoe, to be replaced for cooking purposes by metal pots and pans introduced by Euro-Americans.[1] Matthew S. Makley in his recent history of the Washoes notes that the federal government's attempts to force Washoes to assimilate had resulted in their changing in order to survive: "[T]hey entered the American wage economy, switched to a new currency, and adopted new clothing, all while learning a new language and new customs and trying to fit into a new culture." Cultural changes included new uses for the traditional Washoe baskets, which increasingly were made for sale to collectors (98).

Native basketry assumed growing importance within the burgeoning interest in Native cultural crafts. The Arts and Crafts Movement, building on existing systems of women's clubs, fostered an increase in the curio trade while encouraging the making of crafts in schools. Handmade items were valued in a world increasingly industrial as the movement gained prominence from around 1880 through the first two decades of the twentieth century, a period approximating Louisa Keyser's adulthood. Given the association of Native baskets with a period before the arrival of Europeans, basketry was viewed as reflective of traditional rather than modern art, thus occupying a major place in the curio market. As Wendy Kaplan has noted, "Indian baskets or ... baskets made in the Indian style, were used in Arts and Crafts interiors as waste containers, letter trays, and sewing baskets. Often they had no specific function within a room but were placed on tabletops or mantelpieces simply because of their association with techniques and the use of natural materials" (171).

Dual Views of the Native American

Once the Native American was no longer viewed as a major threat to white dominance, white Americans tended to view Native Americans through two lenses. One perception was of them as poor, lazy, alcoholic, a figure to be scorned or, at best, pitied. This view, while obviously stereotyping, did reflect the impoverished state to which many had been driven by United States policies that followed genocide with attempts to force the Native Americans who survived onto reservations; and, supposedly to reclaim many of them by remaking the Native peoples in the image of the conqueror, although without the conqueror's wealth and power.

The second lens offered a romanticized vision of Native American as Noble Savage. The male was a brave warrior on horseback with feather bonnet and bow and arrow. The female was a comely Indian princess in buckskin. Both lived close to nature, an embodiment of the primitivism that posited virtue as the corollary of a life led simply, with few needs to amplify human vices. As Marvin Cohodas has noted, "Once they no longer posed a threat, their past could be rewritten to suit the needs of the present," providing "a means of dissociation from the degradation of current Indian life" (112–13).

This dual vision would inform the basket-making career of Louisa Keyser, not by her choice, but by that of her employers/patrons, Abram and Amy Cohn.

The Washoe

The Washoe, whose world centered (and continues to center), both spiritually and geographically, around Lake Tahoe, were primarily hunter-gatherers who had never fit the image of the Noble Savage, which more closely, although very imperfectly, reflected the Plains Indians. The Washoe, for instance, did not use horses. Nor were they a very warlike people. Their tendency, when faced with the early arrivals of Euro-Americans, was to wait and watch. They were prepared to assist these new people crossing their land, guiding Captain John C. Frémont on his exploration of the West in the 1840s and even leaving food for struggling members of the Donner party that was snowed in with tragic consequences while trying to cross the Sierra Nevada mountains during the winter of 1846–47 (Downs 72–73).

The discovery of gold in California in 1848 precipitated a great increase in people crossing Washoe country in search of gold. That stream of wealth-seekers increased when silver was also found in western Nevada in 1858—the Comstock Lode. Mines lacerated the land. Towns such as Virginia City, Gold Hill, Silver City, and Carson City grew up complete with hotels, saloons, brothels, and churches. Ranchers and farmers followed with their cattle and pigs, plowing and planting the land that had supplied sustenance for the Washoes. Wildlife declined in numbers. And the traditional life of the Washoe became increasingly difficult to maintain.

As increasing numbers of settlers, miners, and others spread throughout Washoe country, survival options for the Washoes were limited. Some men sought jobs on ranches. To meet the demand for logs as towns grew, lumber camps were established, offering Washoe men employment as lumberjacks felling trees or teamsters hauling logs. Deer largely disappeared with the clearing of land, but rabbits remained. Given that ranchers and farmers viewed jackrabbits as pests, there was no impediment to the Washoes continuing to hunt them. Some use of horses was adopted, which made it easier to pursue their quarry. James Downs reports that a man on foot could perhaps shoot as many as seventeen rabbits in a day, but a skilled hunter accompanied by a family member or friend with a horse to haul the rabbits back home could take as many as fifty (82–83).

Women continued the life of the gatherer as much as possible. Piñon nuts were still accessible, and the edges of barley and wheat fields (and the fields themselves after harvesting) offered a significant quantity of seeds to a careful gatherer. Many women, however, sought employment within the new towns tending settlers' children, cooking, and doing laundry. It was the latter role that brought Louisa Keyser to the attention of the proprietor of a men's clothing shop in Carson City, Nevada.

The Basket Maker

Louisa Keyser, whose original name apparently was Dabuda, was born sometime around 1850 near the future town of Sheridan, Nevada, and was a member of the Washoe people of Nevada and eastern California. Her mother may have died giving birth to Dabuda, as no record of the mother has survived. Louisa identified her father's name as Da-da-u-on-ga-la. As a young girl she learned, along with cooking and other domestic duties, to find basket-making materials and make baskets (Gigli 5). She married Assu, with whom she had two children. Both died in childhood. Assu also died early, although no dates survive for any of these births or deaths. At this time Louisa was working for miners and their families cooking and doing laundry (Gigli 5).

Somewhere around 1888 Louisa married Charlie Keyser, who was a master arrow maker; it was at this time, according to Jane Green Gigli, that Dabuda took the name "Louisa Keyser" (5). Only one sibling, Jim Bryant, whose wife, Scees Bryant, would become a follower of Louisa's basket-making methods, lived into adulthood, although he also would predecease Louisa (Cohodas 130n.24).

Louisa's third name was Dat So La Lee, although when and under what circumstances this name arose remain unclear. Gigli has summarized the three main theories for the origin of the name: (1) that the name means "big hip," according to Abe Cohn, and thus was somewhat descriptive of

Louisa, who became quite heavy; (2) the claim by Dr. S.L. Lee, who had known Louisa for many years, that she had taken a version of his name out of friendship, with the difference in their names explained by Louisa's pronunciation; (3) that she was referred to as "LaLee," and would respond by saying "Dat's so! LaLee." Gigli points out that the third version was far less commonly offered than the others. Since it was not uncommon for a Washoe to take the name of an employer or friend, the second explanation seems most likely, especially since she would have been unlikely to choose a name that mocked her physical appearance (6–8). Regardless of the origin of "Dat So La Lee," she preferred "Louisa Keyser," although the Cohns used "Dat So La Lee," probably because the "Washoe" name was more useful for marketing purposes (Cohodas 107).

By the late 1890s, Louisa was working for Abe Cohn and Abe's wife, Amy, as a laundress and likely performing other household tasks as well. Abe was proprietor of the Cohn's Emporium Company men's clothing store in Carson City, Nevada. Skilled as an entrepreneur and marketer, Abe was branching out from clothing into the curio trade with a special interest in baskets. Local collectors such as the aforementioned Dr. Lee, the most respected physician in Carson City; and Eugene Mead, superintendent of the local Indian school, provided a ready market. Abe's perception of the marketing potential in Native baskets was abetted by Amy's growing interest in Native American culture. So when Louisa presented baskets for sale to Abe, both he and his wife recognized quickly her basket-making ability. The Cohns offered her an appealing deal given the level of poverty among the Washoes: she and her husband, Charlie, were offered a home, food, clothing, and medical care in exchange for Louisa's full-time and exclusive employment making baskets for Abe to sell. Louisa was to weave her baskets publicly, which would entice customers to purchase her baskets, and the baskets became Cohn property. She was to be, in more modern terms, the Cohns' resident artist. It was a deal she could not refuse, and it set her on the path to becoming one of the most honored basket makers in American history (Gigli 5; Cohodas 92–93).

Marketing Dat So La Lee

The Cohns recognized in Louisa an unusually creative artist. Louisa was influenced by the Pomo, who lived north of San Francisco, and the Maidu of California's Central Valley, both of whom were known for the quality of their baskets. Pomo basket makers excelled in baskets that included a variety of geometric designs in black and red along with creative stitching and, especially for gift baskets, shells and feathers (Yenne

129). The Maidu, once among the largest Native tribes in California, were denigrated by Captain Frémont and other white Americans, along with the Washoe and Paiute, as "Digger" Indians because they dug for roots and other plants to eat (Chaffin 237). Maidu baskets often have repeated symbolic patterns representing animals or plants. Some are conical in shape (Dixon 266–76). The creative innovation most associated with Louisa—the type of basket known as the *degikup*, which is defined by Cohodas as "a spheroid objet d'art, finely stitched with complex designs in red and black on a light background" (92)—reflects structurally the work of Maidu basket makers (Cohodas, "Washoe Basketweaving" 162). Undeterred by the decline of basketry occasioned by increased distribution of mass-produced containers on reservations and elsewhere, Louisa drew on traditional basket styles to develop her own creative vision. The growing tourist trade facilitated by the spread of railroads and the burgeoning interest in traditional arts and crafts served as counterweights to help arrest this declining focus on traditional crafts at the same time that Louisa was making herself increasingly valuable to the Cohns.

Louisa's *degikup* is a coiled basket with a small round base that expands considerably in the middle and concludes at the top with an opening equal in size to the bottom of the basket. She used light colored willow for her background and stitched (that is, wove in narrow strips to form designs) in black and red, drawing the black stitching from brown fern roots that were buried in mud for weeks and the red from the bark of the western redbud (Gigli 23–24). Complementing Louisa's skill in making baskets, as Makley has stated, was her "intimate knowledge of plants, growing conditions, and harvesting techniques" (Makley 25–26).

Louisa initially wove variations on the same pattern but by 1905 was varying her patterns considerably (Cohodas 104). She also varied the size of her baskets. The basket titled *Beacon Lights*, completed in 1905 and considered one of her masterpieces, was, at thirteen inches high, almost twice the normal size of her earlier baskets. At the other extreme were mini baskets that she began weaving as an occasional break while working on large baskets and regularly gave to Amy Cohn as gifts.

The result of this artistry, as Marvin Cohodas has stated, was that "Louisa Keyser single-handedly transformed Washoe weaving, establishing many of the directions the new curio style would take" ("Washoe Basketweaving" 162). Elsewhere Cohodas writes: "Louisa Keyser thus deserves credit for originating the popular curio style of Washoe fancy basket weaving, both because she introduced the finely stitched, two-color *degikup* and because she inaugurated individuality and innovation for others to follow" (105). Makley adds similar praise: "Widely acknowledged by collectors and scholars alike as the work of true genius, her productions pushed Washoe

Louisa Keyser, also known as Dat So La Lee, poses between two of her master-pieces, *Light Reflected* (left) and *Hunting Game in a Proscribed District* (Nevada Historical Society).

basketry into a new realm, one that existed at the confluence of tradition and assimilation" (100).

One would think that the Cohns would have been delighted with Louisa's creativity, and they were. However, they also decided that they had to hide the fact of her innovations beneath the cloak of tradition. Tourists, adherents of the Arts and Crafts Movement, and collectors of various sorts wanted tradition, curios that reflected the past—a past romantically re-envisioned as the era of the brave warrior and his Native princess—not an impoverished contemporary culture. So the Cohns had to find a way to benefit from the innovative, creative, nontraditional artwork of Louisa Keyser while presenting her very original creations as the products of past tradition. It was fundamentally a marketing strategy that the Cohns needed to develop, one that fit the bifurcated vision of the Native American held by a great swath of the white population. This dual vision is even present in written accounts of Louisa by Amy Cohn herself and others. Louisa, as photographs show, was quite heavy and dressed very simply. Weight, of course, has nothing to do with intelligence or creativity, but where Louisa was concerned there was much drawing of contrasts as if of something most unusual, that an individual who looked like Louisa could create such beautiful baskets. Amy Cohn, writing in 1900, describes Louisa as possessing "child-like blandness" and acting in childlike ways but also possessing perfect hands and great artistic ability. Writing in *New West* in 1912, Clara McNaughton marvels "'that such delicacy of touch and artistic creative genius could dwell in such a tenement'" (Cohodas 116).

A Fake Biography

This desire for a marketing strategy led to a falsification of Louisa Keyser's life that would endure and be promulgated in almost all written accounts of her life for decades, and even, to some extent, until the present. The most important correction to the falsification of Louisa's life has come through the work of Marvin Cohodas, especially in his deeply researched "Louisa Keyser and the Cohns: Mythmaking and Basket Making in the American West," an article already referred to several times in this account of Louisa Keyser and the basis for the following discussion of ways in which her life was falsified. Concerning what the Cohns asserted about Louisa, Coholdas argues, with convincing evidence, that they said little that was true (94). These false "facts" of her life were easy to make stick because Louisa did not read or write, so she offered no written account of her life; and she was a generally reticent individual who was not about to share her life story with a lot of people. In addition, the biography that the

Cohns fabricated meshed with two realities of Louisa's non–Native con-
temporaries: (1) they knew little of actual Native American history and culture and (2) they viewed Native peoples largely within a vision populated
by stereotypes.

So the Cohns offered to the public a basket maker who alone among
the Washoes carried with her the Washoe basket-making tradition, the
result of a Paiute victory over the Washoes in battle that led to a Paiute
prohibition on Washoe basket making. Abe Cohn, however, supposedly
guaranteed protection to Louisa so that she could carry on this forbidden
tradition that she had inherited as the daughter of a great Washoe chief
and the recipient of her mother's position as medicine woman of the Washoes. Louisa therefore was not only an Indian princess (an image that many
whites loved) but also a revered medicine woman with all of the spiritual
attributes and arcane knowledge that such a position was held to include. It
mattered not at all to the Cohns that such a battle with its prohibition had
never occurred, or that Louisa's father was not a chief; in fact, the Washoes did not have chiefs. As for her mother, the Cohns had no idea who she
had been. The myth of the mysterious basket maker fit nicely, though, with
the growing desire for traditional Native artifacts while also merging into
the dual view of Native Americans past and present previously mentioned.
Unlike the many poverty-ridden individuals of the present, Louisa embodied a nobler age and offered a small piece of that traditional artistry and
nobility to those who purchased her baskets from the Cohns. The concept
of the Indian princess so appealed to Amy Cohn that she would dress up as
one to lecture about Native culture, on occasion with Louisa posing in the
background with her baskets. Louisa's name in the publications that Amy
wrote and during the whole marketing enterprise, despite her preference
for her English name, was consistently Dat So La Lee, which fit much better
into the myth that the Cohns had woven (101–06, 113).

As Louisa's baskets began to sell, Amy composed a certificate for each
basket that included an explanation of its symbolism and started writing
pamphlets about Louisa's creations for the Emporium Company around
1900. Much later, Cohodas suggests about 1918 (99), Amy began to keep a
ledger to record information about the baskets. This record-keeping exercise is valuable as it offers data on when the baskets were created. However, much of the information is fabricated, not just dates—which could
be somewhat excused as an honest but faulty effort after the fact to recall
creation dates—but also the meaning of the designs that Louisa wove into
the baskets. Amy, unsatisfied with a description of the aesthetic nature of
the designs, imposed on them cultural and historical meanings that Louisa had never intended, meanings that often did not at all fit the actual culture and history of the Washoes. The designs, for example, were said to

include a family crest that never existed, and often were interpreted by Amy as referring to scenes of war and religious rituals that, as Marvin Cohodas has pointed out, refer to male activities that women would not have woven into domestic objects such as baskets (111). Interpreting the meaning of Louisa's designs would be fraught with uncertainty even with the best of intentions. Gigli mentions that the ethnologist S.A. Barrett in 1915 surveyed Washoe basketry and concluded that the designs were mainly decorative rather than symbolic. However, Gigli also recognizes that artists "are influenced by nature's own patterns" but cautions that one should be wary of "meanings read into primitive works by sophisticated viewers" (11). That there is "meaning" within Louisa's basket patterns seems most likely, but Amy used considerable creative projection in describing such meanings.

The Cohns even manipulated Louisa Keyser's age in order to create an image that would serve their marketing interests. The story that they concocted had Louisa meeting the explorer Captain John C. Frémont in 1844 and receiving brass buttons from him as an apology for a horse belonging to one of his soldiers having kicked Louisa's nephew. In addition, as Abe continued developing this narrative of Louisa's meeting with Tremont, he claimed that not long before Louisa died she took him to the spot in Eagle Valley where this incident supposedly occurred. In order to make this meeting with Tremont possible, her birth was moved back to 1829 from the already false date of 1834 previously stated by Amy Cohn. The 1829 date would have made Louisa past sixty-five when she began making baskets for the Cohns and close to the century mark at her death. The consensus today is that she probably was born about 1850 plus or minus a few years (Cohodas 122–23).

The biographical revising of Louisa's life also posits an earlier relationship between Louisa, then known as Dabuda, and the Cohn family. According to this fictional narrative, Abe's father, Harris Cohn, who owned a general store in Monitor, California, hired Louisa to help around the house and take care of Abe, then a child. Again Cohodas sets the record straight, drawing on some earlier sleuthing by Norton Stern as reported in the *Western States Jewish Historical Quarterly* in 1983. Stern discovered that the elder Cohn did not own a store in Monitor. Cohodas adds that Louisa was only a few years older than Abe and therefore an unlikely choice to tend the child. Also, earlier accounts in the Emporium publications claimed that the Cohns had not met Louisa prior to employing her to handle their laundry (123).

Despite all of the false reporting that the Cohns engaged in, Louisa and Amy Cohn were quite friendly. Louisa gave Amy gifts of many baskets, especially the miniature baskets that became part of Amy's collection of miniatures. Louisa seemed to be fine with traveling with the Cohns, especially with Amy. The two women traveled together to Tahoe City,

California, on the western shore of Lake Tahoe in 1900 to display Louisa's baskets. Later that summer, they went to the California State Fair in Sacramento and the Nevada State Fair in Reno on marketing ventures. Louisa's baskets were subsequently featured in a San Francisco magazine, *The Saturday Wave*. These efforts proved so successful that Amy brought Louisa back to Tahoe City in 1903 to open a curio store called The Bicose. These joint marketing efforts continued, including a trip to the Industrial Arts Exposition in St. Louis in 1919. Louisa apparently was a willing participant, if largely a silent one, in Amy's lectures on Washoe culture. At times, Amy would dress as an Indian princess and lecture on Washoe baskets and culture, concluding her presentation by bringing Louisa onstage for a *tableau vivant* (Cohodas 96–98, 113–14, 126).

It was not unusual for white and Native American women to develop close relationships, even approaching the emotional level of sisters. As Glenda Riley has documented in her *Women and Indians on the Frontier, 1825–1915*, frontier women not only engaged in commercial transactions with Native women but also hired them as nursemaids for their children, a relationship similar to what Abe Cohn falsely ascribed to Louisa. Such a relationship obviously evinced a high level of trust on the part of those who so employed Native women. Many of the nursemaids taught their charges a great deal about their own customs and culture, and the children for their part often developed great affection for the women who took care of them. The giving of presents was a normal activity between white and Native women who formed friendships, as occurred in the relationship between Louisa and Amy. These sorts of close relationships were far more common between frontier women and Native American women than between males, with frontier men tending to continue seeing Native males as adversaries even when no hostilities existed between them (173–78).

The marketing strategies, coupled with Louisa's genuine talent and her position as essentially a full-time basket maker, did create a large and rich market for her baskets and a sufficiently large enough supply of baskets to at least partly satisfy the demand for them. Abram Cohn's records indicate that she created 120 large baskets and enough miniature baskets to total about 300 overall (Gigli 6). Louisa's baskets, as Makley states, "directly fueled the local Indian arts market and eventually spread well beyond the eastern Sierra, attracting the interest of wealthy collectors from around the United States." Among those collectors was Gotlieb Adam Steiner of Pennsylvania, who purchased *Beacon Lights*, often considered her finest masterpiece, in 1914 for $2000. The purchase made national news, with the *San Francisco Examiner* of April 4, 1914, labeling the price the highest ever for a Nevada basket. Steiner added to his collection two years later with two more of Louisa's baskets (98).

The Enduring Legacy

Amy died in 1919, shortly after the St. Louis trip. The Bicose closed the same year. The following year, Abe married Margaret Jones, a woman with far less interest in Native American culture generally and basket making specifically than Amy had possessed. Abe maintained his business relationship with Louisa, apparently without much involvement by Margaret. Always the marketer, Abe arranged for a film to be made of Louisa gathering materials for her baskets and weaving them in 1922. The famous photographer Edward Curtis photographed Louisa in 1925 as well as Louisa's basket-making grand-niece, Tootsie Dick (Cohodas, "Washoe Basketweaving" 162). On December 6 of that year, Louisa, after suffering from dropsy, died with Charlie by her side in their Carson City home. She was buried in the Stewart Indian School Cemetery. Her husband died three years later. Abe continued to sell Louisa's baskets, even decorating the outside of a new store specializing in Native American objects, the Kit Carson Curio Store, that he established in Carson City in 1928, with a large mural of Louisa. Abe died in 1934, and his widow continued to operate the store into the mid–1940s in order to sell off the remaining merchandise. Louisa's remaining baskets were finally sold in 1944 and 1945, after which Margaret closed down the business.

Louisa Keyser, more broadly known to the public as Dat So La Lee, left behind no written account of her life and creative career. In fact, what written account was left for future generations has been found, as indicated above, to have been almost completely false. What has survived, however, is the creativity embodied in the baskets that she wove. A plaque at the cemetery in Carson County, Nevada, where she is buried states, "GATHERING WILLOW, FERN AND BIRCH WITH THE AID OF HER HUSBAND, SHE WOVE INTO HER MASTERPIECES THE LEGENDS OF HER PEOPLE AND THEIR LOVE OF NATURE. HER BASKETS ARE UNSURPASSED FOR ARTISTIC CONCEPTION AND SYMBOLIC IMPORTANCE."

Dixie Westergard provides a partial list of museums in which Keyser's baskets can be viewed: the Field Museum in Chicago, Yale University Museum, Nevada State Museum, Carnegie Museum in Pittsburgh, Nevada Historical Society, and Smithsonian Institution (39–41).

Louisa surely never saw herself as a leader, perhaps not an artist either, although she was both. Her creative, original contributions to the making of baskets have been, and remain, her legacy. The artist still lives in the art. And that art, if not priceless, is highly valued in monetary terms as well as for the creativity that went into it—and for its historical importance within the tradition of basket making. In 1978, four of her baskets were stolen from the Nevada Historical Society Museum in Reno. One of the baskets was found within two years, but the other three did not turn up until twenty years after the theft. Louisa Keyser's baskets, upon their retrieval, were valued at as much as $300,000 each (Hebert). Such a sum surely would have shocked Louisa Keyser. Most likely the continued artistic and historical value placed on her baskets also would have amazed her. Amy and Abe Cohn saw something special in the baskets woven by this Washoe woman, and even their attempt to hide the degree of her originality and creativity under the veneer of tradition could not obscure her extraordinary accomplishments.

NOTE

    1. Except when otherwise indicated, references to Marvin Cohodas are to his article "Louisa Keyser and the Cohns: Mythmaking and Basket Making in the American West."

REFERENCES

Adovasio, J.M. "Prehistoric North American Basketry." *Collected Papers on Aboriginal Basketry*. Ed. Donald R. Tuohy and Doris L. Rendall. 1974. Carson City: Nevada State Museum, 1984. 98–148.

Chaffin, Tom. *Pathfinder: John Charles Fremont and the Course of American Empire*. New York: Hill and Wang, 2001.

Cohodas, Marvin. "Louisa Keyser and the Cohns: Mythmaking and Basket Making in the American West." *The Early Years of Native American Art History: The Politics of Scholarship and Collecting*. Ed. Janet Catherine Berlo. Seattle: U of Washington P, 1992. 88–133.

_____. "Washoe Basketweaving: A Historical Outline." *The Art of Native American Basketry: A Living Legacy*. Ed. Frank W. Porter III. Westport, CT: Greenwood P, 1990. 153–86.

Dixon, Roland B. "Designs of the Maidu Indians of California." *American Anthropologist* New Series 2 (1900): 266–76.

Downs, James F. *The Two Worlds of the Washo: An Indian Tribe of California and Nevada*. New York: Holt, Rinehart and Winston, 1966.

Gigli, Jane Green. "Dat So La Lee: Queen of the Washo Basket Makers." 1967. *Collected Papers on Aboriginal Basketry*. Ed. Donald R. Tuohy and Doris L. Rendall. Carson City: Nevada State Museum, 1974. 1–27.

Hebert, Linda. "Dat So La Lee." V.I. Reed & Cane. basketweaving.com.

Kaplan, Wendy. *"The Art That Is Life": The Arts & Crafts Movement in America, 1875–1920*. 1987. Boston: Bullfinch P, 1998.

Makley, Matthew S. *The Small Shall Be Strong: A History of Lake Tahoe's Washoe Indians*. Amherst: U of Massachusetts P, 2018.

Orr, Phil C. "Notes on the Archaeology of the Winnemucca Caves, 1952–58." *Collected Papers on Aboriginal Basketry*. Ed. Donald R. Tuohy and Doris L. Rendall. Carson City: Nevada State Museum, 1974. 47–59.

Riley, Glenda. *Women and Indians on the Frontier, 1825–1915*. Albuquerque: U of New Mexico P, 1984.

Stern, Norton B. "Abram Cohn of Carson City, Nevada, Patron of Dat-so-la-lee." *Western States Jewish Historical Quarterly* 15.4 (1983): 291–97.

Turner, Erin. "Dat So La Lee." *Wise Women: From Pocahontas to Sarah Winnemucca, Remarkable Stories of Native American Trailblazers*. Guilford, CT: Two Dot, 2009. 12–20.

Westergard, Dixie. *Dat-So-La-Lee: Washo Indian Basketmaker*. 1999 (place and publisher not given).

Yenne, Bill. *The Encyclopedia of North American Indian Tribes: A Comprehensive Study of Tribes from the Abitibi to the Zuni*. 1998. East Bridgewater, MA: JG Press, 1998.

4

Susette La Flesche (Inshtatheamba, Bright Eyes) (1854–1903)

Susette La Flesche was born at a time when her people, the Omahas, were encountering a mammoth change in their world and therefore facing life-altering choices, none of the choices seemingly good. Born to the last tribally chosen chief of the Omahas, Susette quickly found herself between and within two very different worlds. She spent her life attempting to chart her course within these worlds while always committed to trying to help her Omaha people. Even when she seemed most to have adopted the customs, attitudes, and even the dress of whites, she retained her self-identity as Omaha and worked to bring peace, justice, and opportunity to her people.

Some of Susette La Flesche's decisions, with the wisdom of hindsight, can readily be seen as questionable if not completely wrong. Certainly, some of what she came to espouse proved ultimately to be counterproductive to the Omahas. Yet also with the wisdom of hindsight one can see that at times she made choices that appeared to her to offer the only way forward. However right or wrong she was, Susette La Flesche led a life of great courage and dedication, giving of herself emotionally and physically to right the wrongs inflicted upon her people and to direct them onto the only path that she could see offering hope.

Susette La Flesche was intellectually brilliant and enormously talented. She excelled as an orator, advocate, artist, and journalist at a time when it was almost impossible to imagine a Native American woman in those roles. She was a person of great passion and moral vision, determined to give herself to the cause of justice. An individual should be judged not only within the broad sweep of history but also within the context of her times. From the latter perspective especially, Susette La Flesche deserves to be remembered and honored as a true heroine.

The Old World

The world into which Susette La Flesche was born in 1854 was still largely, but only briefly, the world that the Omahas had occupied for hundreds of years. The Omaha country as identified by commissioners appointed by the Secretary of War in 1834 ran from the Platte River north to the Niobrara River, with the Missouri River on the east and Pawnee territory toward the west. It was a vast tract of land comprising much of present-day northeastern Nebraska. Omahas still hunted buffalo and followed traditional rituals, among them the Turning of the Child ceremony for a child who had reached a sufficient age to walk, to speak, and to understand at least a little of what was occurring. Susette underwent the ceremony, which, among other rituals, involved being lifted and faced consecutively in all four directions in order to be prepared for her journey through life. She received new moccasins symbolizing the beginning of her journey. She also received a new name, Inshtatheamba, which means "Bright Eyes" (Wilson 2–6). The English translation would be the name by which she would become famous. How much of the ceremony she remembered is not known, but her identity as Omaha remained fixed in her despite the many modernizing changes that she would undergo.

Susette's half-brother, Francis, would later write in a book about his time attending the local mission school and how the Omahas in those days still lived in traditional dome-shaped earth lodges, spent their infancy in cradle boards, were trained to speak the Omaha language correctly, and learned to follow Omaha principles of courtesy and respect (xvi–xvii). However, change was coming, for in the year of Susette's birth the Omahas agreed to a treaty with the United States government in which they ceded most of their traditional land, retaining approximately 330,000 acres, mainly in what today is Thurston County, Nebraska, for their reservation. That land total would be sharply reduced as the century progressed.

That Susette would come to incorporate multiple cultures into her own life is unsurprising given her multicultural heritage. Susette's mother, Mary Gale, was the daughter of an Omaha-Iowa woman, Nicomi, and an army surgeon, Dr. John Gale. Gale left his wife but before his death established a trust fund for Nicomi and her daughter, instructing a friend, Peter Sarpy, to administer it. Sarpy subsequently built a house for them and later married Nicomi (Wilson 8–10).

Susette's father, Joseph La Flesche, had a French father also named Joseph who was a trader for the Hudson Bay Company. His mother, Watunna, was either an Omaha or Ponca, two closely related tribes whose interaction would lead to Susette's entry into activism on behalf of Native Americans and establish her fame. The younger Joseph worked for Peter

Sarpy at Sarpy's trading post at Bellevue, the site of the Omahas' principal village south of the current city of Omaha, where he met Mary Gale. Joseph spent much time among the Omahas, although he also traveled with his father hunting, fishing, and trading while learning the languages of several Indigenous peoples. He became steadily committed to the Omahas and concerned about their future survival. Named Inshtámaza in Omaha, which means "Iron Eye," Joseph associated closely with the Omaha chief, Big Elk, learning from him and earning his respect and admiration as a hunter, trader, warrior, and interpreter. Big Elk formally adopted Joseph, declaring him his eldest son (Big Elk's natural son being in ill health) and successor. Upon Big Elk's death in 1853, Joseph became the principal chief (Wilson 8–17).

Joseph and Mary had five children: Louis (1848), Susette (1854), Rosalie (1861), Marguerite (1862), and Susan (1865), the latter becoming a highly regarded physician serving her Omaha people. Joseph also had two sons and a daughter by a second wife, Tainne (multiple wives being acceptable in Omaha culture): Francis (1857), Lucy (1865), and Carey (1872). According to Dorothy Clarke Wilson, Tainne also had given birth to a daughter who did not survive; and Joseph much earlier had been married to an Otoe woman who, along with her son, had died (68, 72).

No Good Options

While Susette was growing up, her father, Joseph, was choosing among options, that, as would soon be the case with his eldest daughter, offered no truly good solutions. What Joseph saw about him was a changing world in which his Omahas faced great problems that called their very existence into question. Land to the west had been opened to homesteaders, whose appetite for land was readily visible and growing. Buffalo were heading toward apparent extinction, and the Poncas (closely related to the Omahas) were virtually starving. In 1863, Washington authorized removing the Winnebagos from Minnesota, transferring a large northern portion of Omaha land to them. Two years later, the lower house of the Nebraska Territorial Legislature voted to move all Native Americans out of the territory, a step never completed but that contributed to the precarious nature of Omaha life.

Joseph had traveled widely enough among whites to understand the military power that they possessed as well as their numbers and wealth. So amid the changes that were occurring, he had to decide whether to cling to the old ways or seek accommodation with the new. Would it be better for his people to resist change or embrace at least some of it? Joseph chose the latter approach.

Shortly after replacing Big Elk as the principal chief of the Omahas, Joseph traveled to Washington, D.C., with other Omaha chiefs and tribal leaders to sign the treaty of 1854. The Omahas were to receive annual payments ranging from $40,000 down to $10,000 for forty years, with the President, however, able at his discretion to determine how much would be paid in money and how much in goods and services, a provision that offered endless freedom to shortchange the Omahas. Other benefits stipulated in the treaty included moving expenses for the Omahas to relocate farther north, a grist and sawmill, a blacksmith shop, and continuation of the mission school run by the Presbyterian church with a new school building to be constructed on the much-reduced reservation (treaty reprinted in Giffen, 11–23). Actually receiving the money promised, however, would prove difficult (Wilson 18).

Having agreed to the treaty, Joseph, who apparently discerned no viable option to agreeing, set out to remake Omaha life in order, as he saw it, for his people to compete in a white-dominated world. Perhaps his strongest reform was in the area of education. He believed that Omahas would not be able to live productively in the changing world without becoming educated in the subjects taught in the mission school, including, of course, reading and writing English, which Joseph himself was not able to do (Wilson 23–33).

Susette meanwhile was passing through childhood between two cultures. As was the case with Joseph's other children, she went to school, attending the mission school on the reservation. Her responses to school were mixed. She did quite well academically, mastering English, learning to write well, drawing with considerable skill, and so enjoying reading that books were, as Wilson writes, "her closest companions" (91). Yet she was shocked upon seeing her older brother Louis with his hair cut short and dressed in white people's clothes (Wilson 30). Louis would die while still a student at the school in 1860. The death understandably had a profound effect on Susette and the entire family. Years later, she would write of his death in *Oo-mah-ha Ta-wa-tha*, describing how their father lay all night cradling his dead son in his arms and seemed never to be the same again (Giffen 64–67).

Susette was caught in the middle of two worlds, liking some from each but still very much considering herself an Omaha. Wilson notes that she was Susette La Flesche, the name she was called at school, dressed in a calico skirt and long-sleeved blouse for six days per week; on Saturdays, she returned home as Inshta Theamba, or Bright Eyes, doing chores around the house and helping to watch her younger siblings. On school holidays, she liked to visit Memetage, her grandmother Nicomi's half-sister, who still largely lived in the old way. There, in Memetage's lodge, she could be Inshta

Theamba, for from the first she had not much liked the large square house her father had built (Wilson 28, 49, 72).

An important turning point for both Susette and her father occurred in 1866 or 1867 when it was suggested to Joseph that he surely was qualified to become an honorary chief in the Honhewachi order, and that his eldest daughter should be made a Nikagahi wa-u, which is a woman chief. Joseph initially agreed, and the four-day ceremony began.

Alice C. Fletcher, an ethnologist specializing in Native American culture and holder of the Thaw fellowship at Harvard's Peabody Museum of Archaeology and Ethnology, and Francis La Flesche, who also became an ethnologist and, in addition to collaborating with Fletcher, worked as an anthropologist in the Smithsonian's Bureau of American Ethnology from 1910 until 1929, describe in detail the Honhewachi in their monumental *The Omaha Tribe*, which comprises most of the *Twenty-Seventh Annual Report of the Bureau of American Ethnology* for 1905–06 (493–509).

Admission to the Honhewachi was limited to men who had accomplished at least one hundred laudatory "acts and gifts," especially "those benefiting the tribe and those made to a very poor man or woman." The order involved more than extraordinary charitable behavior, however, for it also had a deep philosophical underpinning of a cosmic perspective on people's very existence. The name of the order etymologically refers to "in the night" and "dance," the latter in the sense of "dramatic rhythmic movements for the expression of personal emotion or experience, or for the presentation of mythical teachings." Night (including nighttime's heavenly bodies) is viewed as representative of the feminine cosmic force and therefore the creative force. Day and the sun represent the masculine cosmic force, having been given birth by night.

The man chosen to be admitted to the Honhewachi would choose a young woman to have tattooed on her body symbols of night and day, and she would become a Nikagahi wa-u. For both Susette and her father, the tattooing of her would prove to be the most consequential detail of the entire ceremony and a reflection of the type of choices that both made regarding the two worlds in which they were living. According to Dorothy Clarke Wilson's account, the ceremony was well along before Susette learned of the tattooing. It happened on the night before Susette would undergo the procedure when Memetage pointed to the spot on her forehead and showed Susette the star extending from her throat to her chest. That night, the young woman determined to go through with the ritual, accepting the "mark of honor" if it would help her people, a goal that she would never lose. Her father, though, was having serious second thoughts, and they were directed more toward his daughter's future than toward the honor that he would ultimately reject. He realized that his daughter would have to live "in a white man's world" and should not be permanently and visibly marked with symbols of the past. Once Joseph made his decision known, the ceremony ended. It was obviously a decision that angered the more traditionalist of the Omahas, although it was made by a man who still revered many aspects of Omaha culture but also looked with open eyes at what the future held (100–02). And it would be a decision that had great ramifications for Susette.

Susette as Bright Eyes the Orator

Susette La Flesche's formal education seemed to be coming to an end with the closing of the mission

Susette La Flesche (Bright Eyes) dressed in modern Eastern attire but always Omaha at heart (courtesy Nebraska State Historical Society Photograph Collections).

school in 1869. Funds were withdrawn from the Presbyterian school and education was to be provided henceforth at day schools under the control of the government. These schools, however, were designed only for younger students, so Susette, in her middle teens, was too old to qualify. Her love for reading and learning remained unabated, though, and it was supported, despite the unavailability of formal education for Susette, by the Rev. William Hamilton, a longtime friend of her father who, despite the missionaries having been ordered to leave the reservation, remained. His library, though not extensive, he made available to Susette, who devoured the Bible and Shakespeare as well as theological works that Hamilton owned. Then a former teacher of hers, Miss Nettie C. Read, who at the time was teaching at the Elizabeth Institute for Young Ladies in Elizabeth, New Jersey, informed Susette that she had recruited people to pay for her education at the Elizabeth Institute (Wilson 107–11).

Little has been documented concerning Susette's time at the Elizabeth

Institute, which has since closed, but her success there is demonstrated by her graduating with honors and receiving two books as awards: *Yesterdays with Authors* (1872) by James T. Fields, and *Personal Reminiscences of Cornelia Knight and Thomas Raikes* (1875), edited by Richard Henry Stoddard, both inscribed from "N.C. Read," who had become the school's principal. Neither book has anything to do with Susette's Omaha background, but they symbolize her academic achievements and also were surely valued as reading material by a woman who loved reading but had the opportunity to acquire few books. Read, very much a friend and mentor beyond the confines of the school, had welcomed Susette into her home to spend vacations (Wilson 116–17). By the time of Susette's return to Nebraska in 1875, she had acquired a strong "modern education" and appeared very much a cultivated Eastern woman in her early twenties.

Nonetheless, Susette's desire to help her people had not waned, and she attempted to put her education to work teaching. A teaching opportunity arose in Indian Territory, an area originally comprising present-day Kansas, Nebraska, Oklahoma, and part of Iowa but gradually reduced until it consisted of approximately the eastern half of current Oklahoma before being consolidated with Oklahoma Territory to form the state of Oklahoma in 1907. Susette received a job offer but after her father's initial support, opposition from Two Crows, such a close friend of Joseph's that Susette viewed him as an uncle, vetoed her accepting the position. She was more successful in acquiring a position on the Omaha Reservation after pointing out to Indian Bureau authorities that reservation rules called for preferring a qualified Omaha over a white person for positions. Her hiring in 1877 did not occur, though, until she had passed an examination to earn a teaching certificate from Nebraska and a certificate of good character (Wilson 121, 131–32, 145–46). As a teacher, she earned $20 per month and was given a somewhat dilapidated house as a day school. She usually slept in the building, kept it up, and added Sunday School to increase her modest earnings, out of which she purchased an organ in order to add music to the curriculum (Green 49).

While Susette was teaching, continued change was coming to the Omahas and to Native Americans in general. The Omahas went on a buffalo hunt in 1876. Joseph had only reluctantly approved the continuation of the hunts, realizing that the buffalo, which had supplied so much that was both life- and spirit-sustaining to Native Americans, appeared to be rapidly approaching extinction and that the Omahas would have to turn elsewhere for what they needed to meet their daily needs. The hunt proved terribly unsuccessful as the Omahas found many dead buffalo but no live ones. It would be their final buffalo hunt.

At the same time, Omaha tribal government was disintegrating.

Joseph, no longer the Omaha leader, was the last true Omaha chief. Leadership had devolved to a small number of chiefs controlled by the resident agent. Poverty and hunger afflicted the Omahas, who nevertheless remained peaceful. Not so every tribe, as the Battle of Little Big Horn in that same year demonstrated. Such a battle, however, would not be the Omaha way.

As bad as the situation was for the Omahas, it was even more dire for the Poncas, a reality that would lead Susette into internationally recognized activism on behalf of the Poncas and to lasting fame as Bright Eyes. The Poncas were closely related to the Omahas and historically agrarian and peaceful. They had migrated from the Midwest into present-day southern South Dakota and northern Nebraska. In 1858, the Poncas agreed to cede to the United States most of the lands that they claimed in return for an area between the Niobrara River and Ponca Creek (a tributary of the Missouri River) in northern Nebraska. They also were to receive annual payments varying from $12,000 to $8,000 for a period of thirty years. Other provisions included $20,000 to support them for their first year on their new reservation, schools, and various shops and mills. A contemporary history of the Poncas occurs in Helen Hunt Jackson's *A Century of Dishonor* (97–113).

For the Poncas, life continued to become more difficult. In 1868, the federal government, apparently inadvertently, included the Ponca Reservation in land given to the Sioux, a traditional enemy of both the Poncas and Omahas. With Sioux attacks on Poncas increasing, the government decided to move the Poncas to Indian Territory. The forced move occurred in 1877 although no preparation had occurred in the new land for the Poncas. Many died amid extremely difficult living conditions, including an outbreak of malaria. Then in January 1879, a band of about thirty Poncas led by one of their chiefs, Standing Bear, left Indian Territory for Nebraska, seeking refuge with the Omahas. Accompanying Standing Bear in a box was the body of his son, who had recently died. Standing Bear wished to bury him at home among family members who had previously passed. They reached the Omaha Reservation in March more than three months after starting off on their journey. Joseph welcomed the tired and hungry refugees, but any security that the Poncas may have felt among the Omahas soon vanished as Secretary of the Interior Carl Schurz ordered General George Crook, a veteran "Indian fighter" but also an individual generally sympathetic to the plight of Native Americans, to arrest Standing Bear and his party preliminary to returning them to Indian Country (Wilson 156–63).

Here is where Susette La Flesche's life began to take a new and remarkable turn. Susette had responded sympathetically and angrily when the Poncas had been compelled to leave their homeland in 1877. She wrote to the Commissioner of Indian Affairs, Ezra Hayt, objecting to the power of the federal government to order Native Americans to go wherever the government wished with no right of appeal. This would be far from the only letter that Susette wrote to government officials, as she addressed additional complaints regarding actions against Omahas as well as Poncas to the President of the United States, Secretary of the Interior Schurz, and Commissioner Hayt (Wilson 150–53).

After Thomas Henry Tibbles, then assistant editor of the Omaha *Herald*, with at least indirect encouragement from General Crook, had solicited attorneys John L. Webster, former president of the Nebraska Constitutional Convention, and A.J. Poppleton, the attorney for the Union Pacific Railroad, to take up the Poncas' cause, Tibbles received from Susette a letter chronicling the relevant details of the Poncas' plight (Wilson 168–80). In May, Susette would pen another important letter, this one on behalf of the Poncas still on their reservation after she and her father had visited them to ascertain their condition. The letter, ostensibly from White Eagle, the Poncas' head chief, but actually written by Susette, was addressed to Tibbles and the lawyers authorizing them to represent the remaining Poncas (Wilson 204–05).

Susette's attitude toward whites during the campaign to rescue the Poncas demonstrates an extraordinary ability to be argumentatively powerful, politically astute, philosophical, and diplomatic at the same time, an ability that would soon stand her in good stead during her speaking tours of the East and Great Britain. Tibbles published a book originally titled *The Ponca Chiefs: An Account of the Trial of Standing Bear* (later republished as *Standing Bear and the Ponca Chiefs*) in 1880, with Susette writing the introduction under the byline "Inshtatheamba (Bright Eyes)." She states in the introduction that she wishes that every home might have a copy of Tibbles' book, for "people are the power which move the magistrates who administer the laws." She laments that "for years the petitions of my people have gone up unnoticed, unheeded by all but their Creator," but now someone of the readers' race (Tibbles) has arisen "to arouse the nation from the sin of its indifference." She immediately thanks God that it has been indifference, not hatred, which has kept from "an oppressed and unfortunate race, justice and mercy" (3–4). She gives the oppressors the benefit of the doubt. It is not hatred, or, as one might say, racism, but indifference. What people need to do is to start paying attention and therefore caring. They are not evil people, but people who have not been watching. By this time Susette has lived among whites, gone through their schools, visited their homes, and spent her still young life absorbing the directives of her father regarding how to live in a future world. The attitude expressed toward them appears to be a sincere attempt to see things as they are from her perspective even if that is not how they are in reality.

Tibbles meanwhile has become in some respects the indispensable man for the Poncas. His background was diverse and rich in experiences. He was born near Athens, Ohio, on May 22, 1840, into a family that included nine children; at the age of eleven, then living in Iowa, he ran away from an existence as a bound apprentice. He later was involved in the Abolitionist movement, lived with several Native American tribes, studied at Mount Union College in Ohio, married Amelia Owen, became a newspaperman, then a Methodist minister, then a newspaperman again. In the latter role he entered into the battle to secure at least a measure of freedom for the Poncas (Wilson 167–77). At the age of sixty-five in 1905, he wrote his autobiography, covering the years from his birth to the early 1890s. The book, however, was not published until 1957 as *Buckskin and Blanket Days: Memoirs of a Friend of the Indians* after being edited by Theodora Bates Cogswell, who as a child had known Tibbles, and whose brother had married Tibbles' daughter Eda. Tibbles died in 1928, about a week before his eighty-eighth birthday.

The attorneys that Tibbles had recruited issued a petition for *habeas corpus* against General Crook with eight Poncas including standing Bear signing it with their marks. Standing Bear was the chief plaintiff. A writ of *habeas corpus* is brought to attain the release of a person or persons from unlawful restraint. The general legal view at the time was that Native Americans did not have standing to bring such a writ, or, indeed, to take any legal action against the government, for only "persons" as defined in law could make such legal challenges.

The issue was to be decided before Judge Elmer Scipio Dundy, a United States District Judge for the District of Nebraska from 1868 until his death in 1896. On the eve of the trial, which began on April 30, 1879, Susette first met Tibbles. She later visited his home and met his wife, Amelia, and their daughters, May and Eda (Wilson 187–88). A highlight of the trial was a speech by Standing Bear after the closing arguments, briefly summarized in *Standing Bear and the Ponca Chiefs* (93). Standing Bear's earlier testimony was translated by W.W. Hamilton (79–90).

Judge Dundy's decision, filed on May 12, was a landmark decision, although in the short term it had a limited impact on government behavior toward Native Americans. He found that the *habeas corpus* act defines participants as "persons" or "parties" rather than as "citizens." He points out that according to standard usage, a "person" is any human being. Finally, he declares conclusively that the plaintiffs are "persons" and therefore included within the meaning and application of the *habeas corpus* law. The writ, therefore, he says, was "properly issued" and that the Poncas are within the jurisdiction of the law. Then, applying the "right of expatriation" possessed by all people, Judge Dundy declares that the Poncas have the right to leave the reservation and live elsewhere. As a result, Standing Bear and his associates must be released from custody (the decision reprinted in *Standing Bear and the Ponca Chiefs* 95–111).

This victory, though, was a small step in the larger battle to achieve true freedom for Native peoples. In June, Tibbles traveled East to lecture and raise funds to support a legal battle to allow the Poncas, Omahas, and other tribes to live where they wished. While Tibbles was absent, Susette received an invitation from the Omaha Ponca Committee, a group of ministers and other citizens organized to support the Ponca cause, to speak at Bishop Clarkson's Episcopal Church in Omaha. Despite her considerable reluctance to speak before a large group, Susette accepted the invitation. Tibbles had returned in time to attend her presentation. Although she was extremely apprehensive about speaking and, in Wilson's words, had "broken down" from the emotion that she felt regarding the sufferings of not only the Poncas but also her own Omahas, her passion and conviction far outweighed her obvious unease and won the congregation overwhelmingly to her side (205–11).

Tibbles described Susette's initial oratorical performance many years later in his *Buckskin and Blanket Days*:

> There stood the little figure, trembling and gazing at the crowd with eyes which afterwards thrilled many audiences. They were wonderful eyes. They could smile, command, flash, plead, mourn, and play all sorts of tricks with anyone they lingered on.

Aware of her fear of speaking, Tibbles observes that "hers was a graceful, appealing fright that never lost its dignity." He adds that "her breakdown thrilled the audience like an electric shock" (211–12).

The Omaha Committee was deeply impressed and insisted that Susette accompany Tibbles, who had signed to return to the East for a lecture tour. At the time, the Omahas learned that a bill had been introduced in Congress to remove them to Indian Territory. Realizing the danger for her own people as well as for the Poncas, Susette not only decided to participate but persuaded her father to allow her to do so. Joseph agreed providing that his son Francis would accompany her. In October, the group, which also included Standing Bear (for whom Susette and Francis would interpret), and the Rev. W.J. Harsha, pastor of the First Presbyterian Church in Omaha, set out (Wilson 211–13). On the lecture tour, Susette, in the eyes of the public, would permanently become Bright Eyes.

The most thorough account of the speaking tour, as is true for many aspects of Susette La Flesche's life, is provided by Dorothy Clarke Wilson, whose biography, though short on specific documentation, is based on extensive research. The tour began in October 1879 and lasted until April

1880 with the first presentations in Chicago. Bright Eyes, for that quickly became how she was referred to, her half-brother, Frank, and Standing Bear wore what was referred to as "citizens" clothes rather than their more Native attire. The exception was that Standing Bear would wear more traditional clothes when on stage. Still tortured at the prospect of speaking publicly, Susette carefully prepared her addresses, reading her speeches clearly and in a natural manner that proved very effective at conveying her controlled emotion and her sincerity. When asked by a reporter what she hoped to accomplish, she replied, as quoted by Wilson, "'To make known the wrongs done to my people.'" She continued, clarifying the "wrongs" and how to correct them. Her people should be able to control their own money, enjoy the rights guaranteed by the Constitution, be protected from assault and murder, be able to retain their land, and be granted citizenship (217–22).

The next stop was Boston, where Standing Bear learned that his brother, Big Snake, had been shot and killed by a soldier on the Ponca Reservation. In addition, Tibbles was informed that his wife, Amelia, had died of peritonitis. Although both men were devastated by the news, they decided to stay because so many people were depending on them to make the speaking tour successful.

The quartet of Standing Bear, dignified and stately, speaking in his own language, Francis interpreting for him, Susette presenting her own personal views, and the more charged emotionalism of Tibbles received usually favorable press coverage and captured the hearts and minds of most of those in the audiences that usually filled the halls and churches where the group appeared. Their appearance in Music Hall, for example, not only filled the seats but also the aisles, corridors, and stairway, still leaving large numbers of people in the streets attempting to enter. Among the dignitaries also on the platform were Boston's mayor, Frederick Prince, and the governor of Massachusetts, Thomas Talbot (Wilson 231–32).

During the Boston leg of the tour, Susette met Helen Hunt Jackson. Jackson had attended one of the public gatherings at which Susette and Standing Bear had spoken, an experience that dramatically changed Jackson's life. She would accompany the Ponca group for much of the remaining tour, become a close friend of Susette, engage in exhaustive study of Native Americans, and author what would become a groundbreaking book, *A Century of Dishonor*, as she writes in an author's note in the book, "to show our causes for national shame in the matter of our treatment of the Indians" (11).

Another famous individual that Susette met in Boston was the poet Henry Wadsworth Longfellow. Tibbles describes the encounter in *Buckskin and Blanket Days*. H.O. Houghton of Riverside Press invited Susette to his home so that Longfellow could meet her. Longfellow took her hand, gazed carefully at her, and said, "'*This* is Minnehaha." They talked at length, after which the famous poet stated that he wished he could speak "'with the simplicity, fluency, and force used by that Indian girl'" (218). The "Minnehaha" reference is to a character in Longfellow's epic poem *The Song of Hiawatha*, the beautiful young woman that Hiawatha falls in love with. Although the 1855 poem was published when Susette was an infant and obviously not the model for Longfellow's character, she became associated with the poem and, as Norma Kidd Green points out, "became the Symbol of the 'Beautiful Indian Maiden'" for many Easterners (62).

It was also during the Boston stay that Susette became acquainted with the anthropologist Alice C. Fletcher. Fletcher and Susette became good friends, and Fletcher began a lengthy and close professional relationship with Francis La Flesche. Susette also not only met but shared the platform with Oliver Wendell Holmes, the writer and Harvard professor of anatomy and physiology; and Wendell Phillips, a famous abolitionist who had served as president of the American Antislavery Society. The Boston portion of the tour concluded on December 3, where Susette became the first woman ever to give a speech at Faneuil Hall (Tibbles, *Buckskin and Blanket Days* 219).

The Ponca party continued on to New York and Philadelphia, with heavy newspaper coverage that focused on both the content of the presentations and the speakers' physical appearance. Tibbles' *Ponca Chiefs* came out during this time under the pseudonym "Zyliff" and with the introduction by Susette, signing it as "INSHTATHEAMBA (Bright Eyes)," and a dedication by Wendell Phillips to "THE PEOPLE OF THE UNITED STATES" (2). While in Philadelphia, the party was summoned to testify before a Senate committee investigating the Poncas' removal. Susette appeared before the committee on February 13, 1880. She spoke of the sufferings of the Poncas and how, despite that, they had remained peaceful, and of how Standing Bear had said "it was of no use to resist; they had committed no crime, had done no wrong, but the government was strong and they were powerless and could not resist" (testimony printed in Kilcup 172–74). The Washington stay included an evening at the White House with President and Mrs. Rutherford Hayes.

After balancing public lectures with Senate testimony, the group continued to Baltimore. Susette by this time was extremely tired. Tibbles describes her lying motionless, "cold as death," after a reception. Susette's response to expressions of concern, however, was that it would be better for her to die than "that all the Indians should be exterminated." However, the group's agent provided by the Omaha Committee informed the Committee that continuing with the lectures and receptions would result in Susette's death. The decision by the Committee was that the party should return home and rest (*Buckskin and Blanket Days* 220–21).

Back in Nebraska, Susette wrote "Nedawi," a story for children, which was published in the magazine *St. Nicholas* in January 1881. The story features a young girl modeled partly on Susette herself, including an incident involving Susette's rescuing of a wounded bird and the direction that Joseph gave her to set it safely in the grass and give it back to God (Kilcup 174–79; Wilson 37). "Nedawi" would not be her final creative attempt in writing to mine her past. Drawing upon stories told to her by her father, mother, and grandmother, she contributed a series called "Omaha Legends and Tent-Stories" to the children's magazine *Wide Awake* in 1883. The first story, "The Babes in the Woods," about two children deserted by their father who has murdered their mother, but who ultimately not only survive but thrive and save a tribe from starving, also appears in Kilcup's anthology (181–86). Susette also contributed the introduction to *Ploughed Under, the Story of an Indian Chief*, a novel that Tibbles and William Justin Harsha, son of an Omaha clergyman, collaborated on. In the introduction, Susette argued against stereotypes and that Native Americans are like all other humans and deserve to be recognized as persons and as citizens (Kilcup 179–80).

By the fall of 1880, Susette and Tibbles were again in the East, speaking in Boston, other Massachusetts towns, and Portland, Maine. As the new year arrived, Helen Hunt Jackson's *A Century of Dishonor* was published, and the Senate continued debating the fate of the Poncas, ultimately finalizing a plan to grant the Poncas land in severalty on either the old Dakota Territory or on the new reservation in Indian Territory. The Interior Department, however, interpreted the legislation to limit Poncas to their current choice, meaning that the Poncas on the new reservation could possess land there but not in their previous homeland. It was seen as a mixed victory. Standing Bear could remain where he was, but the Poncas would be split in two geographically (Wilson 274–79).

Then the Journalist

Susette was not finished as a public speaker and lecturer after her two tours of the East, but gradually her public utterances began to appear more on the printed page and less on the stage or platform. Her private life also changed, as she married Thomas Tibbles in the mission chapel on July 23, 1881. Although mutual fondness and respect were certainly part of their relationship, Wilson appears correct in stating that a factor in her accepting Tibbles' proposal was her judgment that she could better serve her people as Mrs. Thomas Tibbles, although to many people, especially her family, she would still be Susette La Flesche, and to her reading and listening public, as well as to her husband, she would remain Bright Eyes (281, 287).

Not long after their marriage, the couple moved to Omaha, where Tibbles was working as a freelance journalist, mainly for the Omaha *Herald*. Some of Susette's most valued friendships from her Eastern tours continued. Alice Fletcher arrived in Nebraska in September 1881 and with the assistance of Susette, Tibbles, Standing Bear, and Joseph's cousin Wajapa among others embarked on her ethnological studies, also preparing a petition on behalf of fifty-five Omahas requesting that they be given title to the land on which they had been homesteading (Wilson 287–98). Communications with Helen Hunt Jackson continued, and Susette rejoiced in Jackson's publication of the novel *Ramona* in 1884 but was struck with great sorrow when her friend died the following year.

Much was occurring in many directions during the 1880s. There was a trip to England and Scotland by Susette and Tibbles in 1887–88 during which they experienced extensive coverage in the London papers, lectured as many as five times per week, were welcomed in high society, and were hosted most nights in private homes (Wilson 318–24). Some aspects of the tour grated on her, though, such as the "deference paid to royalty" and being referred to, as she was by the Reverend Dr. Frazier, head of the Presbyterian Church in England, as "'the Princess Bright Eyes from America'" (Tibbles, *Buckskin and Blanket Days* 297–99).

The year 1888 brought with it the death of Susette's father. Joseph developed a fever and just three days later, on September 24, died at the age of sixty-seven. The last of the true Omaha principal chiefs was buried in the cemetery at Bancroft, Nebraska, a new town created in the early 1880s near the Omaha Reservation. Susette's sisters Susan and Marguerite and half-sister Lucy graduated from the Hampton Normal and Agricultural Institute in Virginia, with Susan enrolling in the Woman's Medical College of Pennsylvania and ultimately becoming a physician serving Omahas and others in Nebraska. Marguerite became a teacher in the government school on the reservation. Half-brother Carey spent his adult life on the reservation, farming and holding a number of other jobs, including teaching and serving as a police officer (Green 168–71). Rosalie taught on the reservation and along with her husband, Edward Farley, managed "the pasture," which was unallotted reservation land that non–Omahas could use for their cattle for a fee (Green 82–96). Rosalie was the only La Flesche child other than Louis to predecease Susette, dying in 1900.

During the 1880s, enormously significant pieces of legislation impacting Omahas and other Native American peoples became law. In 1882, with ardent lobbying by Alice Fletcher, an allotment bill was passed and signed into law dividing the Omaha Reservation into homesteading parcels that Omaha individuals would hold in protected trusts for twenty-five years, after which they would have permanent ownership, receiving "fee simple title" to the land (the right to use, control, and dispose of it). Only then would the land be subject to local tax. Alice Fletcher in 1883 was appointed to implement the law granting Omahas their lands "in severalty," that is, individual ownership. Two years later, Congress clarified the issue of citizenship, declaring that the Omaha owners were entitled to citizenship. In 1887, Congress passed the General Allotment Act, also known as the Dawes Act after Senator Henry Dawes, its strongest proponent, expanding the concept of allotment and extending citizenship to all Native Americans who accepted an allotment of land, although the act would be implemented over time for specific reservations at the discretion of the President of the United States (Hoxie 235–36). Universal citizenship for Native Americans, however, did not occur until 1924.

Susette and her husband favored citizenship because they thought that it would enable their people to benefit from the protection of the law. They also, like many well-intentioned people, thought that allotment was a generally positive development because, faced with the opposite, the power of the federal government to move Native Americans wherever it wished whenever it wished, land ownership would provide stability and certainty. But Susette also recognized that in conforming to the white people's way of life, much of the Omahas' culture was being lost. She wondered, as Wilson points out, whether she was making a mistake and how future generations would evaluate her actions (368–71). History has shown, of course, that allotment became both a tool for whites to use in taking for themselves much of the land that had once been tribal lands and the groundwork for federal termination and assimilation policies. The fixed acreage allotments left much of reservation land unallotted, and much of the unallotted land eventually yielded to white ownership. Within a few decades of allotment, the approximately 300,000 acres that the treaty of 1854 assigned to the Omahas had shrunk to about 30,000 acres (Wilson 367). Susette had been faced, as had her father, with bad choices and had made the only choice that she could see giving her people a chance at survival. The fault lay not with the father's and daughter's choices, but with a country and government that offered only bad options.

To a great extent, the allotment legislation and the European trip ended the period of Susette's life devoted to public speaking, yielding to a broader perspective reflected in her journalism. As Erin E. Pedigo notes in her Master of Arts thesis, *"The Gifted Pen": The Journalism Career of Susette La Flesche Tibbles (1854–1903)*, Susette's journalism career has been almost entirely ignored, even in the extensive biography by Dorothy Clarke

Wilson. That is unfortunate, for as Pedigo rightly states, "always writing about the marginalized, always telling the truth, and never losing her integrity in the profession were her hallmarks" (128–30).

Susette's writing for the *Omaha Morning World-Herald* occurred in 1890–91 when she and her husband were sent by the paper to cover the rise of the Ghost Dance at Pine Ridge Agency in South Dakota. Lakota ceremonial dances had been outlawed in 1883, and when a spiritual dance that frightened whites named the Ghost Dance had been brought from Nevada where it had originated with the Paiute Wovoka to Pine Ridge, whites were afraid that the dance portended a violent uprising. A supposed outcome of the dance was that whites would disappear and dead Native Americans, the buffalo, and the former way of life would reappear.

Arriving at Pine Ridge, Susette and Tibbles attempted, as good journalists do, to ascertain what exactly was happening by interviewing those who knew, namely Lakotas. Consequently, they differed considerably from most reporters, who were more than willing to supply the sensationalist stories that their newspapers wanted to print, even if they essentially had to make up the stories. Because that was not the way that Susette and Tibbles operated, they faced hostility from colleagues and anger from their own newspaper. When their sound and truthful reporting earned praise from other sources, however, their own paper appeared to get on board with their approach (Pedigo 81–83).

Susette's careful attention to truth and her efforts to share it with readers shines through these *World-Herald* articles. "Why They Are Starving," which appeared on December 18, 1890, for example, examines how crop failures had led to great hunger among the Lakotas. In "Drama among the Sioux" (19 December 1890), Susette tries to correct the misconception that all Native American dancing is related to impending war (Pedigo 85–87). Ten days later on December 29 came the tragedy at Wounded Knee Creek during which at least 150 Lakota men, women, and children, including the chief Big Foot, also known as Spotted Elk, were killed by the United States military. Back at the Agency, an Episcopal church was turned into an emergency hospital for wounded survivors. Susette attempted to assist them and recorded her experience in "Horrors of War," which appeared in the paper on January 2, 1891. Among the images that she conveyed were "a woman sitting on the floor with a wounded baby on her lap," "a young woman shot through both thighs and her wrist was broken," "a little boy with his throat apparently shot to pieces" (quoted in Pedigo 94). Hugh J. Reilly has labeled Susette "America's first female Native American war correspondent" (117), but the label is misleading. What happened at Wounded Knee was not a war, and Susette was not there. She did, however, report on the reality of what was occurring prior to and after Wounded Knee. The articles that she wrote for the *Omaha Morning World-Herald* would be her final major effort to tell the rest of the world about the world of Native Americans.

By 1893, Thomas Tibbles had become politically connected to the Populist movement, which was motivated to a great extent by income inequality, distrust of big business, and the financial panic of 1893 that resulted in many bank failures and business closures. When Tibbles received an invitation to become the House of Representatives correspondent for the Populist paper the *American Noncomformist*, which was published in Indianapolis, he and Susette moved to Washington, D.C., in 1893. Susette, apparently more because of her husband's passion than her own, joined him in supporting the cause and became the Senate correspondent for the paper, writing under the "Bright Eyes" byline. When she was not following Senate debates and writing accounts of Senate actions, she was enjoying herself at concerts, lectures, and art galleries while also painting (Wilson 355).

According to Amanda L. Paige, who has collected many of Susette's Populist newspaper articles and published twelve of them online, eight from the *American Noncomformist* and four from the *Lincoln Independent*, "she published about fifty articles, which range from straight factual reports of events in the Senate to more 'interpretive pieces'" in the *American Noncomformist*. Given the topical nature of these pieces, and the anonymity into which many of the political figures of the time have fallen, much of this material, if not "dull" (Pedigo 115), lacks the historical interest and sense of personal engagement on the part of Susette that one finds in her pieces for the *Omaha Morning World-Herald*. One of the most interesting subjects that she writes about, as Pedigo recognizes, is the income tax debate, a subject that she gives several pages to in her thesis (115–17). Congress passed a 2 percent tax on incomes over $4000, but the tax was declared unconstitutional the following year. Paige includes Susette's article "Debating the Income Tax," published on June 7, 1894, in her collection. "Granny Hoar Grunts," from May 24, 1894, expresses great sympathy for the hard work and often meager financial rewards that characterize the lives of farmers and farmers' wives. Also cited with respect and compassion are factory workers, children who should be playing rather than working to earn "enough bread and butter to keep them alive and warm," and "girls with pale, pinched faces." Although Susette is not writing about Omahas, Poncas, or other Native Americans, the common thread remains compassion for those who are suffering and an attempt to improve their lives.

Susette and her husband returned to Nebraska in the summer of 1895, taking up residence on the farm where they had sporadically lived on the reservation. They were not there for long, however, as Tibbles accepted the editorship of the *Lincoln Independent*, the official paper of the Populist Party. In October, they moved to Lincoln, where they would live for five years. Susette was less engaged in writing for this paper than the former one. Both Paige and Pedigo (122) state that there are only four extant articles by her. If that is the case, all four are included in Paige's online collection. One article harkens back to the United States Senate while the others discuss control of the country's universities by millionaires and corporations, the unjust social system in England, and the law's role in establishing social and economic inequalities. The four articles were published over a period of just a few months, from October to December 1895.

Susette's health began to deteriorate, and Tibbles took her back periodically to the farm before returning there permanently sometime after Rosalie's death in 1900. Tibbles continued with his editorial duties by mail, often traveling to Lincoln (Wilson 365–66). During these final years, Susette collaborated with Fannie Reed Giffen on a book, *Oo-mah-ha Ta-wa-tha* (*Omaha City*) for the 1898 Exposition in Omaha. The book includes stories that Susette's parents, Joseph and Mary, had related. Susette wrote for the book an account of the death of her brother, Louis (64–67), and added a translation into the Omaha language of the twelfth article of the Treaty of 1854 (57), which prohibits alcohol on the reservation. Most importantly, Susette contributed the illustrations, including full-page depictions of a chief wearing a war bonnet and a young Omaha girl. Her sketches of Omaha life appear throughout the book. The preface by the attorney John L. Webster states, "The illustrations by Inshta Theumba (Bright Eyes) are believed to be the first artistic work by an American Indian ever published" (8). Unfortunately, little of Susette's artwork besides these illustrations survives.

By May 1903, Susette was nearing death. She spent her final days in bed with her husband caring for her. At times she was incoherent. Death came on May 26 with family members, including her mother, beside her. On the night before Susette's funeral, John G. Neihardt, future author of *Black Elk Speaks* (1932), agreed to Tibbles' request that he sit up with him during the night. Several times during the night, Tibbles would jump up and suggest that they go into the bedroom to look at Susette. Tibbles would dip a cloth into cold water and wipe Susette's face, probably, Neihardt thought, to keep her from changing color. "'Isn't she beautiful?'" Tibbles would ask Neihardt (Wilson 372–75). Susette was buried in the Bancroft cemetery near her father and other family members. A marker was later located at her grave stating, "She did all she could to make the world happier and better." Green writes of Susette and her physician sister Susan that they had taken very different paths, "Yet they both maintained a loyalty to their origin and proved that they could learn new ways, that they could walk a goodly distance along the white man's road beckoning to their people to follow" (121). No matter how far along that road Susette walked, she never completely left her people behind, and, at the end, she came home again.

References

Brown, Marion Marsh. *Susette La Flesche: Advocate for Native American Rights.* Chicago: Childrens Press, 1992.

Clark, Jerry E., and Martha Ellen Webb. "Susette and Susan La Flesche: Reformer and Missionary." *Being and Becoming Indian: Biographical Studies of North American Frontiers.* Ed. James A. Clifton. Prospect Hill, IL: Waveland Press, 1989. 137–59.

Dando-Collins, Stephen. *Standing Bear is a Person: The True Story of a Native American's Quest for Justice.* Cambridge, MA: Da Capo P, 2004.

Fletcher, Alice C., and Francis La Flesche. *The Omaha Tribe.* In *Twenty-Seventh Annual Report of the Bureau of American Ethnology to the Secretary of the Smithsonian Institution.* Washington: Government Printing Office, 1905–06.

Giffen, Fannie Reed. *Oo-mah-ha Ta-wa-tha (Omaha City).* Illustrations by Susette La Flesche Tibbles. Lincoln: Published by the Authors, 1898.

Green, Norma Kidd. *Iron Eyes's Family: The Children of Joseph La Flesche.* Lincoln: Johnsen Publishing Company, sponsored by the Nebraska State Historical Society, 1969.

Hoxie, Frederick E. *This Indian Country: American Activists and the Place They Made.* 2012. New York: Penguin Books, 2013.

Jackson, Helen Hunt. *A Century of Dishonor.* Digireads.com Publishing, 2012.

Kilcup, Karen L., ed. *Native American Women's Writing 1800–1924: An Anthology.* Malden, MA: Blackwell, 2000

La Flesche, Francis. *The Middle Five: Indian Schoolboys of the Omaha Tribe.* Lincoln: U of Nebraska P, 1978.

Paige, Amanda L., ed. *The Newspaper Writings of Susette La Flesche: A Selected Edition.* American Native Press Archives and Sequoyah Research Center, University of Arkansas at Little Rock. ualrexhibits.org/tribalwriters/artifacts/Newspaper-Writings-Susette-La-Flesche.html.

Pedigo, Erin E. *"The Gifted Pen": The Journalism Career of Susette La Flesche Tibbles.* Thesis. U of Nebraska–Lincoln, 2011. DigitalCommons@University of Nebraska–Lincoln.

Reilly, Hugh J. *The Frontier Newspapers and the Coverage of the Plains Indian Wars.* Santa Barbara: Praeger, 2010.

Tibbles, Thomas Henry. *Buckskin and Blanket Days.* 1957. Lincoln: U of Nebraska P, 1969.

_____. *Standing Bear and the Ponca Chiefs.* Ed. Kay Graber. Lincoln: U of Nebraska P, 1995.

Wilson, Dorothy Clarke. *Bright Eyes: The Story of Susette La Flesche, an Omaha Indian.* New York: McGraw-Hill, 1974.

5

Zitkala-Ša
(Gertrude Simmons, Gertrude Bonnin) (1876–1938)

Zitkala-Ša was a woman of many talents and accomplishments: writer, musician, orator, political organizer and lobbyist, tireless champion of Native American rights, including the right to vote. She not only bridged the worlds of traditional Sioux culture and Euro-American modernity but also committed herself to a pan–Indian vision that transcended without denying tribal affiliation.

Zitkala-Ša's political awakening came during her years at an off-reservation boarding school, where she recognized the cultural transformation that such schools intended while simultaneously both rejecting that transformation into an imitation white person and accepting the academic education that she would shortly use in pursuit of her goal of maintaining traditional cultural identity while fostering acceptance of Native Americans within a changing world. Her attempts to solidify traditional culture and at the same time encourage Native peoples to become—and be accepted as—citizens of the United States proved to be a challenging balancing act that gained Zitkala-Ša both acclaim and criticism.

Some later activists tended to reject Zitkala-Ša's efforts as overly assimilationist without adequately appreciating her skill at fitting method to audience within a transitional time in Native American history. As a result, she was largely forgotten after her death until a revival of interest in her life and work in the 1970s and beyond. That renewed consideration of her efforts has led to serious analysis about her from a variety of perspectives, including multicultural and gender.

"The School Days of an Indian Girl"

Zitkala-Ša, named Gertrude at birth, was born at Greenwood, Dakota Territory (now in southeastern South Dakota), on the Yankton Reservation, on February 22, 1876, four months before the battle of Greasy Grass, a river known to non–Natives as Little Bighorn. Her mother was a Yankton Sioux named Taté I Yóhin Win, which means "Reaches for the Wind" according to Agnes M. Picotte in her foreword to Zitkala-Ša's *Old Indian Legends* (xii). Her father, a Frenchman named Felker, left, or was told to leave, apparently after beating David, one of three surviving half-brothers of Gertrude, before or shortly after Gertrude's birth. Felker was the third of Taté I Yóhin Win's husbands, the first two having died, and she gave Gertrude her second husband's name, Simmons (Lewandowski 18).[1]

The Yankton and Yanktonai were originally the mid-groups of Sioux, with the Dakota to the east in Minnesota and Wisconsin, and the Lakota to the west. By the seventeenth and eighteenth centuries, however, all of the groups of Sioux had begun migrating as a result of various pull and push forces, including the arrival of Euro-American traders and settlers, declining game to the east, and greater land and game resources to the west (Gibbon 1–6). It is unclear which of the Siouan dialects young Gertrude spoke, either Nakota, as Picotte claims, or Dakota, a dialect that the Yankton also spoke and which Gertrude later would write in when she was not writing in English. The name that she later adopted for her public persona, Zitkala-Ša, is in a third dialect, Lakota (P. Jane Hafen, Introduction to *Dreams and Thunder* xiv).

At the age of six, Gertrude entered a Presbyterian bilingual school at the Yankton Agency where she began to learn English if she had not previously started speaking it. Accounts of an exotic world of apple orchards enticed Gertrude to long for a journey east to attend White's Manual Labor Institute, run by Quakers in Wabash, Indiana. It was a long journey for the eight-year-old Gertrude, one that her mother strongly opposed. Her brother David had returned from three years at the Hampton Institute in Virginia, an experience that probably added to Gertrude's desire to attend a similar school.

When Gertrude arrived at White's in 1884, the school was only about a year into its existence as an Indian school after previously serving as an orphanage. The focus there, as at many such institutions, was on religious conversion and homemaking (farming for the boys). Students also would learn to read, write, and speak English. Music, especially religious hymns, helped to inculcate Christian principles, the school officials and teachers hoped. Gertrude spent two periods of time at White's Manual Labor Institute, from February 1884 to March 1887, and from December 1890 to the fall of 1893 when she was dispatched back to Yankton and also to Pine Ridge Reservation as a recruiter. Between her two stints at White's, she spent some time at the Yankton Presbyterian school and at the Santee Normal Training School in Nebraska.

Gertrude would convey some of her experiences at White's and her

Gertrude Simmons (Zitkala-Ša), in the back row, third from right, with school-mates from the Santee Normal Training School, Nebraska. Gertrude is about fourteen years old (courtesy Center for Western Studies, Augustana University).

bitterness toward the school a few years later in a series of heavily autobiographical stories with a few details altered. In her seven-part "Impressions of an Indian Childhood" and the seven-part "The School Days of an Indian Girl," signed as Zitkala-Ša and published in the *Atlantic Monthly* during January and February 1900, the author describes her motivation for wanting to attend White's Institute, several traumatic experiences there, and her rebellious responses to the transformative vision of the institution, along with details of her family relationships.[2] "Impressions of an Indian Childhood" describes her mother as angry and resentful toward the "palefaces" who had stolen their land, forcing the mother and her family to move to the Yankton Reservation, where Gertrude's sister died from the exhausting trip about two years before Gertrude's birth. The reader learns enticing stories that two white missionaries on a recruiting trip tell about picking apples (which the child had seldom eaten) and about trips on trains (which she had never ridden on nor even seen) (83–86). Ultimately, the mother recognizes the importance of an education in the changing world and gives her permission for her daughter to attend the school. At one point in the story, the author glances forward to the woman she has become, stating that "it was not yet an ambition for Letters that was stirring me" (84).

"The School Days of an Indian Girl" depicts the author's early disenchantment, which begins during her train ride to Indiana, where, dressed simply in her normal child's Yankton attire, she resents being watched by white children who pointed at her moccasins, which embarrasses her and almost brings her to tears (87). Shortly after arriving at the school, she is tossed in the air and caught by a woman, an apparent attempt at familiarity but one that badly frightens and insults young Gertrude. She falls asleep that first night, sobbing (89).

Worse is soon to come for Gertrude, as she faces having her hair cut short. Hiding under her bed to escape, she is pulled out and tied into a chair. As she feels a scissors touching her neck and cutting at her braids, she longs for her mother, who had taught Gertrude that hair was cut short only to mourn the death of a loved one or on captured enemies as a sign of cowardice (90–91).

Zitkala-Ša continues to describe harsh disciplinary treatment, the unrelenting regimentation of school life, and the illnesses and even death that classmates face due to ineffective medical attention. In the fourth part of the account, she recalls returning home after three years at the Institute to find young men and women who had attended boarding school in the East dressed in white men's clothes or tight dresses that Gertrude considers immodest (99). She hears them speaking English and notes that she herself knows English as well as they. When her cousin Dawée refuses to take her to a party with these young people, she cries, and her mother attempts to console her by offering "an Indian Bible" given to her by a missionary, the only book that she has in their home, but Gertrude feels more like burning the bible than reading it (99–100). The white people's clothes, their language, and their religion coalesce in Gertrude's resentment of what she has endured over the past three years and the attempts at cultural transformation that comprised the primary focus of her education.

Nonetheless, in December 1890 Gertrude returned to White's Manual Labor Institute for a second term after an absence of almost four years. Her interim experiences at the Yankton school and the Santee Normal Training School in Nebraska do not figure in "The School Days of an Indian Girl." The final section of "The School Days of an Indian Girl" moves rapidly through those three years, which seemingly were far more fulfilling for Gertrude than her earlier years at the Institute. Upon completing this second term, she acknowledges that she is proud of her first diploma, and against her mother's wishes decides to continue her education by attending college.

In addition to Gertrude's accomplishments in language, writing, and literature, she had developed a serious interest in music at White's Institute. She learned to play the piano and violin, skills likely enhanced by private instruction according to Lewandowski (21). She also participated in singing and oratorical activities at the school. Such was the respect that the staff and teachers had for Gertrude that she was selected to return to Yankton as a recruiter in the fall of 1893, a role that she also performed at the Pine

Ridge Reservation in South Dakota. She also was chosen to give a commencement address in June 1895. Her topic was "The Progress of Women," a subject that would merge for Zitkala-Ša with the welfare of Native peoples during her decades of political and cultural activism. By this time, one of the new students at White's Institute was Raymond Bonnin, who eventually would become Zitkala-Ša's husband.

The Pen and Violin

Gertrude enrolled in Earlham College in Richmond, Indiana, another Quaker school, in the fall of 1895. The college was academically progressive, offering the same curriculum to both males and females, with a rich repertoire of extracurricular activities. As Lewandowski points out, courses included traditional humanities subjects such as English and the classical languages Greek and Latin as well as what were seen as newer disciplines, including biology. Gertrude joined G Clef and the Phoenix Society, music and literature clubs respectively. She helped to create a student literary magazine called *Anpao* and published a poem titled "A Ballad" in the Earlham newspaper, the *Earlhamite*. Her public performances included a piano recital and vocals (21–23).

One of the highlights of Gertrude's time at Earlham College was her participation in a statewide oratory contest at the English Opera House and Hotel in Indianapolis in March 1896. She performed a revision of her earlier "Progress of Women" retitled "Side by Side," which had won first place in an oratory contest at Earlham. Her speech on behalf of Native American equality conveyed history as most members of the Indianapolis audience would never have heard or read it before. "The audience sat hushed and unprotesting," Lewandowski writes, "as she rigorously overturned every prevailing national narrative of America." Gertrude came in second in the contest, falling short of the top honor when a Southern judge failed her on the intellectual content of the speech (Lewandowski 23–27).

Gertrude returned to Earlham, however, as a conquering heroine, with the president of Earlham College among those congratulating her. Unfortunately, she was unable to earn her degree, withdrawing after two years due at least in part to illness.

Despite Gertrude's negative feelings about her own schooling at White's Institute, she accepted a position in July 1897 at the Carlisle Indian Industrial School in Pennsylvania, which began a long and complicated relationship with the school's founder, Richard Henry Pratt. Her early responsibilities included recruiting back at Yankton in August. By September she had returned to Carlisle where she continued to indulge her musical interests by singing at Carlisle ceremonies, leading the Minnehaha Glee Club, and playing the violin on a school tour. She also taught at the school.

During the summer of 1898 after Gertrude's first year at Carlisle, she continued her violin studies in Harrisburg under a Professor Taube. In August, she stayed for a time with the prominent photographer Gertrude Käsebier in New York City. Both Käsebier and fellow photographer Joseph Keiley photographed Gertrude in a variety of poses. Käsebier's portraits show Gertrude's multiple personas: as an Indian in traditional Indian clothing, and as a modern, late-nineteenth-century woman, in one photograph staring into the camera while she rests her violin on her lap, the bow leaning against her right shoulder. According to Susan Rose Dominguez in her doctoral dissertation, "The Gertrude Bonnin Story," the first written example of Gertrude's use of the name "Zitkala-Ša" appears on the back of one of Käsebier's photographs of her (147).

By 1899, Gertrude was in Boston, where, with the financial support of a grant from the Commissioner of Indian Affairs, she was taking violin lessons from Eugene Gruenberg, who played with the Boston Symphony Orchestra and headed the violin department of the New England Conservatory of Music. Beautiful, talented, and by Boston standards exotic due to her Yankton background, she continued to attract photographers, with the world-famous Fred Holland Day photographing her in Boston. There she also met the journalist Joseph Edgar Chamberlin, who welcomed her into one of his homes and established a connection with *Atlantic Monthly* editor Bliss Perry for her (Lewandowski 35–37). She turned to pen as well as the violin, writing the series of autobiographical essays: "Impressions of an Indian Childhood," "The School Days of an Indian Girl," and "An Indian Teacher Among Indians." Perry published them in the January, February, and March 1900 issues of the *Atlantic Monthly*. The budding author signed the publications "Zitkala-Ša," choosing a native name (in Lakota "Red Bird") to fit the subject matter. In doing so, she was clearly choosing one identity over another, the one that would dominate her life, without totally rejecting the other, more assimilationist persona.

In the third of these narratives, "An Indian Teacher Among Indians," the author, now identifying herself as Zitkala-Ša, writes of her chosen direction: "to spend my energies in a work for the Indian race" (104). This account of her teaching experience offers a forceful rejection of the Carlisle School and therefore is attitudinally consistent with her two previous narratives that sharply criticized White's Institute. She accuses white teachers of caring about "self-preservation quite as much as Indian education" (111). Her self-analysis also is unflinching as she writes that she had rejected her faith and separated herself from "mother, nature, and God" (112). Finally, she resigns her position at Carlisle.

Having resigned her teaching position and condemned Richard Pratt's life work, Zitkala-Ša nonetheless neither broke totally from Carlisle nor severed completely her relationship with Pratt. In March 1900, therefore, Zitkala-Ša toured with the Carlisle Indian School Band, playing violin solos. Dressed in buckskin, she recited "The Famine" from Henry Wadsworth Longfellow's *Song of Hiawatha*. Her performance and the tour were well received, and she was invited after a Washington concert to meet with Longfellow's daughter. She also participated in a special performance at the White House for President and Mrs. McKinley, the latter presenting her with a bouquet of violets (Lewandowski 46–49).

Zitkala-Ša at this point in her life clearly saw herself as a writer with a literary career beckoning, a career that she could merge with her commitment to aiding her race, as she had termed her calling in "An Indian Teacher Among Indians." *Harper's Monthly* published "The Soft-Hearted Sioux" in March 1901, her first explicitly fictional piece, and "The Trial Path" in October. In "The Trial Path" (127–31), a young woman listens to her grandmother tell a story of love and redemption concerning the auditor's grandfather.

"The Soft-Hearted Sioux" (118–26), a more complex story than "The Trial Path," further attacks the educational and conversion goals of Indian schools in its account of a young man who returns home after nine years at school, attempts to convert his people to Christianity, but ends up failing his parents, committing a crime against a white man, and being condemned to death. The story, with its rejection of Christianity in very personal terms, angered Pratt, further damaging their relationship. Zitkala-Ša decided to return to Yankton and continue her literary efforts there among the people she was hoping to help.

At Yankton, she completed her first book, *Old Indian Legends*, which was published in October 1901 by Ginn and Company of Boston. *Old Indian Legends* consists of retold stories from Zitkala-Ša's Sioux background. She writes in the preface to the original publication that she has attempted to convey the spirit of these legends into English, America's second tongue. She further notes that she has found multiple versions of these legends (5), perhaps justification for her incorporating contemporary issues and perspectives into some of the narratives. In preparing *Old Indian Legends*, Zitkala-Ša strives to become, as Dexter Fisher has pointed out, "the literary counterpart of the oral storytellers of her tribe" (vii), and in doing so is writing as much for a white audience as a Native American one, declaring in the preface that the "old legends of America belong quite as much to the blue-eyed little patriot as to the black-haired aborigine" (5).

Zitkala-Ša taught at the Crow Creek Agency school in South Dakota in 1902 and continued writing. The short story "A Warrior's Daughter" (132–40) was published in *Everybody's Magazine* in April 1902. It depicts a young woman as warrior saving her beloved. The story offers a theme that will remain an important principle for Zitkala-Ša: that if progress in improving the Native American's lot is to occur, one must turn to women more than to men in order to achieve that success. Zitkala-Ša's feminist view would only grow stronger over the years.

Zitkala-Ša also penned articles, defending Native rituals in "The Indian Dance: A Protest against its Abolition," in the *Boston Evening Transcript* and the autobiographical "Why I am a Pagan" in the *Atlantic Monthly*. The latter is highly spiritual but clearly anti–Christian, as Zitkala-Ša speaks of "the jangling phrases of a bigoted creed" and "the new superstition" (116–17). When Zitkala-Ša included this essay in her later *American Indian Stories* in 1921, she changed the title to "The Great Spirit," dropped the final line ("If this is Paganism, then at present, at least, I am a Pagan"), and added a new closing paragraph that reinforced the positive dimensions of accepting "the Great Spirit." Between the original publication and the appearance of the book, Zitkala-Ša had embraced Christianity, although never for her did Christianity exclude Native beliefs.[3] Writing of Zitkala-Ša's *American Indian Stories*, which primarily consists of stories written between 1900 and 1902, Dexter Fisher points out that the volume "represents one of the first attempts by a Native American woman to write her own story without the aid of an editor, an interpreter, or an ethnographer" (vi).

On a personal level, Zitkala-Ša reestablished a relationship with Raymond Bonnin, whom she had met at White's Institute, and on May 10, 1902, married Bonnin, a relationship and partnership that would endure for the rest of her life. The marriage also coincided with the conclusion of Zitkala-Ša's greatest period of creativity as a writer. In the future, she would devote herself and her writing primarily to campaigning for equal rights for Native Americans, including the right to vote.

A New Life

The recently married Bonnins moved to the Uintah and Ouray Reservation in northeastern Utah, home to the Northern Utes, in December 1902 as Raymond took up his new position in the Office of Indian Affairs as a purchasing agent charged with acquiring cattle and farming equipment for the Utes. They arrived at a reservation in turmoil due to efforts by the United States government to force the division of land into allotments of forty to eighty acres for farming, with the remaining land available for purchase by whites. Although the Bonnins purchased a parcel of land, they quickly realized that the situation on the reservation demanded strong action to end what essentially was a raid on Ute land that would lead to the loss of three and one-half million acres of Ute land by 1909 (Lewand-owski 66).

Zitkala-Ša gave birth to a son on May 28, 1903. He was given dual names of Ohiya, meaning "Winner," and Raymond after his father. Ohiya would be their only child. They also took in an orphaned boy named Oran Curry and an elderly man known as Bad Hand, or Old Sioux.

Raymond resigned from the Indian Service in 1909, and the family moved to the Standing Rock Reservation in the fall. Standing Rock strad-dles North and South Dakota. At Fort Yates, the reservation headquarters near the eastern boundary of the reservation in North Dakota, Zitkala-Ša began work as an issue clerk.

After her early burst of literary success, her musical and oratorical accomplishments, and her acceptance into the artistic communities of the Northeast, the years in Utah and the Dakotas seem to mark a sharp downward turn concerning any clear direction for Zitkala-Ša. Certainly her responsibili-ties as a wife and mother limited her opportunities to further develop her tal-ents or acquire a permanent, substantive position befitting her abilities.

At Fort Yates, though, Zitkala-Ša developed a relationship that would become an important part of her life, if a controversial part: her involve-ment with the Catholic Church. The Benedictines operated a mission at Fort Yates, and Zitkala-Ša admired the priests and nuns who worked at the mission and formed a close friendship with one of the priests, Father Mar-tin Kenel. She referred to being converted, but whether that conversion was formally enacted remains unclear, with considerable debate still occurring regarding her primary religious allegiance, as she had formed friendships with Mormans and attended events sponsored by the Church of Latter-Day Saints while at Uintah (Dominguez 192–93; Lewandowski 69–70, 220n.29).

In the spring of 1910, the Bonnins returned to Utah, where they set out to farm the land that they had previously purchased. With the zeal of a new convert, Zitkala-Ša expressed her disapproval of the Utes' practice of tradi-tional dances, including the Sun Dance, and their failure to observe Sun-day, concerns that she expressed along with her desire to bring the Utes to Catholicism in a correspondence that she began with Father William Ketcham, Director of the Bureau of Catholic Indian Missions in Washing-ton, D.C. (Lewandowski 70). Given a project that Zitkala-Sa was soon to embark upon, her denigration of the Sun Dance is difficult to understand.

The Sun Dance Opera

Zitkala-Ša's choice of life among the Utes rather than among her own Sioux is consistent with a pan-Indian rather than tribal vision that she developed more fully in the future as her political activism grew and her involvement in national organizations expanded.

Despite Zitkala-Ša's lament that Utes were practicing the Sun Dance and other traditional dances, she attended a Sun Dance herself during the summer of 1910 with Raymond. At the dance, they encountered William Hanson, a Mormon who was teaching music at the nearby Uintah Academy and whom Zitkala-Ša had met about two years earlier. She described the Sun Dance in detail to Hanson, and soon proposed that they bring their respective knowledge of the Sun Dance and creative talents together to compose a Sun Dance opera. Hanson's dual interests in Native culture and music apparently made entering into the partnership an easy decision for him to make (Lewandowski 71; Hafen xix, 125–28).

The collaboration on *The Sun Dance Opera* continued over the next two and one-half years, with the premiere occurring in February 1913 in Vernal, Utah. As Lewandowski notes, non–Native Americans experienced in performing played the leads, and Utes created the costumes and performed songs and dances. Old Sioux, who had become a member of Zitkala-Ša's family, led some of the dances. The opera was performed several times through 1914, including performances staged by the Brigham Young University Music Department. Zitkala-Ša introduced some performances with a lecture. Local reactions were positive, and the historical importance of the opera is considerable. It is usually considered the first Native opera because of its authorship and celebration of Native culture (Lewandowski 83–85). The Sun Dance, although outlawed throughout the United States, had never disappeared; because of the prohibition, however, some details were softened (piercings, for example, were deleted) and the dance sometimes was performed more or less in secret (Mails 1–11). The Sun Dance is especially associated with the Sioux, and Zitkala-Ša took the Lakota version as the basis for the opera.

Zitkala-Ša and Hanson's *Sun Dance Opera* was prepared for the stage and for a white as well as Native American audience. Zitkala-Ša brought to the enterprise not only considerable knowledge of Sioux music and rituals but also great experience as a musician. She would play Native music on her violin—music and instrument combining, like so much in her life, the two worlds that she inhabited—while Hanson transcribed the music, essentially converting it into Western music, and they would add lyrics. The process, as P. Jane Hafen describes it in her introduction to the opera in *Dreams and Thunder*, "was a little like forcing a proverbial square peg into a round hole" (126–27).[4] In creating *The Sun Dance Opera*, Zitkala-Ša was repeating an effort represented in her *Old Indian Legends*: transforming what had existed in the oral tradition and in Native languages into the written tradition in English.

Some level of verisimilitude was introduced into the opera by the use of Ute performers, who entered the stage to sing and dance at various times during the performance (Hafen 127). The plot of the opera, less historically realistic, is a love triangle. The hero, Ohiya (named after Zitkala-Ša's son), a Sioux, is in love with a Sioux woman, Winona, and ultimately wins her against a disreputable Shoshone named Sweet Singer.

The Sun Dance Opera was the last great creative expression of Zitkala-Ša as writer. While she did not permanently set aside her creative pen, as she wrote additional short stories as well as some poetry, she primarily would place her writing talent at the disposal of what was for her a greater calling: securing enhanced opportunities for Native Americans in the United States through her involvement in and leadership of pan-Indian organizations.

The Society of American Indians

Fayette Avery McKenzie, an Ohio State University sociologist, future president of Fisk University, an expert on government Indian policy, and a lifelong advocate for an improved life for Native Americans and African Americans, urged creation of an organization by and for Native Americans. At his invitation, a group of prominent leaders met in 1911 to form the American Indian Association, soon to be known as the Society of American Indians (SAI). The society's members tended to be middle class, educated at off-reservation boarding schools such as Carlisle, fluent in English, largely accepting of Christianity and assimilationist goals, pan-Indian regarding their reach, and committed to securing citizenship for Native Americans and exercising the political power that citizenship would bring (Hoxie 225–29).

While the Society of American Indians was establishing itself, Zitkala-Ša and her family were embarking in February 1913 on another move, this time to Fort Duchesne south of Whiterocks, Utah, where Raymond Bonnin had a new job as a property clerk at the agency. She and Ohiya traveled to Nauvoo, Illinois, to enroll Ohiya in the Spalding Institute for Small Boys. The fact that Spalding was a Catholic school run by the order of Benedictine nuns was surely an important factor in her choice, as Catholicism had become an important part of her life even while she continued to honor her traditional spiritual values and rituals.

Zitkala-Ša in 1914 not only became a member of the Society of American Indians but also joined the advisory board of the organization. The following year, she became increasingly involved in the SAI, first as a member of the board of its *Quarterly Journal* and then as a contributing editor. During these early years with the SAI, Zitkala-Ša experienced personal losses: the deaths of her mother on Christmas Day, 1914; and her father-in-law, Joseph Bonnin, a week later on New Year's Day, 1915. She also was becoming heavily engaged locally, forming a sewing group to supply clothes to those who were struggling financially and a meals program. Although her greatest creative triumphs were behind her, she continued writing poetry, submitting several to the SAI *Quarterly Journal*.

In 1916, Zitkala-Ša's poem "The Indian's Awakening" was published in the SAI journal, by then retitled the *American Indian Magazine* (*AIM*). The poem takes Zitkala-Ša back to her school days and a vision in which her spirit is renewed, her determination to use her life wisely reinforced (164–67). She published the poem over the name Zitkala-Ša. That decision, along with her involvement in the SIA (including her successful effort to establish a local chapter at Fort Duchesne) and the content of the poem itself, reflects her renewed commitment to improving life for America's Native peoples.

That focus on the welfare of Native Americans led Zitkala-Ša into a variety of issues in the second decade of the twentieth century, including the Utes' loss of land and irrigation failures, and the increased use of peyote at Uintah and elsewhere. The Uintah Reservation had been reduced from its original 4,000,000 acres to about 360,000 acres by 1909 and water was being diverted by government canals (Lewandowski 109). The loss of Native lands through a variety of disreputable methods carried out by federal and state governments, and the attempt to preserve what little remained, was a battle that Zitkala-Ša would return to often.

Her opposition to peyote use, however, would prove much more controversial, as that battle pitted Zitkala-Ša against other Native Americans more than against whites. Although used in religious rituals, peyote's intoxicating effects convinced Zitkala-Ša that it led to immoral behavior; she also denounced the practice as not truly traditional but a practice imported from Mexico. This would be another battle that she would not quickly give up on.

Zitakala-Ša began lecturing on the evils of peyote use, as she saw them, including her fear that peyote use endangered young Indian women, making them more susceptible to sexual exploitation. Her lectures took her not only through Utah but also to Nevada and Colorado. She continued her efforts at the annual SAI conference in Cedar Rapids, Iowa, in the fall of 1916. The anti-peyote faction carried the day at the conference, with the SAI formally condemning peyote use (Lewandowski 108–13).

A poem by Zitkala-Ša from this time, "The Red Man's America," which she published in the *American Indian Magazine*, incorporates her views on peyote into a parody of "My Country 'Tis of Thee." *The Menace of Peyote*, a pamphlet written by Zitkala-Ša, was published in 1916 with the financial support of the General Federation of Women's Clubs (GFWC), which had originated as a Christian suffrage movement. Zitkala-Ša developed a strong relationship with the organization. The alliance fit well with her growing belief that true change would have to be ushered in by women, a stance that made Zitkala-Ša not only an activist on Indian affairs but also a significant figure in early feminism (Lewandowski 113, 156–76).

In the same year, Zitkala-Ša was elected secretary of the Society of American Indians and worked closely with its president, Arthur C. Parker, a Seneca archaeologist. On a personal level, Zitkala-Ša lost a member of her family in December when Old Sioux died. Internationally, the dominant concern was World War I, which the United States was soon to become part of after Germany resumed unrestricted submarine warfare in January 1917. Shortly after the U.S. entered the war, the Bonnins moved to Washington, D.C., arriving in May of 1918.

Zitkala-Ša had become one of the most prominent members of the Society of American Indians. Then at the 1918 SAI conference in Pierre, South Dakota, in September, Zitkala-Sa was named both secretary and treasurer. She also became editor of the *American Indian Magazine* (Lewandowski 120–22). Her commitment to working on behalf of Native peoples had solidified even more since her move to Washington, as evidenced by the manner in which she had started signing correspondence: "yours for the Indian cause" (Hafen xxiv, 154n.6).

Along with other efforts, Zitkala-Ša's campaign against peyote continued. She allied herself with the Indian Rights Association (IRA), a primarily Quaker organization founded in 1882; and the Board of Indian Commissioners, which was housed in the BIA as a watchdog to prevent corruption and which had been sending missionaries to the reservations since the 1870s. The collective anti-peyote movement brought sufficient pressure to bear on state legislatures that anti-peyote legislation was enacted in thirteen states, including South Dakota, Utah, Iowa, New Mexico, and Wyoming.

Success in the Congress of the United States, however, proved more difficult, although efforts continued. Congressman Carl Hayden of Arizona introduced legislation that came up for a hearing in February 1918 before the House Subcommittee on Indian Affairs. Dueling testimony occurred between Zitkala-Ša, urging passage, and the famous ethnologist James Mooney, who worked at the Smithsonian Institution, had studied Native American culture for decades, and strongly endorsed peyote as a religious, almost sacramental substance. Both engaged in a no-holds-barred attack on each other.[5] Zitkala-Ša attempted to counter Mooney's cultural claims for peyote by fixing its introduction to Native Americans as quite recent, for example, first encountered by Plains Indians in the late nineteenth century. Zitkala-Ša's arguments successfully undermined Mooney's efforts and Mooney himself as a supporter of harmful, hallucinogenic drugs at odds with Christian values.

The House Subcommittee issued a report in May of 1918 titled "Prohibition of the Use of Peyote among Indians," and recommended a ban on peyote that did not occur. Today Zitkala-Ša might see her efforts as yielding a partial victory. Peyote is listed under federal law as a Schedule I controlled substance, but its harvesting and use are permitted for religious purposes under the American Indian Religious Freedom Act of 1978 and the American Indian Religious Freedom Act Amendments of 1994.

The Battle for Citizenship

Although acquiring the right to vote for the Indigenous population of the country consumed much of Zitkala-Ša's attention during the closing years of the second decade of the twentieth century and the opening years of the third, she continued to push Native American rights on a number of fronts while also reclaiming something of her earlier literary focus. Safeguarding Native lands was a priority to which she devoted much attention. Zitkala-Ša's short story "The Widespread Enigma Concerning Blue-Star Woman," published in her *American Indian Stories*, is a powerful indictment of federal Indian land policy (143–54). Even when gaining a small portion of what one deserving person—Blue-Star Woman—merits, she ironically and inadvertently gains it at the expense of other Native people. It is a sad story, but if it seems hopeless, Zitkala-Ša was not. She kept up the fight. Zitkala-Ša believed that more Native Americans, as she had done, should learn to use English well. Then they could more effectively communicate their own stories and more effectively achieve their goals. She made this argument, linking using English with retaining their lands, in her "Letter to the Chiefs and Headmen of the Tribes" (199–200) in the winter of 1919.

Zitkala-Ša's association with the SAI, however, was coming to an end. At the SAI conference in October 1919, Thomas Sloan, a peyote advocate, was elected president of the organization over the incumbent, Charles Eastman, and Raymond Bonnin, whom Zitkala-Ša had nominated when it appeared that Eastman would lose. She was re-elected to her dual roles as secretary and treasurer but resigned from the SAI. The organization struggled on for a few more years amid declining membership, ending in 1923.

Zitkala-Ša's departure from the Society of American Indians included the conclusion of her tenure as editor of the *American Indian Magazine*. Closing the door on that literary endeavor, however, was followed by her opening of another literary door. In 1921, she saw her second book published. *American Indian Stories* included the pieces that she had written about twenty years before for the *Atlantic Monthly*. She also included in the volume such additional selections as "The Widespread Enigma Concerning Blue-Star Woman," "A Dream of Her Grandfather," and "America's Indian Problem." The book included at the end a letter from Helen Keller praising Zitkala-Ša's earlier book, *Old Indian Legends*. In the brief story "A Dream of Her Grandfather" (141–42), the narrator speaks of the granddaughter of a Dakota medicine man. The granddaughter has a dream vision that concludes with the granddaughter filled with hope for her people (142). Although far from being a great work of literature, the story affirms Zitkala-Ša's own sense of optimism that she can make a difference for her own people.

The essay "America's Indian Problem" concludes the volume. In the opening section, she emphasizes that the time to act is now. Success in ensuring that "the American Indian shall have his day in court" will come "through the help of the women of America," an especially apt declaration given Zitkala-Ša's growing association with the General Federation of Women's Clubs. She goes on to state that there must be a concerted effort to create opportunity for Native peoples so they can occupy a meaningful place in the life of the country. The avenue through which to accomplish this, she notes, is by enfranchisement (155–56).

The effort to attain citizenship for Native Americans was perhaps the most important focus of Zitkala-Ša's life. It was, she believed, necessary to escaping an auxiliary role in American life and achieving full membership in society, able to wield political power that comes with citizenship. At the same time, she believed that citizenship must and could come without sacrificing traditional culture.

During World War I, Zitkala-Ša had supported the war effort, at least in part because she believed that Native Americans' participation in the war would foster support for granting them citizenship. Twenty-five percent of adult male Native Americans served during the war (Lewandowski 125–26). That number included Raymond Bonnin, who enlisted and, although too old to serve in combat, worked in the Food Provisions Unit of the Quarter Master Corps in Washington.

In November 1919, citizenship was granted to all Native Americans who had served in the military and been honorably discharged. This was a first step, and, although far short of the full citizenship for all that Zitkala-Ša wanted, had to have given her more reason to hope for her ultimate success.

A variety of publications that appeared in the *American Indian Magazine* at this time demonstrate Zitkala-Ša's arguments for citizenship. In

"Indian Gifts to Civilized Man," she recounts military service by males and the work Native American women were performing at home to aid the war effort (184–86). In an editorial in *AIM*, Zitkala-Ša again reminds the country of the Native Americans' patriotism, appeals for their representation at the post-war peace conference in Paris, and explicitly states her request for citizenship (191–92). "America, Home of the Red Man" again emphasizes Native American contributions to the war, including combat duty and financial contributions to Liberty Loans and war funds of various organizations such as the Red Cross and Y.M.C.A. (193–95). If war service merits citizenship, so does commitment to democracy. In "The Coronation of Chief Powhatan Retold," Zitkala-Ša delves into the early seventeenth century to demonstrate that the origins of American democracy are to be found in tribal history (196–98).

Zitkala-Ša continued to lend her pen and voice to securing the twin goals of citizenship and land security. In her pamphlet *Americanize the First American: A Plan of Regeneration* (1921), she refers to Indians isolated by noncitizenship on reservations as "virtually prisoners of war in America," urges the revocation of the almost unlimited power of officials in charge of reservations and calls for the extension of opportunities to the first Americans through citizenship (242–44). In the concluding section of the pamphlet, an essay titled "Bureaucracy Versus Democracy," Zitkala-Ša proposes a number of changes, among them that the Bureau of Indian Affairs be transformed from a controlling instrument to an agent of protection against individuals endangering Native Americans' liberty and property, and that citizenship be granted to every Native American born in the United States (245–46).

As Lewandowski points out, some modern readers have seen the pamphlet, especially its title, as assimilationist, but he correctly points out that Zitkala-Ša is calling for both "Indian participation in American and world affairs" and "the preservation of Native religion and culture." "The ultimate goal," he writes, "is unfettered existence outside of federal government control and the overwhelming influence of white society" (161). It is important to note that Zitkala-Ša especially makes her appeal in *Americanize the First American* to women, hardly a surprise given her alliance with the General Federation of Women's Clubs and her appeals elsewhere to women (244). Feminism was seldom very far from Zitkala-Ša's mindset when pushing for change.

In November 1923, Zitkala-Ša arrived in Oklahoma along with Charles H. Fabens, an attorney with the American Indian Defense Association (AIDA), an organization whose advisory board she would join the following year, and Matthew K. Sniffen of the Indian Rights Association (IRA), to investigate a wave of murders committed against Osages, dozens of whom were murdered between 1921 and 1925 for their wealth that came from oil lands. Out of this investigation came their pamphlet *Oklahoma's Poor Rich Indians: An Orgy of Graft and Exploitation of the Five Civilized Tribes—Legalized Robbery*, written by the three investigators and published by the Indian Rights Association. The report recommended that control over Indian property should be transferred from Oklahoma courts to the Department of the Interior, which was seen as the lesser of two evils (Debo 329–30).

The pamphlet, as Marion Gridley has noted, played an important role in the establishment of a commission led by anthropologist Lewis Meriam of the Institute for Government Research, and ultimately to the Meriam Report (86), which helped to alter federal policy in a variety of areas, including abolishment of the practice of allotment, which the report blamed for exacerbating Native American poverty, and which was finally ended with the Indian Reorganization Act of 1934. The report also was critical of Indian boarding schools and highlighted the need for improved medical facilities on and off reservations (Lewandowski 181).

Meanwhile, the fight for citizenship was moving toward a significant if imperfect victory. The Indian Citizenship Act, introduced by Representative Homer P. Snyder of New York, was passed in the House of Representatives on March 18, 1924. The Senate adopted an amendment by Senator Robert La Follette of Wisconsin removing the original House stipulation that Native Americans must request citizenship and approved the legislation on May 15. The House accepted the Senate version on May 23, and President Calvin Coolidge signed the bill into law on June 2. The Indian Citizenship Act reads:

> *Be it enacted by the Senate and House of Representatives of the United States of America in Congress assembled,* That all non-citizen Indians born within the territorial limits of the United States be, and they are hereby, declared to be citizens of the United States: *Provided* That the granting of such citizenship shall not in any manner impair or otherwise affect the right of any Indian to tribal or other property [archives.gov].

The law allowed dual citizenship: in the United States and in their own sovereign tribal nation. However, that sovereignty was not absolute. States, until later forbidden to do so, were allowed to deny the vote to those who did not meet official requirements, a loophole that allowed Arizona, Utah, and New Mexico to limit Native American suffrage. BIA control over reservations also continued. Nonetheless, Zitkala-Ša had seen her efforts to bring about universal Indian citizenship enacted into law, even if the law was in some places partly subverted. When Zitkala-Ša was listing her major accomplishments around 1929, she included "Helped get Act through Congress granting citizenship to all Indians" (quoted in Lewandowski 171).

The National Council of American Indians

Zitkala-Ša had left the Society of American Indians, but she was far from finished with national organizations. This time the organization, the National Council of American Indians (NCAI), founded in February 1926, was her own creation, and she served as its president, extending her conviction that meaningful change must come through the leadership of women. Her husband functioned as secretary and treasurer. Reflecting Zitkala-Ša's priorities, the organization had as its motto "Help Indians Help Themselves in Protecting Their Rights and Properties." The NCAI was very much a family enterprise, as the primary source of revenue was the Bonnins themselves: Zitkala-Ša's writings and Raymond's income as a law clerk. Membership fees were nominal: $1.00 for individuals and $1.50 for the local branches, which were called "tribal lodges." Zitkala-Ša turned much of her attention to Congress, urging fulfillment of the rights of citizenship.

The NCAI entered forcefully into political races in order to support those who had championed Native rights and defeat those who had stood in the way, for example, helping to defeat Senator John W. Harreld of Oklahoma, chairman of the Senate Committee on Indian Affairs, who, Zitkala-Ša believed, had been insufficiently supportive of Native rights and property. Her efforts precipitated substantive actions, such as correcting BIA abuses on the Cherokee Reservation in North Carolina and inducing the U.S. Senate to hold hearings on corporal punishment in Arizona's Indian schools (Lewandowski 177–79).

Zitkala-Ša wanted to speak to Native Americans throughout the country. She attempted to do precisely that by establishing the *Indian Newsletter* in 1929, which she distributed to reservations. The newsletter informed its readers of national concerns, educated them as to their rights, and kept her readership informed on what was happening in the halls of Congress. In the same year, she published the essay "What It Means to Be an Indian Today" in *The Friends' Intelligencer* of January 19, 1929. Zitkala-Ša demonstrates in her essay the disparity between Native Americans' official status, which had significantly changed with the conferring of citizenship, and the reality of their condition, which included for a great many poverty, ill health, reduced land holdings, substandard education, and lack of political power (Lewandowski 179–80).

Success or Failure?

By 1935, Zitkala-Ša was almost sixty years old, in declining health, and trying to continue with limited financial resources. Maintaining the

National Council of American Indians no longer proved financially, physically, or emotionally possible, and Zitkala-Ša closed down the Washington office in 1934, taking NCAI materials to their home in Virginia, a state they had moved to about a decade earlier. Despite her difficulties, Zitkala-Sa continued to communicate with Congressional subcommittees regarding issues affecting Native Americans and attempted to bring a tribal constitution to the Yankton Sioux.

These issues and more are reflected in Zitkala-Ša's diaries that she kept during her final years and that are now housed within the Harold B. Lee Library at Brigham Young University. The diaries are discussed within Lewandowski's study of Zitkala-Ša (184–88).

Zitkala-Ša slipped into a coma on January 25, 1938, and was admitted to Georgetown Hospital. On January 26, she died of "cardiac dilation and kidney disease" (Lewandowski 187), the former what is now called dilated cardiomyopathy in which the heart muscle dilates, thus stretching and becoming thinner. The chamber therefore enlarges, but the muscle surrounding it weakens so that the heart does not pump blood adequately. Ultimately, heart failure occurs.

Despite Zitkala-Ša's apparent preference for Catholicism throughout much of her life, her funeral occurred at the Church of Latter-Day Saints in Washington, D.C. John Collier, named Commissioner of Indian Affairs by Franklin D. Roosevelt in 1933, eulogized her, noting that "'The Sioux and all Indians have lost a real leader'" (quoted in Lewandowski 188). Burial was at Arlington National Cemetery because Raymond had served in the military. Other deaths followed quickly: Ohiya in 1939, Raymond in 1942.

Zitkala-Ša's diaries demonstrate that, as she approached the end of her life, she was questioning how much she actually had accomplished. At the beginning of her second diary, on April 1, 1936, she wrote, "'Ten years have passed and I have done nothing at all in all these years! Just a fretful milling around in dense ignorance—that's all.'" The year before, she had lamented in a letter to a friend, Elaine Eastman, "'I appreciate your genuine desire to give me credit for having tried to render service to the Red Race. But though it took a lifetime, the achievements are scarcely visible!!!'" (quoted in Lewandowski 184–86).

Although many of the leading activists of the 1960s and 1970s were initially unaware of Zitkala-Ša, her reputation has grown steadily. Tadeusz Lewandowski, in his outstanding study of Zitkala-Ša, points out that "her published work bears direct comparison to the ideas put forth by Indian activists in the late 1960s and 1970s when the Native American civil rights movement emerged and gained national attention" (192). In fact, he devotes his final chapter to arguing convincingly that she was "a forerunner of Red Power who asserted the moral, cultural, and religious superiority of Sioux over white civilization" (189). P. Jane Hafen writes, "When that eight-year-old left the reservation for boarding school, she began a process in which her tribal self—her identity as a Yankton Sioux— became subsumed by a broader identity as Indian. She used the skills she had learned in the non–Indian world to fight for Indian rights, a commitment that stemmed from her memories of those long ago days on the plains. She remained, as she always signed her letters, 'yours for the Indian cause'" (139). David Martínez, in *The American Indian Intellectual Tradition: An Anthology of Writings from 1772–1972*, sees Zitkala-Ša as epitomizing—along with Charles A. Eastman, Carlos Montezuma, and Arthur C. Parker—"the Progressive Era Indian intellectual" (198). He also includes two of Zitkala-Ša's publications in the anthology: *Americanize the First American* and *Oklahoma's Poor Rich Indians*. In an anthology of nineteenth-century American women essayists, *In Her Own Voice*, edited by Sherry Lee Linkon, Zitkala-Ša appears within a much broader, national context.

Had Zitkala-Ša failed? The answer today is clear.

Notes

1. I am greatly indebted to Tadeusz Lewandowski's *Red Bird, Red Power: The Life and Legacy of Zitkala-Ša* for factual information on Zitkala-Ša throughout this chapter.

2. Unless otherwise noted, references to Zitkala-Ša's publications are to *American Indian Stories, Legends, and Other Writings*, edited by Cathy N. Davidson and Ada Norris.

3. For the original version of "Why I Am a Pagan," see it along with the first two *Atlantic Monthly* narratives in *My Life: Impressions of an Indian Childhood; The School Days of an Indian Girl; Why I Am a Pagan*, published by Hannah Wilson in Lexington, Kentucky, in 2016.

4. Quotations from Hafen and *The Sun Dance Opera*, as well as references to both, are from *Dreams and Thunder*, edited by Hafen with the general introduction to the book and the specific introduction to the opera by Hafen.

5. For a detailed account of the struggle between the two, see Lewandowski, pp. 136–49.

References

Debo, Angie. *And Still the Waters Run: The Betrayal of the Five Civilized Tribes*. Rev. ed. PrincetonPrinceton UP, 1972.
Dominguez, Susan Rose. "The Gertrude Bonnin Story: From Yankton to American History, 1904–1938." Diss. Michigan State U, 2005.
Fisher, Dexter. Foreword. *American Indian Stories*. By Zitkala-Sa. Lincoln: U of Nebraska P, 1985.
Gibbon, Guy. *The Sioux: The Dakota and Lakota Nations*. Malden, MA: Blackwell, 2003.
Grann, David. *Killers of the Flower Moon: The Osage Murders and the Birth of the FBI*. New York: Doubleday, 2017.
Gridley, Marion E. "Gertrude Simmons Bonnin: A Modern Progressive." *American Indian Women*. New York: Hawthorn, 1974. 81–87.
Hafen, P. Jane. "Gertrude Simmons Bonnin: For the Indian Cause." *Sifters: Native American Women's Lives*. Ed. Theda Perdue. New York: Oxford UP, 2001. 127–40.

Hoxie, Frederick E. *This Indian Country: American Indian Activists and the Place They Made.* 2012. New York: Penguin, 2013.

Indian Citizenship Act. Sixty-Eighth Congress of the United States of America: At the First Session. archives.gov/global-pages/larger-image.html?i=/historical-docs/doc-content/images/indian-citizenship-act-1924-l.jpg&c=/historical-docs/doc-content/images/indian-citizenship-act-1924.caption.html.

Johnston, Robert D. *The Radical Middle Class: Populist Democracy and the Question of Capitalism in Progressive Era Portland, Oregon.* Princeton: Princeton UP, 2003.

Lewandowski, Tadeusz. *Red Bird, Red Power: The Life and Legacy of Zitkala-Sa.* Norman: U of Oklahoma P, 2016.

Lukens, Margaret A. "The American Indian Story of Zitkala-Sa." *In Her Own Voice: Nineteenth-Century American Women Essayists.* Ed. Sherry Lee Linkon. New York: Garland, 1997. 141–55.

Mails, Thomas E. *Sundancing: The Great Sioux Piercing Ritual.* 2nd edition. Tulsa: Council Oaks Books, 1998.

Stewart, Omer C. *Peyote Religion: A History.* Norman: U of Oklahoma P, 1987.

Zitkala-Sa. *American Indian Stories, Legends, and Other Writings.* Ed. Cathy N. Davidson and Ada Norris. New York: Penguin, 2003.

_____. *Dreams and Thunder: Stories, Poems, and The Sun Dance Opera.* Ed. P. Jane Hafen. Lincoln: U of Nebraska P, 2001.

_____. *My Life: Impressions of an Indian Childhood: The School Days of an Indian Girl; Why I am a Pagan.* Lexington: Hannah Wilson, 2016.

_____. *Old Indian Legends.* 1901. Lincoln: U of Nebraska P, 1985.

_____. "Our Sioux People." MSS 1704; Gertrude and Raymond Bonnin Collection; 20th–21st Century Western and Mormon Americana; L. Tom Perry Special Collections, Harold B. Lee Library, Brigham Young University.

_____. "The Sioux Cause." MSS 1704; Gertrude and Raymond Bonnin Collection; 20th–21st Century Western and Mormon Americana; L. Tom Perry Special Collections, Harold B. Lee Library, Brigham Young University.

_____. "What It Means to Be an Indian Today." *Friends' Intelligencer* 19 Jan. 1929: 46–47.

_____, Charles H. Fabens, and Matthew K. Sniffen. *Oklahoma's Poor Rich Indians: An Orgy of Graft and Exploitation of the Five Civilized Tribes—Legalized Robbery. The American Indian Intellectual Tradition: An Anthology of Writings from 1772 to 1972.* Ed. David Martínez. Ithaca: Cornell UP, 2011. 225–54.

6

Annie Dodge Wauneka
(1910–1997)

Annie Dodge Wauneka's life could well be a model for countless individuals who face a difficult childhood but strive to overcome it and ultimately achieve great success. Her first significant role in life was herding sheep. She did not know who her biological mother was until her late twenties, and her famous and politically influential father seemingly favored her siblings regarding educational opportunities, although he later came to recognize and encourage Annie's abilities.

Shortly after beginning her delayed schooling, Annie encountered serious illness, the terrible influenza of 1918, which decimated her school, perhaps laying the foundation for how she would spend most of her adult life. It is difficult to imagine anyone giving more completely of herself to improve people's health than was the case with Annie Dodge Wauneka, who labored with considerable success to combat tuberculosis, unsanitary living conditions, and a general lack of access to good health care on the Navajo Reservation. Recognized for her great contributions by the Navajo Nation and beyond, she received the Presidential Medal of Freedom and retains, a quarter century after her death, her position as one of the greatest of Navajo leaders.

Childhood: Sheep and Tuberculosis

Annie Dodge was born on April 11, 1910, near Sawmill, Arizona, on the Navajo Reservation. Her mother, Kee'hanabah, gave birth to her daughter in a hogan, a small house typically made of logs with a dirt floor, windows without glass, and a wood stove. A small door would face the east so that the morning sun could be seen rising. The round hogan itself symbolized the sun, and the position of the door thus was a spiritual matter while also offering the practical advantage of lighting the home in the morning and imparting warmth. Annie remained with her mother until she was about eight months old, at which time her father took her to live with him at his large and impressive home at Sonsola Buttes near Crystal, New Mexico.

Kee'hanabah had been sent to Annie's father, Henry Chee Dodge, as a sort of substitute wife by the family of his two earlier wives, the sisters Nanabah and Asza Yaze, marrying sisters then allowed under Navajo culture. The two sisters had left Dodge as a result of some dispute. When Kee'hanabah was pregnant with Annie, the sisters returned, and Kee'hanabah departed for her home at Sawmill. For the better part of three decades, Annie would believe that Nanabah was her mother and Kee'hanabah was an aunt. Only on Nanabah's death would her father divulge her true parentage (Niethammer, *I'll Go* 3–4; *Keeping the Rope Straight* 33–34). Before then, Annie would often visit Kee'hanabah, and, although family members, including the children that Kee'hanabah had with a later husband, apparently knew who Annie's mother really was, no one shared that knowledge with her (Niethammer, *I'll Go* 32–33; *Keeping the Rope Straight* 16–18).

Annie's father would have a great influence on her, so much so that it is important to understand who he was and what he did. The Rev. Francis Borgman, a Franciscan priest stationed at St. Michael's Mission in Arizona south of Fort Defiance, a close friend of Henry Chee Dodge and the priest who administered the Last Rites to Dodge as he was dying, has presented a detailed biographical account of Dodge, which was published in the *New Mexico Historical Review* the year following Dodge's death. According to Borgman, Dodge was born on February 22, 1860, which made him almost eighty-seven years old when he passed away on January 7, 1947. Borgman states that Dodge was born at Fort Defiance, the son of a Mexican father, Juan Anaya (elsewhere referred to as Juan Cocinas), and a Navajo mother, Bisnayanchi. The father had been captured by Navajos as a child and later served as a translator for Captain Henry L. Dodge, the agent at Fort Defiance, who was killed in 1856 (81–82). Captain Dodge, the son of Henry Dodge, a territorial governor and later United States senator for Wisconsin, had befriended Juan, so when their son was born they named him Henry Dodge after the agent. Young Henry, however, was orphaned while young. A period of Navajo hostility to the white soldiers occurred during this time, and the decision was made to remove the Navajos to the Bosque Redondo, a region along the Pecos River in eastern New Mexico, a forced journey of three hundred to four hundred miles referred to as "the long walk." In attempting to avoid this forced march, Henry's mother, having left Henry with relatives, died while seeking help in a Hopi village, his father having died earlier. When the Navajo war chief Manuelito finally ended his opposition, the Navajos were permitted to return home. Henry reached Fort Defiance in 1868 and was reunited with his mother's sister. He was known by the soldiers there as "Chee," a word that conveyed his reddish color (Niethammer, *I'll Go* 7–11).

In addition to Navajo, Chee began learning English and was so adept at it that he began developing a skill that would serve him well over the years: translating. Popular with the soldiers at Fort Defiance, for whom he served, according to Borgman, as an "errand boy" (84), he also benefited from the support of his aunt's husband, a white man named Perry Williams who worked as an issue clerk at Fort Defiance and hired Chee to work for him in the store as an interpreter (Niethammer, *I'll Go* 11–12), as well as support from the Fort Defiance agent William Arny, who thought that Dodge was the son of the late Captain Dodge (Iverson 88). He also worked for Dr. Washington Matthews, an army surgeon and one of the first ethnographers who focused on Navajo culture (Brugge 94).

Liked and respected for his ability to work well with both Navajos and whites, Henry Chee Dodge advanced quickly. He was appointed to the official federal position of translator for the Navajo people by the age of twenty; he also was named chief herder. By the age of twenty-four, he had been named by Manuelito as his successor as chief, an appointment that required and received the approval of Navajo agent Denis Riordan as well as the consent of the Secretary of the Interior and the Commissioner of Indian Affairs. Dodge also was named chief of police for the reservation, a position for which he apparently was seen as particularly suited after he assisted in investigating killings of two white prospectors and a white settler (Brugge 94). By twenty-six, he was raising sheep and cattle, having claimed a large area of land with good soil and plenty of moisture known as Sonsola Buttes near Crystal in the Chuksa Mountains. After losing hundreds of sheep during a particularly hard winter in 1891, he added another ranch farther south in an area of Arizona called Tanner Springs. Here he could better raise cattle and sheep because of the milder weather. Tanner Springs was not within the Navajo Reservation, but Dodge had sufficient money to purchase the land. In addition, he purchased part ownership in a trading post at Round Rock near Chinle, Arizona (Niethammer, *I'll Go* 14–17; Borgman 85–87; Brugge 95–97).

By the end of the nineteenth century, Henry Chee Dodge was a wealthy owner of much land and livestock and widely respected as a leader that both Navajos and U.S. government officials looked to for advice and guidance. By the time Annie was born, Dodge already had three children: Tom, Ben, and Mary, Tom (who would serve as Tribal Council Chairperson and later work for the Bureau of Indian Affairs) by Asza Yaze, and the others by Nanabah. The actual number of his children, however, is not totally clear, as a St. Michael's Mission census lists six. Dodge's new house, at Sonsola Buttes, was completed by 1903. A far cry from the hogans in which so many of the Navajos lived, the house, designed by a Flagstaff architect, included a modern kitchen and a porch across the front. Additional buildings behind it accommodated guests and workers (Niethammer, *I'll Go* 21; *Keeping the Rope Straight* 4; Brugge 97).

Into this home came Annie, not yet one year old. Although the three older children were sent to Catholic schools, Annie remained at home. Once she was old enough, at about five, she was tasked with daily taking a herd of sheep out to graze. Once they were settled in, Annie left her dog to guard them and would return to the house for a breakfast of fry bread and weak coffee. Then she would take a bottle of water and more fry bread with her for lunch and head back to watch the sheep. Late in the afternoon, Annie would bring the sheep back and put them in a corral for the night (Niethammer, *Keeping the Rope Straight* 3–6).

Like most children, Annie liked to play, making do with what surrounded her. A favorite game involved white stones representing sheep and a black stone that stood for a coyote. The black stone, of course, would attempt to attack and eat the white stones. She also staged ant wars, depositing black ants at red ant anthills and watching the conflict (Niethammer, *Keeping the Rope Straight* 6–8).

If Annie's father saw in her someone best suited for herding sheep rather than attending school, perhaps not intellectually equal to his other children, that attitude would change dramatically over the years. The change began, and with it perhaps the first of several periods in Annie's life that would shape her destiny, when she was eight years old. It was then that Annie began attending the government school at Fort Defiance. Although her father had received little formal education, he had come to value education highly, urging Navajos to send their children to school and modeling with his children what he was urging others to do, so it is not surprising that he finally enrolled his youngest child (Borgman 90).

Unfortunately, Annie was not long at the Fort Defiance school before the influenza pandemic of 1918 struck. Chee Dodge brought his other three children home and locked the gate to his estate in order to try to keep the pandemic at bay. Annie remained at Fort Defiance and did, in fact, become ill. She recovered quickly, though, and with the school quarantined pitched in to help. With most of the staff ill, only Domatilda Showalter, a nurse at the school, was left to care for the ill with Annie assisting. Annie would keep the lanterns clean and filled with kerosene. She also fed with a spoon those who were too sick even to eat their soup by themselves. So many people at the school died that no more coffins were available, so the bodies were wrapped in sheets and placed on a porch in the shade until they could be hauled away on a wagon. Many of the bodies were buried in a mass grave near the school. In the spring, the school temporarily closed, and survivors, including Annie, returned home (Niethammer, *Keeping the Rope Straight* 8–10; Nelson 24). The early days of the coronavirus pandemic of 2020 in New York City would have seemed familiar to Annie.

Although it is unlikely that Annie Dodge Wauneka decided at the age of eight to spend most of her adult life fighting disease and supporting improved sanitation and health care, it is also difficult not to believe that the influenza pandemic left a permanent imprint on her young, impressionable mind and conscience.

When Annie was in the fourth grade at Fort Defiance, another health issue confronted her. Two ongoing and very serious problems on the Navajo Reservation were tuberculosis and trachoma. These two illnesses were constant threats and especially dangerous in the confined environment of a school where they could be easily transmitted from person to person (Iverson 115–17). Annie's fourth grade was interrupted by an outbreak of trachoma, an eye infection that can cause blindness. Annie and other students who had not been infected were transferred to St. Michael's Mission School. There Annie, who had been baptized into the Catholic religion while at Fort Defiance, continued to receive religious instruction that would stay with her throughout her life, leading her to be a regular attendee at Catholic mass. Annie spent about a year and a half at St. Michael's, returning to Fort Defiance after the trachoma crisis had ceased (Niethammer, *I'll Go* 30–31; *Keeping the Rope Straight* 12). St. Michael's was an appropriate school for Annie, given her father's close relationship with the priests at St. Michael's Mission. He often visited there, staying in a room in the rectory. Borgman credits Chee with providing substantial help when the Franciscan fathers attempted to prepare a catechism to instruct Navajos in the Catholic faith. With his excellent knowledge of both Navajo and English, he was able to develop Navajo substitutes for religious phrases that did not have explicit parallels in the Navajo language. Borgman cites as examples *immortality*, *original sin*, and even *God*, for the latter choosing *digin ayoitei*, translated as "the Great Holy One" (90–91).

After completing fifth grade at Fort Defiance, Annie, along with her sister, Mary, transferred to the Albuquerque Indian School run by the Bureau of Indian Affairs (BIA). The railroad leg of the trip, from Gallup, New Mexico, to Albuquerque, was temporarily disrupted when another train collided with the one that the girls were on. The inauspicious beginning, however, did not adversely color Annie's view of her new school.

Annie continued at this school until 1928, making friends from a wide range of tribes, with some Pueblo girls becoming her closest friends. Having known primarily Navajos previously, she learned that the students spoke different languages, necessitating the speaking of English so that they could understand each other (Lapahie). Along with experiencing a more demanding curriculum than at Fort Defiance, Annie became involved in sports, developing expertise in tennis, and learning about classical music, with Beethoven a favorite (Niethammer, *I'll Go* 34).

During Annie's school years, her father was becoming increasingly important as a political leader of the Navajos. Albert Bacon Fall, Secretary of the Interior, during the Warren G. Harding administration, decided to create a Navajo tribal council to represent the whole reservation. Before the council was constituted, Hall was forced out of his position and replaced by Hubert Work. Work kept Herbert J. Hagerman on as a special commissioner to work with the Navajos, and it was Hagerman who led the effort to create a tribal council. The council consisted of twelve delegates representing agencies plus a tribal chairman. Chee Dodge became the first chairman of the Navajo Tribal Council, which held its first meeting on June 7, 1923 (Iverson 133–36). Dodge headed the Tribal Council until 1929, later serving additional terms as chairman; in the immediate aftermath of World War II, for example, once again chairman of the Tribal Council, he would lead a delegation to Washington, D.C., to testify before the United States Senate Committee on Indian Affairs in support of a greater federal commitment to improving education on the Navajo Reservation (Iverson 191). Borgman states that "even when he was not 'ex officio' chairman he still remained the 'Chief,' and very little was done without his council [sic] and advice" (88). Dodge encouraged Navajos to take better advantage of educational opportunities and accept modern methods of health care, including use of area hospitals. He provided important leadership on many other weighty issues as well, among them oil leases on Navajo land, expansion of the reservation, allotment, stock reduction, and range control while also traveling to Washington several times to solicit federal support for the Navajos (Borgman 88–90; Brugge 104–07).

Annie returned home in 1928 after completing her eleventh grade. It would be her final year at the school in Albuquerque. Her next role, albeit a temporary one, was to help run the Dodge household with Nanabah and Asza Yaze. However, Annie had met a young man named George Wauneka at the Albuquerque school, and with the agreement of her father and Nanabah, they were married in a Catholic ceremony. Then, in October 1929, they were married in a traditional Navajo ceremony at Tanner Springs (Niethammer, *I'll Go* 38–43). Annie was only nineteen, and her life might have proceeded along a traditional Navajo path as a wife and mother. That, however, would be only part of her path. She would soon find another purpose in life through a growing bond with her father, who would increasingly recognize other talents that she had and involve her in his political life, which would ultimately place her alongside her father among the greatest of Navajo leaders.

Entering Politics and Fighting Tuberculosis

Annie and George initially lived at Sonsola Buttes for about two years, but when Annie's sister, Mary, expressed her unhappiness living at Tanner Springs, Chee brought Mary and her husband, Carl Peshlaki, back to Sonsola Buttes and sent Annie and George to Tanner Springs to run that ranch, under, however, the strict supervision of Chee. They lived in a modern, sandstone house rather than a traditional hogan. The house had running water and electricity, a front porch, and several rooms, although as children started arriving the house must have felt cramped at times (Niethammer, *Keeping the Rope Straight* 23; *I'll Go* 41–43, 72–75; Nelson 35–38).

Annie and George's first child, Georgia Ann, was born in 1931. Nine more would follow her: James Henry, who died in infancy (1932), Marvin (1934), Henry (1935), Irma (1936), George Leonard (1939), Timothy (1942), Franklin (1945), Lorencita (1946), and Sallie (1950). Several of the births were difficult, and some of the children were born with disabilities (Niethammer, *I'll Go* 58, 67, 72–73). The final birth was especially difficult and life-threatening for Annie. George helped Annie, who had gone into labor but was clearly in trouble, into their truck and raced to a nearby trading post. Sallie Lippincott Wagner, who ran the trading post with her husband, tells in her book *Wide Ruins: Memories from a Navajo Trading Post* that the baby had been born before their arrival but "Annie had retained the placenta and was in agony." Sallie called the Ganado Hospital and was told to rush Annie there, which she did, loading Annie and baby into the back of her station wagon and arriving, according to the doctor, just in time to save Annie's life. Annie needed blood transfusions, which she received from her husband. In gratitude for the life-saving assistance, the parents named the baby after Sallie (45–46). When the children were old enough, Annie, remembering her own experience, sent them to St. Michael's Catholic school (Nelson 40).

At the same time that Annie was beginning her life as a wife and mother, she also was stepping into the world of politics, with her father leading her. Chee Dodge would stop by to check on how the ranch was operating and then take Annie, and sometimes George as well, to a local chapter meeting at Klagetoh or Wide Ruins, chapters corresponding somewhat to counties. At other times, he would call a meeting at Tanner Springs. There Annie would be tasked with preparing mutton stew and coffee, but she also would listen to the political discussions. At one meeting of the Klagetoh chapter, Annie listened to a government agent discuss the 1933 level of stock reduction, which required sharp reductions in stock in order to avoid the overgrazing that was causing serious soil erosion. Annie realized that the individual who was translating from English into Navajo was making significant errors. At the end of the meeting, she told her father about the mistranslating and he exploded in anger that she had not spoken up at the time. This would be an important turning point for Annie, motivating her to enter far more actively into the political life of the Navajo Nation (Carolyn Niethammer, *I'll Go* 43–45, 53–54; *Keeping the Rope Straight* 24–28). Before long, Chee was having Annie do any interpreting that was required (Niethammer, *I'll Go 62*).

With Annie becoming increasingly visible at official functions, and as the daughter of perhaps the most respected Navajo leader, it was not surprising that she would be called upon to take a more prominent role in the life of the Navajo Nation. Her local Klagetoh chapter elected her to the Grazing Committee, which had the serious and sometimes difficult responsibility of mediating conflicts over rangeland rights while also overseeing basic cattle functions such as branding and vaccinating. The next step was her selection to be secretary of her chapter (Niethammer, *I'll Go* 62–63).

The long life and career of Chee Dodge came to an end on January 7, 1947. Hospitalized in Sage Memorial Hospital in Ganado, Arizona, he learned that death was imminent. With his children at his bedside, he instructed them: "'Do not let my straight rope fall to the ground. If you discover it dropping, quickly one of you pick it up and hold it aloft and straight'" (quoted in Niethammer, *Keeping the Rope Straight* 37). His son, Tom, had served as Tribal Council chairperson but by this time was employed by the Bureau of Indian Affairs. The person who had become increasingly involved with Navajo leadership was Annie, and she did indeed pick up the rope.

Annie decided to seek a position on the Tribal Council. Her father and brother had both chaired the council and, as Peter Iverson has pointed out, used the position to push for, among other changes, better health care for Navajos (198). Annie's early encounters with diseases on the reservation had embedded in her a commitment to the same cause, although she was deeply aware of many other important issues as well. So, despite being busy with her ranch and children, Annie pursued her place in Navajo leadership. The election occurred over two days, March 5 and 6, 1951. Three-fourths of eligible voters participated despite many of them having to travel great distances by wagon. When the votes were tabulated, Annie had been elected to represent the Klagetoh and Wide Ruins chapters. She took her oath of office in the Council Chambers at the base of Window Rock in eastern Arizona, a natural sandstone formation that for Navajos is an important religious shrine. Carolyn Niethammer summarizes her condition at the time: "She was forty-one years old—healthy, politically astute, and more than ready to move into her new life" (*I'll Go 76*).

No longer the shy young woman who sat quietly, listening to her father and other leaders talk of Navajo matters, Annie wasted no time expressing her opinions in her very first council meeting. She offered her views on how the Advisory Council, which presented recommendations to the full council, should function. The following day she criticized the practice of allowing the Bureau of Indian Affairs superintendent to sit in front next to the chairperson and whisper to him, implying that the superintendent was giving orders. In response, the superintendent changed where he sat even if his actual authority may have remained just as great (Niethammer, *I'll Go* 77). In February 1952, Annie, with the Advisory Council members, traveled to Washington, D.C., the first of many such trips that she made over the years to gain federal support for her people. Annie Dodge Wauneka would spend twenty-six years on the Tribal Council and leave behind a legacy greater perhaps than even that of her father.

Annie probably spent more time and energy combatting tuberculosis than on any other single issue during her years on the Tribal Council. The prevalence of tuberculosis on the Navajo Reservation had reached devastating proportions, with the rate of the disease among Navajos fourteen times the national average. Factors contributing to the high incidence of tuberculosis amounted to virtually a perfect storm of causes. Health facilities, hit hard by federal cuts in funds for health services, had declined sharply during the World War II years. Iverson summarizes some of the facility-related problems:

> The nursing staff at the Fort Defiance hospital dwindled from thirty-eight to thirteen and other facilities suffered similar depletions. Hospitals at Fort Defiance, Kayenta, Leupp, Toadlena, and Tohatchi closed their doors. So, too, did the Kayenta Sanatorium [197].

Cultural factors also raised impediments. Many Navajos were reluctant to trust white doctors, preferring to rely on Navajo medicine men to heal them. Staying at home while sick, given the highly infectious nature of tuberculosis, endangered everyone else around the sick person. Hospitals posed a huge cultural shock, requiring the patient to be largely isolated from family, wear hospital gowns, and eat food with which the patient was unfamiliar. For many patients even something as basic as a thermometer was strange. Recovery typically took a long time, perhaps months, of isolation in the hospital, so many patients would leave before being cured. Also, Navajos knew that people died in hospitals, which created considerable fear for those who believed that spirits of the dead could make one ill (Niethammer, *I'll Go* 87–89).

Undeterred, Annie set out to effect change. During her trip to Washington in February 1952, newspapers reported development of a new drug, isonicotinic acid hydrazide, to fight tuberculosis. A group of doctors affiliated with Cornell University, who had previously visited the Navajo Reservation concerning an outbreak of hepatitis, decided to return with doses of the drug donated by the E.R. Squibb Company. The doctors, headed by Dr. Walsh McDermott, also were donating their time. Annie presented in the Tribal Council a motion, which passed, to cover the doctors' travel expenses between New York and the reservation (Niethammer, *I'll Go* 79–80).

The problem with the new drug treatment was the old difficulty of persuading individuals to go to a hospital for treatment. A report to the Tribal Council by the Cornell team in January 1953 stated that the new drug was effective but that large numbers of Navajos infected with tuberculosis were not seeing doctors, leading to the continued spread of the disease. A council member, as related by Annie, stood up at the meeting and asked, "'Where's the lady?' He said, 'You women can take care of the sick far better than we men can. So let's appoint her and get her to work.'" Annie thus found herself the chair of the Health and Welfare Subcommittee of the Community Services Committee. The subcommittee soon became a stand-alone committee, and Annie embarked on, what Carolyn Niethammer writes, would define "the next thirty years of her life, eventually thrusting her to the national platform of Indian health care concerns" (*I'll Go* 84–85). Wade Davies points out in *Healing Ways: Navajo Health Care in the Twentieth Century* that the committee "served as the ideal mediator among Western medical providers, the Tribal Council and Navajo patients because it fostered a simple, straightforward communication. Wauneka had learned well from her father the power and necessity of communication and instilled that principle in the Health Committee" (66).

Annie Dodge Wauneka realized that if she were to help reduce the epidemic of tuberculosis among Navajos, she would have to learn much more about the disease herself. Consequently, she turned to Dr. Kurt Deuschle, a Bureau of Indian Affairs doctor at Fort Defiance involved with the Cornell University project who had presented the Tribal Council with an update on efforts to control the disease. She was impressed with Dr. Deuschle and especially moved by his explanation of the harm done to the patient and others when a person leaves the hospital before completing his or her treatment. How to address this problem was clearly frustrating Dr. Deuschle, and the problem, Annie realized, cried out for her to help solve. A first step in learning more about tuberculosis was to ask the doctor to arrange for her to accompany a nurse as the nurse visited patients (Niethammer, *I'll Go* 87). She also asked to study tuberculosis with Dr. Deuschle, which began essentially a three-month cram course on the disease. She had hands-on instruction that included learning how to read X-rays, especially of lungs, and to examine sputum under a microscope. She assiduously did her homework, reading medical books that Dr. Deuschle provided, and learning about the worldwide reach of tuberculosis rather than seeing the disease as an indication of something uniquely wrong with Navajos (Carolyn Niethammer, *I'll Go* 89–90; *Keeping the Rope Straight* 49–50).

Having learned much about tuberculosis, Annie set out to educate fellow Navajos. Driving her pickup (her constant method of transport), she visited regional hospitals, starting with one in Colorado Springs. Her choices were dictated by the number of Navajo tubercular patients in the institution. Wearing her Tribal Council badge (she quickly became known as the "Woman with the Badge"), she explained to the patients what she had learned about the disease, translating medical terminology into colloquial language, for example, the tubercle bacillus (the rod-shaped bacterium that causes tuberculosis) into Navajo words that mean "bugs that eat the body." Showing rather than just telling, Annie would have the patients go to the hospital laboratory, where they could see their X-rays and, using a microscope, their sputum. Understanding the loneliness of the patients far apart from their families, Annie recorded patients on her tape recorder and later took the recordings to their families. Reversing the process, she then had family members record greetings that she conveyed to their hospitalized loved ones. Similar trips to hospitals and sanatoriums in the Tucson and Albuquerque areas followed, with Annie spending about a week at each site (Niethammer, *I'll Go* 90–92; *Keeping the Rope Straight* 50–53).

Most infected Navajos were not in hospitals; in fact, most had not even seen a physician, opting, if they saw anyone, to seek help from a medicine man. The task of locating hundreds of individuals spread throughout the reservation, many living off dirt roads that were barely passable, especially in bad weather, was enormously challenging, but Annie did not hesitate. Often traveling alone, she covered huge tracts of land to locate stricken Navajos. Combining tact and persistence, she kept at it, explaining what tuberculosis was to Navajo families and encouraging individuals to seek modern treatment. Many days turned into nights with Annie far from home, but Navajo generosity was commonplace, so she would be welcomed to spend the night, typically on some sheepskins by the fire. By this time, Annie's determined efforts to improve Navajo health had carried her reputation well beyond the Navajo Reservation. Walter Cronkite, for example, featured her on his *Twentieth Century* series. Slowly but steadily, progress was being made. In the spring of 1954, Dr. Deuschle reported that fewer Navajos were leaving hospitals prior to completing treatment, and some who had earlier left had returned (Carolyn Niethammer, *I'll Go* 93–96; *Keeping the Rope Straight* 53–57).

Numbers can often hide the individual story. One of the individuals that Annie Dodge Wauneka not only helped but, by his own admission, saved, was Albert Hale. Hale was elected as president of the Navajo Nation in 1994, serving until 1998. He later served in the Arizona State Senate and the Arizona House of Representatives. In an introduction to Carolyn Niethammer's *Keeping the Rope Straight: Annie Dodge Wauneka's Life of Service to the Navajo,* Hale recounts how he contracted tuberculosis as a child. Efforts by medicine men failed to help, and Hale grew increasingly weak. Annie Wauneka, however, had been going hogan to hogan to help residents understand tuberculosis and convince them to accept treatment, Hale writes. One of those people convinced by Annie was Hale's mother, who persuaded a man to drive her son to the hospital. That, according, to Hale, saved his life. But he also credits Annie with saving his life a second time. Hale quit high school but attended Klagetoh chapter meetings. At one meeting, Annie spoke directly to Hale and even shook her finger at him, demanding that he return to school and "make something of yourself." Hale did, graduating from college and law school before enjoying a long, successful career in political leadership serving especially his fellow Navajos (xiii–xv). On February 2, 2021, however, Hale, having survived the epidemic of tuberculosis as a child, died of complications from COVID-19.

Annie Dodge Wauneka realized that communicating with medicine men, the traditional Navajo healers, would be essential. Although committed to her Navajo culture and traditions, Annie also recognized the importance of many of the new ways, especially regarding health. Annie communicated directly with medicine men and Bureau of Indian Affairs doctors in order to strike a balance. That balance included such practices as allowing tuberculosis-infected patients who did not need immediate hospitalization to experience a traditional sing ceremony before being taken to a hospital, permitting a healing ceremony inside the patient's hospital room in addition to standard tuberculosis treatment, and, in general, encouraging both physicians and medicine men to respect each other. She also sought to teach the Navajo healers about the disease. Gradually, Annie made progress in a manner that neither denigrated traditional practices nor kept Navajos with tuberculosis from seeking modern medical help (Niethammer, *I'll Go* 98–101; *Keeping the Rope Straight* 59–65).

Annie continued educating herself about tuberculosis and attempting to educate others. She attended conferences, investigated health care services in other areas, including Alaska, made films featuring local Navajos speaking Navajo in order to present information on tuberculosis and other health issues, conducted a weekly radio show on station KGAK in Gallup, New Mexico, testified before Congress, and encouraged establishment of additional hospitals and clinics to serve Navajo patients. In order to assist communication among "white" doctors, medicine men, and Navajo patients and family members, Annie wrote a glossary "defining Navajo medical terms in English and the white man's medical terms in Navajo" (Nelson 52). The glossary paralleled her father's earlier effort to translate Christian terms into Navajo expressions.

The opportunity for sustained progress was enhanced when the health care program for Native Americans was transferred from the Bureau of Indian Affairs to the Public Health Service in 1955. The Public Health Service created a new Division of Indian Health, later renamed the Indian Health Service (IHS). The IHS contracted with the Department of Public Health and Preventive Medicine at Cornell University to establish a clinic on the Navajo Reservation and conduct a five-year study to identify a best-practices health system for the reservation. Annie worked with the Cornell team to select the site for the clinic, settling on the Many Farms-Rough Rock district. The project was well received by the community, with the Cornell team estimating that about 90 percent of the area population at some point in the five years (1956–1961) of the study made at least some use of the clinic. The X-ray and laboratory facilities helped to reduce the incidence of tuberculosis in the area. The IHS on the whole, however, elicited a mixed reaction from Annie and other Navajo leaders, as they saw the IHS as insufficiently committed to consulting tribal leadership (Davies 73–95). The IHS, as Wade Davies, points out, continued to rely primarily on Navajo leadership to recruit patients for medical care. Davies adds, "Perhaps Annie Wauneka fulfilled this role better than any other tribal leader" (96).

The Indian Health Service had more funding than was available before the transfer of responsibility from the BIA, which allowed for the creation of several new hospitals, health centers, field stations, and, in 1961, the Gallup Indian Medical Center. Although certainly not the lone individual responsible for such growth in health care facilities, Annie, perhaps more than anyone else, was the constant force for change; in the words of Peter Iverson, "from the outset, Wauneka cajoled and countered, prodded and pleaded to achieve results" (200). And the results came. In the Many Farms-Rough Rock area, along with improvements in other areas during the 1950s, such as a decline in infant mortality and increases in overall patient as well as outpatient numbers and in women giving birth in hospitals, tuberculosis rates declined by 60 percent from 1952 to 1960 (Iverson 200). In an address to the Tribal Council on January 15, 1959, Annie spoke about how tuberculosis had been reported to be the number one killer of Navajos, but that it had been reduced to the sixth most common cause of death. But, she said, "I am not happy because 1,500 entered sanitariums the past five years; a little bit over 900 are cured as arrested cases, and are among us; [but] very few deaths" (*"For Our Navajo People"* 156).

Advances in reducing tuberculosis in the Navajo Nation were still too slow for Annie. She had relied on education, compromise, persuasion, and making health care opportunities more available. Another approach, she concluded, was necessary. Despite the traditional Navajo opposition to compelling action, she decided that in order to save more lives, requiring rather than merely persuading would have to be implemented. Arizona, New Mexico, and Utah had enacted legislation allowing involuntary confinement of tuberculosis patients, but no such power existed on the Navajo Reservation. Annie argued before the Tribal Council that involuntary hospitalization must also be available on the reservation. To make this possible, the council would need to request that the Public Health Service ask for such authority from the Secretary of the Interior. The vote by council delegates was fifty-nine for and six against making the request. The regulation finally took effect in November 1961. Tribal courts could commit patients to an IHS facility, from which the patient could be transferred to a sanatorium off the reservation. The patient, however, was guaranteed the right to a traditional healing ceremony before commitment, which would offer emotional support to the individual (Niethammer, *I'll Go* 116–19; Davies 96–98).

Another example of Annie Dodge Wauneka's commitment to fostering good health while also respecting traditional Navajo culture was the Navajo Health Authority (NHA), which the Tribal Council created in 1972 with Annie serving on its board (Davies 139–40). Over the years, the Navajo Nation would move toward greater control of its own health care programs as the NHA yielded to the Navajo Division of Health and the current Navajo Department of Health. In 1974, Project HOPE (Health Opportunity for People Everywhere) turned Sage Memorial Hospital in Ganado, Arizona, over to the Navajo Nation Health Foundation, which was a community organization in Ganado. As with the NHA, again Annie Wauneka agreed to serve on the board, which consisted mainly of Navajos from the area (Davies 148–49). In accepting the role, she may have been remembering how the hospital had probably saved her life and that of her youngest child, Sallie.

Annie continued her efforts to reduce the prevalence of tuberculosis among Navajos. As the years passed, she could see the disease shrinking as a killer of Navajos. Tuberculosis deaths among the Navajo population declined in the 1950s, 1960s, and 1970s. By the 1980s, tuberculosis still afflicted Navajos disproportionately compared to the United States average, but it no longer caused a high number of Navajo deaths, with tuberculosis absent from the top ten causes of Navajo mortality (Davies 154–55).

Annie Dodge Wauneka is congratulated by President Lyndon Johnson upon receiving the Presidential Medal of Freedom, the nation's highest civilian honor, on December 6, 1963. President Lincoln meditates above the recipient in the State Dining Room of the White House (courtesy LBJ Presidential Library, photograph by Yoichi Okamoto).

Keeping the Rope Straight

Annie Dodge Wauneka's involvement with tuberculosis earned her considerable renown on the Navajo Reservation and nationally. It may also have been the effort in which she had the most success. However, it was far from the only area in which she strove to make a difference in the life of Navajos. Throughout the rest of her life, in a multitude of ways, she sought to keep straight the rope that her father had bequeathed to her.

In addition to tuberculosis, there were other health issues that captured Annie's attention and her commitment. Foremost among them was alcoholism. Annie herself did not drink, but she understood well the serious problem that many Navajos had with alcohol. Although alcohol could not be sold legally on the reservation, it was readily available. When an Alcoholism Committee was established by the Tribal Council in the early 1960s, Annie was chosen to lead it. Shortly before the committee was constituted, the issue had been brought home in a very personal way for Annie when her brother Ben had been beaten to death, apparently in an alcohol-related incident. Ben had just been released from jail, where he had been incarcerated for drunkenness. At the time, over 80 percent of arrests on the reservation were connected to alcohol-related behavior. In December 1962, Annie reported to the Tribal Council on behalf of the Alcoholism Committee. The committee had been examining not only behavior but also causes. The conclusion that the committee came to was that the primary cause of excessive drinking was despair, itself precipitated by, among other factors, poverty, unemployment, and inadequate education that impeded acquisition of good jobs. Clearly, Annie understood that alcoholism was a complex matter related to a number of other conditions in Navajo Nation (Niethammer, *I'll Go* 122–27).

Another important health issue was sanitation. Shortly after the Public Health Service had been given responsibility for health care on the Navajo Reservation, Dr. James Shaw, head of the Indian Health Services' Navajo office, reported that a majority of Navaho illnesses were preventable infections. As with tuberculosis, this issue led Annie to engage in more traveling hogan to hogan in order to encourage basic sanitation, which was often quite difficult because of the lack of readily accessible fresh water and the physical details of many hogans, which typically had a dirt floor and open windows. She encouraged safe storing of food in containers, boiling water to drink, careful washing of dishes in clean water, adding wooden floors, screening windows to prevent flies from entering, covering food that was being eaten outside, and improving personal hygiene. Annie worked with departments of education in Arizona and New Mexico to develop a sanitation and personal hygiene program to be taught in the schools. Yet knowing well that most families did not have the money to upgrade their hogans, she urged the Tribal Council to appropriate funds to assist in the upgrading. The council initially refused, but Annie worked hard to raise a public demand for action. The Tribal Council finally agreed, appropriating $300,000 to help residents improve their housing and sanitation (Niethammer, *I'll Go* 108–12; *Keeping the Rope Straight* 68–75; Nelson 56–57). The IHS also entered the picture, constructing sewage and water supply systems (Davies 75). By 1968, Annie, continuing to expand her areas of interest and expertise, was serving on the board of directors of the Navajo Tribal Utility Authority, which provided reservation power, water, and sewer services (Niethammer, *I'll Go* 177).

If there was a health crisis on the reservation, Annie most likely would be engaged in trying to address it, from infant mortality rates (twice as high as in the general U.S. population) to an outbreak of bubonic plague related to prairie dogs. If an indirect approach was necessary to address a problem, Annie was more than capable of finding one. Concerned about babies' health? Initiate a baby contest. While proud parents are showing off their beautiful babies, Indian Health Service doctors and nurses can subtly examine the infants to detect health problems. Late in life, she even tried, though unsuccessfully, to secure approval and funding to open a medical school on the reservation, and failing that, to create one in affiliation with other medical and educational institutions (Niethammer, *I'll Go* 115, 152, 166, 194–98).

Education was a constant concern. In addition to Annie's own commitment to lifelong learning, and her efforts to educate others, she strove to improve formal education in schools. She worked energetically to support Head Start on the reservation and solicit participation from parents. A strong supporter of Girl Scouts, Annie attended Scout meetings to encourage the girls to further their education, especially suggesting training in health care (Nelson 60). After earlier encouraging use of boarding schools, even sending her own children to one, she later switched to favoring community schools. The change in outlook seemed to be in response to problems, today well documented, with boarding schools for Native American children, but also because of improvements on the reservation. For example, the road system had improved, making it easier for buses to transport children to school. Improved housing, with better sanitation, and many now with a healthy water supply, made living at home healthier. A Tribal Council program to provide students with clothing helped ensure that students would not be embarrassed at school because of what they were wearing. That program came after a 1954 report that 2,500 of 17,000 Navajo students were in families that could not afford appropriate school clothes (Niethammer, *Keeping the Rope Straight* 93–96; *I'll Go* 160–66).

By the 1960s, activism regarding women's rights had found an important place in American society, as it did as well in Navajo Nation. Peter Iverson points out that by the 1990s, Navajo politics still was "largely a men's club" (303). That had not deterred Annie, though, who readily expressed her opinions, and did so forcefully and clearly. In the 1970s, she was appointed to a women's commission and set out to do what she had so much experience doing, traveling about to talk with women on the reservation. She learned that women were concerned, not surprisingly, about inadequate housing, medical treatment, alcoholism on the part of family members, and finances. Many wanted to find employment, but jobs were few and those that did exist often required more education than they had. Other concerns included protecting their Native lands, improving tribal government, improving tribal-federal relationships, and maintaining traditional values. Unafraid as usual to bring concerns before the public, Annie spoke at the first Southwest Indian Women's Conference, at Window Rock in 1975, and gave the keynote address at the first Navajo Women's Conference (Niethammer, *I'll Go* 206–09).

Annie was up for reelection in 1978 but went back and forth about whether to seek another term. She finally decided to run but did not actively campaign for herself, losing by just thirteen votes. Despite her loss, she was certainly not devoid of responsibilities, among which were her memberships on a variety of boards: the Navajo Area Health Board, the Navajo Health Authority Board of Directors, the Navajo Health Systems Agency, and the Navajo Nation Health Foundation that was charged with finding financing for the Sage Memorial Hospital. These boards kept Annie in the middle of health planning for Navajo Nation, which had long been at the heart of Annie Dodge Wauneka's life (Niethammer, *I'll Go* 219).

Nor did the council defeat immediately curtail her traveling. In 1980, she went to China as a member of the delegation of Native Americans invited by China. Although a strong advocate for modern medicine and a lifelong and regular mass-attending Catholic, Annie, in preparing for the trip, demonstrated her continued blending of the new with traditional Navajo values. She solicited a medicine man to perform a traditional protective ceremony for her prior to the trip. During her time in China, she suffered from problems with one of her knees and was persuaded to undergo acupuncture, which was an entirely novel medical treatment for her. However, when the delegation was taken to various historical sites, she skipped trips to tombs and a visit to see Mao Zedong's body encased in a glass casket, reflecting the traditional Navajo opposition to being physically associated with the dead (Niethammer, *I'll Go* 222–25). Annie also retained her interest and involvement in reservation politics, campaigning hard for Peterson Zah in his victorious campaign for Tribal Chair in 1982.

Recognition of Annie Dodge Wauneka's accomplishments had started much earlier and continued during the post-council years. A few of the awards that she received: the Indian Council Fire Achievement Award by the intertribal Indian Council Fire in 1959 (an award that her father had received in 1944), the Josephine B. Hughes Memorial Award in 1959 (named for a pioneer in supporting women's rights), Arizona Woman of the Year by the Arizona Press Women's Club in 1959, and additional awards from Project Hope, the Girl Scouts of America, Project Concern, the Public Health Service, the National Community Health Representatives, the Society of Public Health Educators, the International Lung Association Conference in Montreal, and an honorary doctorate from the University of New Mexico in Albuquerque (after which she regularly signed letters as "Dr. Annie Wauneka"). In 1876, the *Ladies Home Journal* named her a Woman of the Year in its category of inspirational and educational leaders. Having visited Washington, D.C., many times, Annie made a final trip there in 1992 to be honored with a special Indian Achievement Award. The University of Arizona awarded Annie an honorary doctor of laws degree in 1996, but by that time she was unable to travel (Niethammer, *I'll Go* 132–33, 209, 239–41).

Probably the two most memorable honors were the Presidential Medal of Freedom and the Navajo Medal of Honor. The former, which is the highest civil honor that the President of the United States can bestow on an individual, was to be presented by President John F. Kennedy. Annie received a telegram from the President on July 1, 1963, with the event initially planned for early November but delayed until December 6. Then on November 22, 1963, President Kennedy was assassinated. President Lyndon Johnson, however, went ahead with the ceremony on December 6. Along with the medal, Annie received a citation that read as follows:

> Vigorous crusader for betterment of the health of her people, Mrs. Wauneka has selflessly worked to help them conquer tuberculosis, dysentery and trachoma. She succeeded in these efforts by winning the confidence of her people, and then by interpreting to them the miracles of modern medical science [quoted in Niethammer, *I'll Go* 139].

The Navajo Medal of Honor, the highest honor given by the Navajo Nation, was awarded by President Zah in 1984 during an elaborate birthday party ordered by Zah to commemorate not only Annie's seventy-fourth birthday but, more importantly, her life's work on behalf of Navajos. Arizona and New Mexico declared the day "Annie Wauneka Day," a scholarship was established to honor her, school buses transported children from across the reservation, many dignitaries attended, Annie was addressed as "Our Legendary Mother," and Annie accepted the medal, as she said, "in honor of my better half, George Wauneka, my family and the memory of my father, Chee Dodge, who greatly influenced my life and in honor of the people who have worked with me." A banquet and speeches followed. Telegrams were read from many, including President Ronald Reagan. Annie's closing comment has remained a commentary on her life and supplied the title for one of Carolyn Niethammer's excellent biographies of her: "'This [award] does not mean I want to stop here. When I get up in the morning, I want to go and do more'" (Niethammer, *I'll Go* 235–37).

Finally, however, Annie would become unable to get up and do more. She was diagnosed with Alzheimer's disease and entered a nursing home in Toyei, Arizona, in 1993, reuniting with George and several of their children, who also were residing there. George died in 1994. In 1997, Annie was diagnosed with leukemia and transferred to a Flagstaff hospital. There she died on November 10. A funeral mass for Annie was held on November 13 in the Catholic church at St. Michael's Mission, the church from which her father had also been buried. The family chose to bury her at the Tanner Springs ranch at a spot where sheep sometimes graze. Annie Dodge Wauneka had gone full circle, the keeper of sheep come home after a lifetime of helping others.

Laura Tohe, an acclaimed Navajo poet and recipient of the 2020 Academy of American Poets Laureate Fellowship, recorded her poem "Within Dinétah the People's Spirit Remains Strong" on July 10, 2020, for the Library of Congress series "Living Nations, Living Words: A Map of First Peoples Poetry." In a catalogue of who the Navajo are, she includes Annie Wauneka, remembered for helping her people develop faith in white doctors' medicine. It is unlikely that Annie Dodge Wauneka will be forgotten anytime soon.

References

Borgman, Rev. Francis. "Henry Chee Dodge the Last Chief of the Navaho Indians." *New Mexico Historical Review* 23.2 (1948): 81–93.

Brugge, David M. "Henry Chee Dodge: From the Long Walk to Self-Determination." *Indian Lives: Essays on Nineteenth- and Twentieth-Century Native American Leaders.* Ed. L.G. Moses and Raymond Wilson. Albuquerque: U of New Mexico P, 1985. 91–112.

Caravantes, Peggy, and Carolyn Dee Flores. *Daughters of Two Nations.* Missoula: Montana Press Publishing Company, 2013.

Davies, Wade. *Healing Ways: Navajo Health Care in the Twentieth Century.* Albuquerque: U of New Mexico P, 2001.

Gridley, Marion E. *American Indian Women.* New York: Hawthorn Books, 1974.

Iverson, Peter. *Diné: A History of the Navajos.* Albuquerque: U of New Mexico P, 2002.

_____, ed. *"For Our Navajo People": Diné Letters, Speeches & Petitions 1900–1960.* Albuquerque: U of New Mexico P, 2002.

Lapahie, Jr., Harrison. "Annie Dodge Wauneka." *Lapahie.com.* web.archive.org/web/20051026140806/http://www.lapahie.com/Annie_Dodge_Wauneka.cfm.

Nelson, Mary Carroll. *Annie Wauneka: The Story of an American Indian.* Minneapolis: Dillon P, 1972.

Niethammer, Carolyn. *I'll Go and Do More: Annie Dodge Wauneka Navajo Leader and Activist.* Lincoln: U of Nebraska P, 2001.

_____. *Keeping the Rope Straight: Annie Dodge Wauneka's Life of Service to the Navajo.* Flagstaff: Salina Bookshelf, 2006.

Tohe, Laura. "Within Dinétah the People's Spirit Remains Strong." "Living Nations, Living Words: A Map of First Peoples Poetry." *Library of Congress.* loc.gov/item/2020785228/.

Wagner, Sallie. *Wide Ruins: Memories from a Navajo Trading Post.* Albuquerque: U of New Mexico P in cooperation with the Albuquerque Museum, 1997.

7

Kathryn Jones Harrison
(b. 1924)

Kathryn Jones Harrison, a former chair of the Grand Ronde Tribal Council and longtime advocate for her people's cultural, educational, and financial well-being, was in significant ways the mother of the modern Grand Ronde Confederated Tribes. She played a major leadership role in giving birth to the modern Grand Ronde, reclaiming her people's identity and official recognition after the United States policy of termination had declared her people nonexistent as an official entity. Then she nurtured the Grand Ronde through their maturation as a viable and ultimately highly successful cultural and political organization. In order for her efforts to yield this phoenix-like rebirth, however, she first had to reclaim herself from the ashes of poverty, abuse, and deprivation.

A Promising Beginning[1]

Kathryn May Jones was born on March 28, 1924, to Henry "Harry" Jones and Ella Flemming Jones. Her father was a Molalla from the Grand Ronde Reservation in Oregon; her mother was the daughter of a Scottish and Italian man and an Eyak woman from Alaska. In something of a precursor to the fate of Kathryn's own cultural heritage, her maternal grandmother's people were virtually eliminated by epidemics and commercial and cultural changes introduced by Russians and their Euro-American successors in Alaska.

Both Ella Flemming and Harry Jones attended Chemawa Indian School in Salem, Oregon, one of the earliest Indian boarding schools and the longest still in existence. When Harry matriculated at Chemawa in 1905, Ella was already a student there. He distinguished himself as a scholar, graduating as the valedictorian and so impressing his teachers that they encouraged him to attend college. He subsequently attended

Capital Business College in Salem, Oregon, and Washington State University in Pullman until he ran out of money when the Bureau of Indian Affairs reclaimed the land that he rightfully owned under the Dawes Act of 1887, which distributed allotments of reservation land to individuals and families. The allotments were held in trust for twenty-five years, during which ownership could not be transferred.

Shortly before the twenty-five-year period would have expired, assigning ownership outright to Harry Jones, the BIA declared him incompetent to own land, supposedly because he could not handle finances effectively, and reclaimed the land as it did with many allotments, then selling the land to Euro-Americans. A House of Representatives subcommittee, in a minority report quoted by Charles Wilkinson, had argued that the purpose of allotment was "to get at the Indian lands and open them up to settlement." How widespread that motivation was is impossible to discern, but along with "surplus" reservation land that was never allotted and subsequently sold to white settlers, Native American landholdings declined nationally between 1887 and 1934 (when the allotment policy ended) from 140 million acres to 52 million acres (Wilkinson 43). Apparently the BIA did not consider spending money to attend college an appropriate expense for a Native American, no matter how talented.

Meanwhile, Ella left Chemawa shortly after Harry graduated in response to an accident suffered by her father in Alaska. He had suffered frostbitten hands and needed help running his fox ranch. She and Harry corresponded regularly and were married on March 23, 1916, in Alaska.

Following the birth of a son, Harold, in 1917, and a daughter, Dorothy, in 1920, and the deaths of two children who did not survive infancy, Kathryn was born in Corvallis, Oregon, where the family had moved after spending some time on the Siletz Reservation in western Oregon. Kathryn was named after a great-great-aunt, Molalla Kate, a niece and adopted daughter of Yel-kus, chief of the northern band of Molalla. In her eighties when Kathryn was born, Molalla Kate introduced the child to Chinuk-Wawa, the standard language of many tribes in the Northwest, as well as traditional Molalla clothing and crafts. The commitment to her Native culture that energized much of Kathryn's later life owed a great deal to her interactions with her great-great-aunt (see Olson 21–31).

The early years of Kathryn's childhood were happy. Other siblings arrived: Marie in 1927, Bob in 1929. Music was an important part of the family, with both parents providing the music: her father on a guitar and her mother on a ukulele. Ella shared with her children stories of life in Alaska and items such as furs and a Russian tea set that she had kept from her life there. The family also made regular visits to Siletz to visit the graves of Kathryn's siblings—Maxine and George—who had died shortly after birth.

The family attended church together, initially a Pentecostal church and later the Full Gospel Assembly Church; and Harry taught Bible stories to the children. In third grade, Kathryn was chosen to play Goldilocks in an operetta of that title, indicating that she was at least reasonably well accepted despite being the only Native American in her class.

In 1933, after the birth of another child, Norma, the family moved close to Siletz, staying for a time with Molalla Kate. Later that year, Harry began to build a log cabin to give his family a home of their own. He also constructed a sweat lodge nearby. In her new school, Kathryn continued to be involved with dramatics, playing the role of a child in *The Old Woman Who Lived in a Shoe*. Harry meanwhile was becoming a respected member of the Grand Ronde community and was chosen to testify for the tribe at a Congressional hearing on the Indian Reorganization Act, which was held at the Chemawa Indian School.

The IRA would prove controversial and, from a Native American perspective, something of a mixed bag. It stopped allotments (allotting small parcels of reservation land to individuals but making much of the rest available to non–Indians), enabled tribes to regain some of the land that had been taken from them under the General Allotment Act of 1887, and allowed the Interior Secretary to expand existing reservations and create new ones. However, although the IRA urged greater tribal self-rule, it pushed tribes to create tribal constitutions and reorganize along federal or state lines, an emphasis that some tribes saw as depressing their own traditions (Wilkinson 60–62, Hoxie 296–309). It is easy to see in Harry's involvement the seeds of his daughter's very extensive future engagement with tribal governance.

Down but Not Out

At the age of ten, in 1934, Kathryn saw her world change quickly. An outbreak of influenza struck Kathryn first in her family. Soon Dorothy, Harold, Harry, and Ella fell sick and were transported to the Bureau of Indian Affairs clinic at Siletz. Ella died on December 13, Harry on December 19, leaving Kathryn and the other children orphans. Kristine Olson recorded Kathryn's feelings after losing her parents: "I just felt so lost.... I didn't know where to go, what to do. All I wanted was to feel Mama's arms, hear her voice. I wanted to sleep all the time because maybe Mama would come to me in my dreams" (47). In an interview in the *Great Tribal Leaders of Modern Times* series, Kathryn admits that after losing her parents, she hated God. That attitude, however, would change dramatically. In the same interview, she details the essential importance of faith and prayer in her life. Her love and reverence for her parents, though, did not change. She states that when she dies and goes to meet her Maker, she will want to know whether she has lived up to what her parents taught her and whether they are proud of her (Harrison).

The next period in Kathryn's life was one of deprivation, struggle, and suffering. The odds were long against her achieving much more than survival, if that. Kathryn—along with siblings Bob, Norma, and Marie—was taken into the Buxton, Oregon, home of Lillian and Carl Watson, who received permission from the BIA to take the children. According to Kathryn, Carl attempted to molest the girls while treating Bob very well. In the summer of 1939, Kathryn matriculated as a sophomore at Chemawa Indian School, where Dorothy had preceded her as a student, finally escaping Lillian's beatings and Carl's sexual pursuit (Olson 52–53).

Kathryn enjoyed considerable success at Chemawa. She performed in plays, wrote for the yearbook and school newspaper, was a cheerleader, and participated in the school's famous musical programs. She performed in the Girls' Septette, enjoying a repertoire that included songs reflecting Native cultural traditions. One of the most moving moments for Kathryn was the traditional end-of-year rendition of "God Be with You Till We Meet Again," as some of the students in fact would not be returning the next year and therefore not meeting again. Kathryn also performed group dances, including the corn dance and other dances that were part of the "Thunder Mountain" pageant near the end of the school year. Students from many tribes worked together on these performances. Melissa Parkhurst observes in *To Win the Indian Heart: Music at Chemawa Indian School* that Kathryn's "ability to find truth and significance in the traditional dances of other tribes would later enable her to help reconstruct the cultural forms of her own people" (129). Parkhurst quotes Kathryn as stating, "'Chemawa is where I gained my self-esteem. I had none when I got there'" (59). She also has stated that enrolling at Chemawa was like dying and going to "Indian heaven." She felt that way, she says, because at Chemawa she encountered individuals she had known before and she was able to indulge her love for reading. She delighted in writing book reports and continued throughout her life attempting to read at least one book per week (Harrison).

In her second year at Chemawa, Kathryn began dating Frank Harrison, a highly talented clarinetist from the Rocky Boy Chippewa Reservation in Montana. She also formed lifelong friends such as Dada Case, who was her Chemawa roommate, and Cecilia Bearchum and June Simmons, all of whom would offer Kathryn much-needed help in later years.

Kathryn graduated in 1942. Frank, however, had been expelled for drinking. Nonetheless, they had maintained their relationship, with Kathryn becoming pregnant. Their attempt to marry was denied because they were underage: Kathryn was eighteen, one year older than Frank. As Frank, who had enlisted in the army, reported to basic training, Kathryn moved to Portland, Oregon, to work as a waitress at the Golden Wheel Restaurant. Kathryn later shifted to a Jell-O factory, where her job was to weigh Jell-O packages. Kathryn and Frank's daughter, Patsy, was born on June 8, 1943; shortly afterward, Kathryn moved in with her sister Dorothy in Wolf Point, Montana. There, on February 16, 1944, Kathryn and Frank were married.

If life seemed promising, Kathryn's fortunes would turn again quickly. Dorothy fell ill of the same illness that earlier had claimed their parents' lives and died in the winter of 1944. Kathryn and her daughter moved into a temporary shelter, and then, during the following summer, moved to Siletz to live with her former classmate June Simmons.

Frank was discharged in September 1945 and returned to the States. By this time he was an alcoholic. Kristine Olson succinctly summarizes the next twenty years of Kathryn Jones Harrison's life: "Her life from 1946 through 1966 was marked by biannual pregnancies and childbirth and backbreaking migrant labor at minimum wage, with no permanent home for an anchor" (69). Kathryn gave birth to nine more children (Jeannie, Frankie, Tommy, Raymond, Roger, Kathy, Diane, David, and Karen). The family moved repeatedly within Oregon and beyond, spending time in the late 1950s in Arizona and the late 1960s in Alaska. Kathryn's jobs included working in a lumber mill, as a migrant farm worker, as a field hand in Arizona, and in a fish cannery in Alaska. During this time, her marriage became increasingly difficult due to her husband's alcoholism, physical abuse of Kathryn, and difficulty holding down a steady job (Olson 69–72).

Also during these years, the Eisenhower administration actively carried out its assimilation policy, an attempt supposedly to assimilate Native Americans into the larger community, but which also involved a termination policy that terminated the very existence of previously recognized Native tribes, a move that simultaneously withdrew the governmental safety net that included a variety of social services and educational programs. Termination as a policy, as David Treuer points out, became "clearly a catastrophe," wiping away any gains made by the Indian Reorganization Act, "as flawed as the IRA was" (277). In 1954, Congress passed the Siletz and Grand Ronde termination bill, which withdrew recognition of the tribes, ended federal programs for them, and brought previous reservation land under the control of the federal government, which then sold most of the land. The Siletz Reservation, which had been the closest to a home that Kathryn had known, ceased to exist; and the Grand Ronde land possessions were reduced to their cemetery, approximately two and one-half acres (73).

The Turning Point

The new decade of the 1970s marked a turning point for Kathryn and, in a larger sense, for federal policy toward Native Americans. Kathryn made the hard decision to leave Frank. She moved from Alaska back to Oregon with the children who were still at home, temporarily living with her Chemawa roommate, Dada Case, before moving close to the former Siletz Reservation. That year President Richard Nixon declared in a Special Message to Congress that federal policies had failed to address the reality that "the American Indians have been oppressed and brutalized, deprived of their ancestral lands and denied the opportunity to control their own destiny." He called for "a new era in which the Indian future is determined by Indian acts and Indian decisions" ("Special Message on Indian Affairs"). President Nixon's special message to Congress signaled the beginning of a change away from termination and other federal policies completely determined by federal authorities. The address helped pave the way to enactment in 1975 of the Indian Self-Determination and Education Assistance Act, which "directed the BIA and the Indian Health Service to contract with tribes for the planning and administration of programs" (Wilkinson 197). These were small but important steps, a tentative new beginning that paralleled Kathryn's own first steps toward reconstructing her life.

Kathryn enrolled in a computer-training program at Lane Community College in Eugene, Oregon, in the fall of 1970 but switched to a nursing curriculum, graduating in 1972 as the first Native American to earn a nursing degree from the institution (Harrison). She accepted a position as a licensed practical nurse at Lincoln County Hospital, but surgery for a prolapsed uterus and gallstones prevented her from continuing in such a physically demanding role. After recovering, she was hired as a counselor in an alcohol rehabilitation program at Siletz. Her interest in working with alcoholics was personal as well as professional, as her husband and her two oldest sons, Frankie and Tommy, suffered from alcoholism. In 1974, Kathryn's marriage finally came to an official end when Frank agreed to sign divorce papers (Olson 88–89). Educated, self-confident, and free to be who she longed to be, Kathryn was ready to help bring about change, not only for herself but also for Native American peoples in the Northwest and throughout the country.

Tribal Leadership and Cultural Identity

With termination increasingly in disfavor with the federal government as well as with Native American tribes, the Siletz determined to seek restoration of their tribal status. Art Bensell, Siletz Tribal Council Chair, encouraged Kathryn to seek election to the Tribal Council, which she succeeded in doing in 1975. The following March Kathryn was a member of a delegation that journeyed to Washington, D.C., to testify before the Senate Committee on Interior and Insular Affairs. The Siletz were strongly supported in their effort at restoration by Oregon Republican Senator Mark Hatfield and Oregon Democratic Representative Les AuCoin. Kathryn's involvement began a long-running association with Senator Hatfield that ultimately would lead decades later to his enthusiastic foreword to Kristine Olson's biography of Kathryn, in which the senator writes of his subject:

> Whether she sought better medical care for Indian children or the protection of the sacred burial sites of her ancestors, Kathryn Harrison was not to be denied and certainly not to be forgotten. It is no mystery to me how she has risen among her people to become a distinguished leader and tribal elder, commanding respect not only among the Grand Rondes but also among people from all walks of life and throughout this country [x].

Senator Hatfield adds that "Kathryn Harrison endows generations of future Native Americans with a legacy that teaches persistence in the face of adversity, consistency against a backdrop of hypocrisy, and, most importantly, love in the presence of animosity" (xi).

The accomplishments that would lead to this glowing testimonial were just starting in 1975, but they would increase quickly, although not without great effort and vision. Kathryn's particular role before Congress, as secretary of the Tribal Council, was to speak about Siletz identity in order to establish that the Siletz were indeed a unified people deserving of formal recognition as a tribal entity. As she spoke of her own personal history and of Native culture, she established an ongoing theme that would guide much of her future work: traditional culture and its importance to Native American identity (see Olson 91–96).

The effort at restoration was successful, with the Siletz regaining federal recognition in 1977. Nonetheless, the victory was bittersweet for Kathryn, who was not in fact Siletz herself but a member of the Grand Ronde, the people to which her father had belonged.

The 1970s was a decade in which much was happening nationally to help create a context in which Kathryn could contribute to substantial progress for the Grand Ronde and also for Native Americans throughout the country. The American Indian Movement, which began in the late 1960s, helped to position Native rights within the broader Civil Rights Movement. The Kennedy Report of 1969, officially known as *Indian Education: A National Tragedy—A National Challenge*, prepared by the Special Senate Subcommittee on Indian Education chaired by Senator Robert Kennedy of New York and later (at the time of the release of the report and after

Kathryn Harrison acknowledges receiving a "History Makers" Award at the Oregon Historical Society on September 27, 2012 (courtesy *Smoke Signals*/ Michelle Alaimo photo).

the assassination of his brother) by Senator Edward Kennedy of Massachusetts, called for greater financial investment in Native American education and greater attention to Native history, culture, and self-determination in that education. During the 1970s, several important pieces of national legislation were passed and signed into law: the Indian Self-Determination and Education Assistance Act mentioned above (1975), the American Indian Religious Freedom Act (1978), and the Indian Child Welfare Act (1978). The legislation recognized the importance of self-determination, improved tribal educational opportunities, respect for Native American religious and cultural beliefs, and placement of Native children in tribal foster homes in order for children to grow up within their traditional culture.

Within this atmosphere of change, Kathryn continued her efforts to combat alcoholism, working for the Coos Bay Detox Center, both at a halfway house for recovering alcoholics and at a sweat lodge called Lampa Mountain. As she neared the age of sixty, a time when many people are thinking of retirement, Kathryn was ready to embark on her greatest "career," helping her Grand Ronde people more directly. She resigned from her position at Coos Bay and returned to the village of Grand Ronde.

Hearing of Kathryn's move, her Chemawa classmate Cecilia Bearchum noted, "'Isn't that just like Jonesy—always wanting to help make something happen'" (quoted in Olson 102).

Back to Her Roots

Kathryn was back at Grand Ronde by 1982, quickly becoming involved in the effort to restore tribal recognition of the Grand Ronde. She began as an enrollment clerk. The position led her to door-to-door canvassing in order to enroll tribal members. She then moved on to become a community organizer, which involved her in grant writing, speaking engagements before a variety of organizations, and fund raising, among other activities. Raising money did not come easily, as Kathryn had to rely on tactics as basic as bake sales and raffles (Harrison). Senator Mark Hatfield, with whom Kathryn had become acquainted during the restoration effort involving the Siletz, urged her to try to get Congressman AuCoin on board. She followed his advice, traveling to Washington, D.C., in 1982 as a member of a Grand Ronde delegation to solicit his support. The congressman initially was not particularly encouraging, instead charging the group with collecting data to substantiate the Grand Ronde identity as a coherent tribal unit and with mustering strong support in the community. Kathryn and her colleagues, however, were not about to give up. Returning to their only remaining tribal land, the Grand Ronde cemetery, they set up shop in a small building on the cemetery grounds to start their research, build support from other tribes, and deal with local concerns. These efforts to collect data, build support, establish government contacts, and engage in effective public relations efforts with the media moved forward with Kathryn Harrison providing strong and effective leadership (Olson 106–09).

Kathryn also served as an emissary to the Oregon tribes—Burns-Paiute, Siletz, Umatilla, Warm Springs—that already enjoyed federal recognition. She met with many public and private organizations in Oregon, from city councils to chambers of commerce, to church and educational groups, to fishing organizations, to name just a few. Some of the organizations' concerns were financial, including the prospect of losing a significant amount of tax base from the land that might be restored to the Grand Ronde. With considerable help from Elizabeth Furse, a law student and experienced Native American rights activist (later a U.S. Congresswoman from Oregon) who had been hired as Restoration Coordinator and who helped prepare the testimony to be presented before Congress, Kathryn made a strong case for restoration. Drawing on her own personal history, she talked about the poverty and suffering caused by termination and the subsequent dispersal of tribal members. Three times Kathryn traveled to Washington to testify. Her testimony before the House Interior and Insular Affairs Committee after the Grand Ronde Restoration Bill was introduced in September 1983 was especially striking. She began by speaking in Chinuk-Wawa, her father's language, before switching to English. By this time, Kathryn had risen in Grand Ronde leadership to become Vice-Chair of the Tribal Council. The website of the Confederated Tribes of Grand Ronde, as of this writing, featured a statement by Kathryn Harrison from her Congressional testimony in its history section:

> It has taken a lot of hard work, depressing and discouraging at times, but, there's always been the feeling that, as extensions of our ancestors, this restoration effort is the carrying out of their visions—and, so we could always reach back to their strengths and wisdom. Because of this, we have seen organizations come and go, yet the Grand Ronde Tribe continues. The roots are there, but we need those roots confirmed by restoration [see Olson 109–21].

In November, Congress approved the bill, and President Ronald Reagan signed the legislation re-recognizing the Grand Ronde on November 22, 1983.

Approximately four months after the restoration victory, Kathryn Harrison was named Interim Chair of the Tribal Council for the Confederated Tribes of the Grand Ronde Community of Oregon, a confederation that included the Chasta, Kalapuya, Molalla (the band to which Kathryn's father had belonged), Rogue River, and Umpqua. The Grand Ronde were an officially recognized people again, but the battle was far from over.

The Grand Ronde were a people without land of their own except for the small cemetery that they had retained. That situation needed to change, and Kathryn Harrison helped lead the way to reuniting her people with their homeland. Kathryn was reelected to the Tribal Council in 1985 and set about achieving two major goals. She worked to gain support for the restoration of Grand Ronde lands, and she sought to regain hunting and fishing rights for her people. Both efforts faced great challenges as local individuals and groups feared losing their own land and their ability to continue fishing and hunting where they wished (see Olson 123–38).

Kathryn achieved an important strategic position to further these ends when she was appointed Vice-Chairperson of the Board of the Oregon State Commission on Indian Services, an organization that had been established by the state legislature. As Vice-Chair, she worked with a wide range of individuals, including Oregon Governor Neil Goldschmidt, members of the state legislature, tribal leaders, and area businessmen. The Grand Rondes established a plan that called for the acquisition of about 17,000 acres, a proposal that immediately elicited opposition, especially from timber interests.

Kathryn worked with her by-now firm allies Senator Hatfield and Congressman AuCoin to draft legislation for Congressional action. Devising a politically astute plan, they developed two bills that they hoped would be seen as compromises less extensive than the original 17,000-acre proposal yet still sufficient to meet the aspirations of the Grand Ronde. One bill would designate 15,665 acres for a Grand Ronde reservation; the other proposed a reservation approximately 5,000 acres smaller. Both bills were introduced in July 1987 but were not acted on. During the following March, supporters of land restoration tried again. The AuCoin-Hatfield Compromise Bill provided for a reservation of about 10,000 acres and included restrictions on logging designed to limit competition with the local timber industry and a requirement that 30 percent of tribal timber revenue be invested in Grand Ronde economic development. The latter provision would help the Grand Ronde become more economically self-sufficient and limit the need for taxpayer-sponsored social services. In addition, the bill provided for exchanging some of the reservation timberlands for Bureau of Land Management lands in order not to negatively impact the local tax base. As summer neared its end, Congress finally passed the legislation, and President Reagan signed it into law. The Grand Rondes were no longer a landless people (Olson 123–33).

Building a Future

Much more than land, however, was required for the Grand Rondes to face the challenge of building a better tomorrow. Revenue for the tribe and its members, ways to combat serious problems such as alcohol and drug abuse, safe and secure housing, improved educational opportunities, and a strong sense of self-identity were among the challenges to be faced, and Kathryn Harrison provided a great deal of leadership and inspiration in facing these challenges.

Still a member of the Tribal Council, Kathryn strongly supported creation of a treatment center to address the problem of substance abuse, a subject about which Kathryn had much personal and professional experience. The center opened in April 1989.

Kathryn, who also sat on the Advisory Board of the Native American Program of Oregon Legal Services (NAPOLS), was instrumental in the joint effort by the Tribal Council and NAPOLS to develop an economic development strategy. She urged the Tribal Council to establish several endowments for education, health, housing, and retirement, the latter helping to ensure a dignified and secure final phase to tribal members' lives. These efforts required that Kathryn work closely with the Oregon legislature as well as with Congressional committees. She also was a member of the Oregon Commission on Indian Services, a commission established by the Oregon State Legislature in 1975 to channel Native American concerns to the appropriate body.

Kathryn's efforts to aid her Grand Ronde people were tragically interrupted near Labor Day in 1991 when her son Frankie suffered a fatal accident while hiking on the Oregon coast. Frankie was just forty-three years old. He was found at the base of a cliff near Otter Crest Outlook, but it took eight days to locate and retrieve Frankie's body. Olson describes Kathryn's action when her family gathered at Kathryn's trailer after the funeral. She entered her bathroom and cut off her braid. "'I cut my mourning hair forever,'" she said, deciding never to let her hair grow long again (139–43). Gradually, however, Kathryn returned to her work on behalf of the Grand Ronde tribe. Her commitment did not waver even when another of her sons, Tommy, was in an automobile accident about four years later and unexpectedly died a few days afterward of internal hemorrhaging.

With timber revenue increasing, the Grand Rondes were able to invest in more land, including the location for the Grand Rondes' Spirit Mountain Casino. By the 1990s, Kathryn was involved in helping to establish a new community center and a dental clinic. In 1992, she was re-elected again to the Tribal Council and shortly afterward Vice-Chair of the Council. She helped to introduce a Head Start Program in the Community Center. She testified with great effectiveness before the Oregon State Senate Judiciary Committee in support of a multi-tribe-proposed bill to protect cultural resources, including burial sites. When the bill was signed into law, Governor Barbara Roberts presented the pen with which she had signed the legislation to Kathryn (see Olson 144–47).

While Kathryn and the Grand Ronde Tribal Council worked to receive state authorization to build a casino, an effort that she devoted considerable time to despite the fact that she personally has stated that she does not gamble (Harrison), she was elected to the Board of Directors of the Native American Rights Fund. By this time, Kathryn Harrison was not only a Grand Ronde leader but also a national leader, working on behalf of tribal sovereignty and Native-American rights.

In 1995, Kathryn was again re-elected to the Tribal Council, the year in which the Grand Ronde casino opened. The Council began to invest part of the casino revenue in additional land, especially land that had once been part of the Grand Ronde Reservation. Kathryn was instrumental in setting major long-range goals designed not only to solve immediate problems but also to create a future that promised fulfillment and security for her people. A pension was established for tribal elders, and financial training programs were started to establish a strong core of able financial planners.

Kathryn was elected chairperson of the Tribal Council in 1996, becoming the first woman to lead the Grand Ronde nation (Harrison). Shortly afterward she signed a contract for a new wellness clinic to be built. Then came construction on a hotel to accommodate visitors to the Spirit Mountain Casino, followed by a new tribal government building. Politically astute, as she had demonstrated countless times in her interactions with state and federal governments as well as with local organizations, Kathryn reached out to the surrounding community in ways that exhibited both her political sensitivities and her commitment to a rich cultural tradition. The Grand Rondes established a charitable fund that drew on casino revenues to disburse grants to community organizations. Recipients ranged from cultural institutions such as the Portland Art Museum and the Oregon Museum of Science and Industry to organizations providing such social services as domestic violence shelters, food pantries, and hospices (see Olson 173–77).

The Grand Ronde approach to constructing the casino and other buildings demonstrated great respect for the surrounding environment. This commitment led to an invitation for Kathryn to address President Bill Clinton's Council on Sustainability in 1998.

The next tribal election—in September 1998—gave Kathryn another term as Tribal Chair. Additional accomplishments under her leadership included a Chinook Language Program, which sought to bring the native Grand Ronde language back more fully into use. The program involved teaching Chinuk-Wawa (considered by many to be a more accurate name than Chinook Jargon) in elementary school and encouraging use of the language at official functions.

Kathryn's involvement continued to expand beyond her own Grand Ronde tribe. Governor John Kitzhaber named her to the Oregon Council for the Humanities, and the Oregon Commission for Women honored her in 1999, the same year in which the Grand Rondes opened a food bank and entered into an agreement with the U.S. Forest Service regarding maintenance of Grand Ronde graves. Also in 1999, Kathryn gave the keynote address at the second annual Chinook Jargon Conference.

When the Grand Rondes opposed possession by the American Museum of Natural History in New York City of a meteorite that had been discovered on Molalla sacred ground, Kathryn traveled to New York with tribal attorneys and council members. The Grand Rondes claimed the meteorite under provisions of the Native American Graves Protection and Repatriation Act (NAGPRA). An agreement was struck to allow the continued display of the meteorite in New York, but Grand Rondes would maintain access to it for cultural purposes and the museum would sponsor an internship program for Native American youth.

Additional tribal efforts came to fruition under Kathryn's leadership, including a housing project for tribal elders, a tribal cultural area, and a Native American Gallery at the Portland Art Museum. By 2001, as Kathryn turned seventy-seven, she felt ready to turn over her formal leadership role. She chose not to seek re-election to the Tribal Council. Honors, however, continued to come. The Institute for Tribal Governance at Portland State University nominated her for the DC Advocacy Institute's Leadership for a Changing World award. In 2003, Portland State University presented her with an honorary doctorate. The Grand Rondes continued to turn to her as a special ambassador, representing her people, for example, at Senator Mark Hatfield's eightieth birthday celebration in October 2003. During the following year, she received another honorary degree, one that took her back many years, as she was honored by her alma mater, the Lane Community College School of Nursing. The Oregon Historical society named her a History Maker in 2012, and Emerge Oregon, a training program for women, gave her the Betty Roberts Woman in Leadership Award. On May 5, 2013, she received an honorary degree from the University of Portland, honoring her for her long service to both her tribe and the state of Oregon. AGE+, a companion organization to the Jessie F. Richardson Foundation, named Kathryn Harrison the recipient of an Ageless Award in 2015. The Ageless Award is granted to individuals aged seventy-five or older who continue to contribute in significant ways to their communities. In 2020, Kathryn's lengthy accomplishments led USA TODAY to include her in its Women of the Century list marking women's "documented and outstanding achievements" since receiving the right to vote in 1920. And as of this writing, Kathryn remains a member of the Board of Trustees of the American Museum of Natural History.

In 2005, she was the subject of a biographical study by Kristine Olson, a longtime friend of Kathryn's, who, starting in 1994 when she was a United States Attorney for the state of Oregon, worked with Kathryn on many tribal and government matters. Although Kathryn Jones Harrison is not likely to be forgotten for many years, if ever, by the Grand Rondes, Olson's book achieved a goal that Kathryn Harrison richly deserves—bringing her accomplishments to the attention of an audience far beyond Oregon.

Asked in 2004 which accomplishments Kathryn was most proud of, she began by citing advances in education, explaining how important it is for people to be well educated in order to enhance their quality of life. Then she talked about efforts to help elders, including good housing and a burial fund so that they would not have to worry about burdening their children with final expenses. She also included buildings, as the Grand Ronde Nation has advanced from one building with one small office for administrative officials, the water faucet and toilet facilities outside, to a variety of buildings serving many of the people's needs. Asked for her ultimate recommendation, she responded with the directive to strive for "balance and harmony" in one's life (Harrison). Kathryn Harrison has achieved that balance and harmony within the twin spheres of her personal and professional lives, becoming not only an irreplaceable leader of the Grand Rondes but also a great American leader as well as the loving parent and grandmother of a very large family. Perhaps others were thinking of both portions of that life in referring to her, as many have done, as the "grandmother of this tribe" (mentioned in Harrison).

Twenty years after retiring from the Grand Ronde Tribal Council, Kathryn Harrison continues to wear well that title of the "grandmother of this tribe." Although she holds no official position within the Grand Ronde, she continues to serve as a sort of oral historian. Well into her nineties, she keeps well informed on tribal matters and offers advice and counsel (Watson). Michael Cherry, the Executive Director of Spirit Mountain Community Fund and a close friend of Kathryn's, describes her as a strong and courageous person revered as a tribal elder, and as an individual of great spiritual depth who has demonstrated resiliency throughout her life. Those who know Kathryn Harrison personally or who simply know what she has accomplished would agree that she remains a Grand Ronde resource and national treasure.

NOTE

1. Throughout this account of Kathryn Harrison, I am heavily indebted to Kristine Olson's *Standing Tall: The Lifeway of Kathryn Jones Harrison*.

REFERENCES

Chemawa Indian School. chemawa.bie.edu.
Cherry, Michael. Personal Interview. 12 Apr. 2021.
The Confederated Tribes of Grand Ronde website. grandronde.org.
Harrison, Kathryn. Interview. Great Tribal Leaders of Modern Times: Kathryn Harrison. The University of Arizona Native Nations Institute. 2004. nnigovernance.arizona.edu/great-tribal-leaders-modern-times-kathryn-harrison.
Hoxie, Frederick E. *This Indian Country: American Indian Activists and the Place They Made*. 2012. New York: Penguin, 2013.
Indian Education: A National Tragedy—A National Challenge (Kennedy Report). National Indian Law Library. 1969. narf.org/nill/resources/education/reports/kennedy/toc.html.
Nixon, Richard. "Special Message on Indian Affairs." 8 Jan. 1970. *The American Presidency Project*. www.presidency.ucsb.edu/documents/special-message-the-congress-indian-affairs.
Olson, Kristine. *Standing Tall: The Lifeway of Kathryn Jones Harrison*. Portland: Oregon Historical Society Press; Seattle: U of Washington P, 2005.
Parkhurst, Melissa D. *To Win the Indian Heart: Music at Chemawa Indian School*. Corvallis: Oregon State UP, 2014.

Patterson, Philana. "State-by-State: *USA TODAY* Network's Women of the Century Marks 100 Years Since the 19th Amendment." *USA TODAY* 13 Aug. 2020, updated 26 Aug. 2020. usatoday.com/in-depth/life/women-of-the-century/2020/08/13/history-constitution-19th-amendment-woman-voting-rights-100-years-election/3351140001/.

Treuer, David. *The Heartbeat of Wounded Knee: Native America from 1890 to the Present*. New York: Riverhead Books, 2019.

Watson, Lisa. Personal Interview. 7 Apr. 2021.

Wilkinson, Charles. *Blood Struggle: The Rise of Modern Indian Nations*. 2005. New York: Norton, 2006.

8

LaDonna Vita Crawford Harris (b. 1931)

LaDonna Crawford was born into modest economic means, relied heavily on grandparents during her childhood, suffered from dyslexia, and lacked the opportunity to achieve higher education. Despite these impediments, she became a partner in every way to a United States senator and Presidential candidate, was the creative force behind Oklahomans for Indian Opportunity and later Americans for Indian Opportunity and achieved national recognition as an activist for not only Comanches but for Native Americans throughout the country. Through her efforts, countless individuals have benefited educationally, economically, and culturally, while tribal governments have profited from her efforts to help create new generations of tribal leaders.

Growing Up with Grandparents

LaDonna Vita Crawford Harris was born on February 15, 1931, in Cotton County, Oklahoma, near the junction of the West and East Cache rivers, on land that was her grandmother's allotment under the Dawes Act of 1887. Her parents, Lily Tabbytite and Donald Crawford, came from very different backgrounds. Tabbytite was Comanche and Crawford Irish. Both left LaDonna for job-related reasons early, Crawford heading to California shortly after her birth, where he eventually owned a dry-cleaning shop and occasionally communicated with his daughter by letter. On the whole, though, he appears to have had little impact on LaDonna (*Voices* 2–3; *Memoir* 23)[1].

Lily Tabbytite had a more lasting relationship with her daughter, despite having to live apart because of her job as an assistant dietician at Fort Sill Indian Health, which required that she reside on campus. As a child, Tabbytite had attended the Fort Sill Indian School for a time but shifted to school in Temple, Oklahoma, as a result of being very unhappy with Fort Sill. Prior to marrying Crawford, she had been married to a Carl Evans, with whom she had a daughter, Billie Carl Evans. Harris fondly remembers how her mother would come to visit her and they would go shopping in Lawton, with her mother buying Harris beautiful clothes (*Voices* 2–4; Memoir 17). An especially perceptive comment by Harris concerns her mother's reserved personality, which Harris ascribes to her moving outside of her community (Memoir 3); the daughter experienced a similar shyness, seemingly the result of a lack of self-confidence perhaps related to her dyslexia and the fact that as a wife she would move far beyond her Native community.

LaDonna Harris records a childhood that involved some academic challenges but that also included much family love and enjoyment on the Tabbytite family farm in Walters, Oklahoma. The farm had lots of animals: cows, pigs, horses, chickens, and turkeys. There also were a vegetable garden, flowers, and peach and apple orchards. She certainly had chores to perform, such as feeding the chickens and turkeys, heating water on her grandparents' wood stove, and washing and drying dishes. Yet she also had time for games with other children, including a favorite, Nioka of the Jungle, which involved pretending to be living in a jungle. She recalls loving to run in the rain and playing in one-half of a chicken house that was allotted to the children as a playhouse. Stealing an occasional watermelon from a neighbor when cousins came to visit did not seem to elicit any serious repercussions (Memoir 13–16).

School was a challenge, especially because of her dyslexia, which was not well understood at the time, causing LaDonna to feel that she was not very intelligent. To compensate, La Donna would memorize information in order to convince teachers that she knew the material. By the time she reached high school, she was entering into extracurricular activities such as the glee club and serving as a flag girl for the band, the latter as a device to get to attend ball games. She also worked on the school yearbook and was nominated for homecoming queen. She loved studying history and was chosen to be one of the speakers at her graduation (*Voices* 13–14; Memoir 31–33). By this time, she was employed at various part-time jobs, including babysitting and working as a soda jerk in a drugstore (Memoir 26). Among the lessons that young LaDonna learned in school was the nature of racism. She had blue eyes and lighter skin than most of her Comanche relatives and friends, learning as a girl that appearing less Indian could make her more appealing to whites. She also felt that schools were saying that she would be more accepted if she became less Comanche and more like white people (Memoir 20–21).

Meanwhile, LaDonna Crawford was spending most of her childhood being cared for and loved by her grandparents. Also in the picture was her great-grandmother, her grandmother's mother, who lived in Cache and was much admired by her great-granddaughter. She was the matriarch of the family, and relatives, to show their respect, would not smoke around her. Harris describes in her *Voices of Oklahoma* interview how she early on came to admire older women and, in turn, to be liked by them. They would "pet me and tell me how pretty I was," she says. She also came to believe that reaching old age demonstrated that they possessed "good medicine." Her great-grandmother, though, had not had an easy life and had lost a child, as had her daughter (LaDonna's grandmother) (5–6).

The grandmother, Wick-ie Tabbytite, probably was the most influential person in young LaDonna's life. She brought into her granddaughter's life not only love and direction but also a sense of belonging to a long cultural tradition. LaDonna's great-grandmother and family had been at the battle of Palo Duro Canyon near Amarillo, Texas, in 1874, which resulted in the military under General William Tecumseh Sherman driving the Comanches' horses off a cliff to prevent the Comanches from successfully fleeing the military. LaDonna's family were among those marched back to Fort Sill in the Comanches' own Trail of Tears. The family also had a connection to Quanah Parker, the legendary chief of the Comanches. Harris states in her memoir that her grandmother was born in a tipi in front of Parker's home, and that Parker remained a hero to her (Memoir 7–11).

Wick-ie Tabbytite converted to Christianity and helped start a Northern Baptist church at Cache, Oklahoma, although when LaDonna was young her grandmother usually attended the Brown Church near Walters. The congregation was Comanche, although the pastor, the Reverend Howes and his wife, were white. The Howes studiously learned about Comanche culture, with Mrs. Howe learning Comanche songs so she could sing them while playing an organ. LaDonna assisted by pumping the organ. LaDonna, however, did not care generally for Christianity, as she felt that other ministers were demeaning Comanche culture. Nonetheless, to please her beloved grandmother, she agreed to be baptized, which occurred in a horse trough (Memoir 19–21).

The grandfather, John Tabbytite, whom Harris refers to as Papa, was a mixture of the traditional and the progressive. He rejected standard Christianity in favor of a peyote-based religion (Harris calls him a "peyote man"), driving his wife to church but waiting for her in the car. He also opposed cameras, believing that taking one's picture could rob the individual of his or her spirit (Memoir 24–25). However, he owned the first car in Cotton County and had a battery-powered radio in the living room on which he would follow the events of World War II, and on which the children could listen to *The Lone Ranger* and *The Green Hornet*. He never learned to read, though, so he would have LaDonna identify the people in photographs that he found in *Look* or *Life* magazines (Memoir 23). As a young man, he had served in the military as a member of an all–Indian troop at Fort Sill. The troop wore elaborate uniforms and rode horses, communicating in sign language because members came from a wide range of tribes (Memoir 9–10; *Voices* 8).

Harris's grandparents thus had an enormous impact on her in many ways. Sarah Eppler Janda in *Beloved Women: The Political Lives of LaDonna Harris and Wilma Mankiller* concludes that Harris learned two basic principles regarding "identity formation" from her grandparents: "first, being Comanche made her different. Second, being Comanche gave her a lens through which to view and respond to the world" (15). Harris's vision of herself and of the world would expand mightily over the years, much to the advantage of a great many people. It would start expanding through a life-altering relationship.

A Partnership

The most significant turning point in LaDonna's life was meeting Fred Harris, who was a year ahead of her in high school at Walters, to which she had transferred from the school in Putnam. LaDonna was living with an aunt in Walters across from the school. LaDonna later recalled that she was impressed by Fred's working at the *Walters Herald* newspaper and that he had two cows of his own. He also had won a prize for a Future Farmers of America speech. Their first date was at what she calls a "juke joint," and Fred later walked her home. It was not an especially exciting date as dates go, but it marked an extraordinarily important beginning for both of them. LaDonna was still in high school when they collaborated for the first time on a campaign, as Fred helped organize her effort to be named the Cotton County turkey queen. Unlike some future campaigns, this one was unsuccessful (*Voices* 15–16; Memoir 28; Janda 17).

Fred Harris was an outstanding student with a bright future despite coming from considerable poverty. In his memoir *Does People Do It?* he describes in detail his impoverished background. He was born in a two-room house on the outskirts of Walters on November 13, 1930. The family moved constantly, with Harris citing nineteen different homes which his family rented during his first seventeen years. At times, the Harrises shared living quarters with another family, including a Comanche family when he was about three years old. His father worked various jobs, including sharecropping and buying and selling cattle. The entire family at one point moved to West Texas for a while to pick cotton. Through it all,

Fred, from the start of his schooling, loved reading, winning the reading prize in first grade for reading the most books. His prize was "a shiny new quarter" (3–12).

While LaDonna was completing her senior year, Fred already had matriculated at the University of Oklahoma in Norman. LaDonna would take the bus from Walters to Lawton, where her mother then owned a house and would drive her daughter to the Harris home north of town. Fred would meet LaDonna there. The courtship went quickly, and marriage followed in 1949 shortly before the conclusion of LaDonna's senior year. They were married in the Baptist church at Porter Hill, the community at the edge of Lawton where Fred's parents lived. Before returning to Norman, both took some time to earn much-needed money: LaDonna working as a waitress in Walters and Fred helping with wheat harvesting (Memoir 29, 34).

Later that summer the newlyweds took up residence in Norman, living in a trailer house. Both worked part-time jobs while Fred attended the university, including working at a floral shop, which at that time included the apartment where LaDonna and Fred were living. What LaDonna especially recalled about that job was creating flower arrangements for funerals, which resulted in a lowering of their rent (*Voices* 16).

Their first child, Kathryn, was born while Fred was still working on his undergraduate degree. LaDonna gave birth at the home of Fred's parents, with Fred's mother, who had been a midwife, assisting the doctor. Fred was still at the university, taking exams, and joined wife and daughter as soon as he had completed them (Memoir 35–37).

LaDonna and Fred continued at the university as Fred attended law school. LaDonna worked a variety of jobs, including as a hostess at the university faculty club, in the periodicals section of the library, and doing clerical work in the Center for Continuing Education. She especially enjoyed the library position and being around so many books. Fred continued to excel academically, eventually graduating at the top of his law school class, and together they managed despite having little money. LaDonna states in her memoir that "we were poor as snakes," but she also views those times as among her happiest. Her mother helped out by buying clothes for LaDonna and Kathryn, her grandmother brought them food from time to time, and LaDonna learned how to do a great deal with hamburger. "I never thought of those times as being hard," she wrote, "because we did it together and it built a relationship that lasted for years" (Memoir 39–42).

It was during the law school years that LaDonna Harris began to develop an expanded awareness of racism that would help lay the groundwork for her future activism. According to LaDonna, the University of Oklahoma law school initially segregated its classrooms by having the first black law student separated by a rope from the rest of the students. Then the rope was removed and a second black student was admitted. The local law school wives' organization asked LaDonna to serve as chairperson of the Decorations Committee for their fund-raiser dance. LaDonna's choices of committee members were the two wives of the black students. Only a few Native Americans were in the law school. At the time, LaDonna did not feel that she was being discriminated against, although she later assumed that, despite the lack of overt actions or statements against her, some people probably did indeed feel real anger against her as a Comanche (Memoir 41–42). Sarah Eppler Janda points out that under Oklahoma law at the time, people of African descent were considered "colored" or "negro," with everyone else being "white." Under that dichotomy, Native Americans would logically be considered "white," but in reality they occupied an undefined, ambiguous state, not African American but not really white either (18–19).

Fred graduated from law school in 1954 and he and LaDonna moved to Lawton where, plans for practicing law with a classmate having fallen through, he joined the law firm of Bledsoe, Niklas, and Chrisman (*Does People Do It?* 41). LaDonna and Fred attended Comanche churches, and Fred continued learning to speak the Comanche language and sing Comanche songs. He also put his law degree to work on behalf of an effort to break the Comanches free from the KCA, which was a political confederation consisting of the Kiowa, Comanche, and Apache peoples created by the Bureau of Indian Affairs. The three tribes were organized into the KCA under what was called the Oklahoma Intercourse Act, but Fred Harris researched the act, found that it did not prohibit any of the tribes from leaving the KCA, and petitioned the federal government to allow a Comanche withdrawal. A subsequent vote was held to decide whether to leave the confederation, and although the issue proved highly divisive, the "yes" vote to leave won (Memoir 46–48).

During the Lawton years, LaDonna and Fred lost a baby girl at birth when she was born with the umbilical cord wrapped around her neck. On a much happier note, Fred sought and won a seat in the Oklahoma State Senate in 1956. LaDonna often accompanied her husband to the Senate and sat beside him. Having campaigned with Fred, she now was increasingly a complete partner for him. It was a time that LaDonna, looking back on, would refer to as her "glory years." They were both young and excited about what they were doing. LaDonna consciously sought to convey a conservative image in her clothes and with her hair pulled back. Fred admired her ability to sense how people were reacting and relied on LaDonna to interpret senators' physical reactions during committee meetings. The close political partnership was especially unusual then as most of the Senate wives largely stayed out of their husbands' political lives. She viewed their partnership as "one of the best things in our relationship," but still self-conscious about speaking publicly, she relied on Fred to be their collective voice. Also during these Senate years they had another child, Byron (Memoir 50–53).

Gradually, LaDonna was becoming more involved in social activism. When Fred was chair of the Mental Health Committee, he asked LaDonna and a staff member to visit a mental health institution and present him with a report. That effort helped lead to state legislation being enacted. It also ushered in what would be a longstanding subject of importance for LaDonna: mental health. When the University of Oklahoma invited Fred to participate in a symposium at the Southwest Center for Human Relations Studies, he asked LaDonna to go in his place. The focus of the symposium was on African American-white relationships, with Native American concerns missing. Given what she recognized as serious issues affecting her people, such as high suicide and school dropout rates, she later led creation of a new organization, Oklahomans for Indian Opportunity (Memoir 54–59).

LaDonna Harris, having come to recognize the racial dimensions of interrelationships among Native Americans, African Americans, and whites, met with about a dozen other people representing all three racial categories in September 1963 to discuss integrating Lawton. They called themselves "The Group" or "The Honcho Group" (members took turns leading the meetings and were referred to respectively as "the Honcho") and set about trying to sensitive people regarding racial justice and effect change often one person or business at a time. The effort continued after Fred had run unsuccessfully for Oklahoma governor in 1962 and successfully for the United States Senate in 1964. The Group elicited the cooperation of the Catholic Church and Fort Sill, the latter, given its large numbers and great economic effect on the local community, could bring considerable pressure to bear. The Group focused on integrating restaurants, housing, even the local swimming pool, as well as opening up jobs to all races. Following a Lawton-Fort Sill race relations conference in the spring of 1967, the Defense Department recognized the positive impact of The Group. According to the Lawton chapter of the National Association for the Advancement of Colored People (NAACP), within three years of The Group's founding approximately 95 percent of public accommodations were serving everyone regardless of race (Memoir 54–56; Janda 22–24).

By 1963, Fred, having been reelected to the State Senate in 1960 but defeated two years later in the gubernatorial race, saw an opportunity to move onto a larger political stage. It was time for the partnership to go national.

Life in Washington

LaDonna was an active partner to Fred during his campaign for the United States Senate during 1963–64. She campaigned without him in such places as Stillwater and Guthrie where she felt discrimination because she was a Comanche. Nonetheless, she persisted. She held coffee klatches, which offered an intimate setting in which she could help voters develop a connection to Fred. Visiting African American communities was an important ingredient in the campaign strategy, as the Harrises had developed relationships there through their involvement in civil rights cases. Despite LaDonna's feelings of unease as a Comanche in some white communities, she openly identified herself as Comanche in campaign literature because, she said, so many Oklahoma residents claimed Native American ancestry. LaDonna, by this time a mother of three, Laura having been born in 1961, found herself able to balance the demands of motherhood, marriage, and campaigner despite the constant travel, which included many trips in small planes. Vice President Hubert Humphrey joined them to campaign in Oklahoma, and even President Lyndon Johnson offered an endorsement. Fred started out as the underdog in the race against the popular and highly successful former Oklahoma University football coach, Bud Wilkinson, but he won, aided by Johnson's landslide victory in the Presidential race against Barry Goldwater (Memoir 66–72).

Fred's victory also owed much to LaDonna, which he has acknowledged. Fred writes in *Potomac Fever* about a family member of the late Senator Robert Kerr, whose death had opened up the Senate seat that Harris was seeking, suggesting that LaDonna was receiving too much attention, which would hurt Fred politically. Fred rejected the advice, stating:

> Our ideas were the same, because we had formed them together. We were—and are—each other's best friends. The Kerr family member was wrong on two counts. LaDonna's presence was good politics; she helped bring the women out to our meetings, and she charmed both them and their husbands. More important for us, we liked being with each other; it made the campaign fun [41].

Washington was a new world for two people who had come from considerable poverty in Oklahoma. They quickly became friends with some of the most prominent and powerful political couples in Washington: the Hubert Humphreys, the Walter Mondales, the Robert Kennedys (near whom the Harrises lived in McLean, Virginia), the Sargent Shrivers, and the Stewart Udalls among others. Occasionally LaDonna and Fred would fly to Hyannis Port, Massachusetts, in the Kennedys' private plane for a weekend. One of the especially memorable vignettes from the Harris-Kennedy relationship occurred when Robert and Ethel's daughter, Kerry, approached

LaDonna and asked whether she lived in a teepee. LaDonna mock-seriously responded by asking Ethel what she was teaching her children (*Voices* 29). Not surprisingly, the couples with whom LaDonna and Fred became especially close shared a strong commitment to social justice.

Some of what occupied LaDonna's time was socializing and doing what Senate wives were traditionally expected to do. LaDonna Harris describes in her memoir hosting parties at her Virginia house, which was, as she says, small "by Virginia and Georgetown standards." They would take down their dining room table and replace it with three small tables so that guests could converse more easily. The Harrises also socialized with journalists in order to help members of the press understand better the Harrises' commitment to certain issues (79–80). LaDonna, along with other Senate wives, met on Wednesdays to create squares of gauze for bandages, which she found extraordinarily boring. She found more meaningful a service that she, Muriel Humphrey, and Joan Mondale provided as they made baby clothes and blankets for servicemembers' children (Memoir 72–74).

What principally interested LaDonna, though, were policy and social action that would improve people's lives. A huge step forward to making a significant difference for people was creation of Oklahomans for Indian Opportunity (OIO). In the summer of 1965, she helped organize a conference at the University of Oklahoma to discuss improving economic and educational opportunities for Native Americans. The inability of Native Americans in Oklahoma to qualify for War on Poverty funds because they were not members of formally recognized reservations severely limited their opportunities. Out of this conference, which has been called "the most important gathering of Oklahoma Indians since the last intertribal council met in 1888 to fight dissolution" (Sachs 411), came the new organization with LaDonna chosen as president. Recognizing that a key to economic advancement is a good education, she determined to try to improve the high dropout rate among Native American children in the state. And the dropout rate, she knew, was related to the children's self-image. Too often, the children were faced with negative comments and the sense that they had value only insofar as they could abandon their own culture and become, in values and behavior, more like white people. Progress required sensitizing teachers and school administrators to what they were doing; a tactic that the organization employed to do that was role-playing in which the students became the teachers and the teachers the students (Memoir 59–60; Janda 37). OIO also contributed books about Native Americans to school libraries in order to increase self-knowledge and self-pride. Such efforts would prove positive, as the dropout rate declined from 75 percent to 35 percent (*Voices* 24–26).

OIO organized CAPs (community action programs) to acquaint

families with available services, and, in a move that some tribal leaders opposed, advocated for tribes electing their own leaders rather than continuing to have the Bureau of Indian Affairs select them. A major belief of OIO was that Indigenous peoples should control more of their own lives (Janda 38–40). Among the very practical programs was an effort to improve diet. Low-income families and individuals qualified for free food, but some items, such as canned meats, were unappetizing. The organization consequently organized women to prepare a cookbook in order to take more advantage of such foods and make them more appealing. OIO even started a pig farm (*Voices* 25).

OIO took a multipronged approach to improving opportunities for a better life, ranging from specific local efforts to improve basic aspects of life to academic research projects. Money, of course, would be necessary for projects large and small. John B. O'Hara, director of the Southwest Center for Human Relations at the University of Oklahoma, offered to house the organization and offered helpful advice regarding establishment of a board of directors and an executive board. He also was instrumental in persuading the Office of Economic Opportunity to change its policy of allotting grants only to reservation tribes. He urged Fred Harris to intercede with Sargent Shriver, head of President Johnson's War on Poverty, to support broadening grant opportunities, thus allowing OIO to apply for grant money. Bureaucracy in this case moved quickly, and by April 1966, OIO was awarded over $240,000 (Anderson 126–30).

With financial support, OIO was able to continue moving ahead to achieve its goals in a wide range of areas that included community economic development, education, food cooperatives, improved housing, enhanced job opportunities, and leadership training. Referral centers were established to help individuals apply for aid and to supply food and clothing to those in need. Field representatives were trained on the Oklahoma University campus in leadership training. Regional coordinators were identified and trained. A growing list of activities to encourage students to stay in school included essay contests, recognition of student excellence, and social gatherings. LaDonna even wrote personal letters to students congratulating them on their achievements. Job trainees were placed with businesses and their salaries paid by OIO for the first thirteen weeks. LaDonna invited Senator Robert Kennedy to speak at an OIO meeting in 1967, which he did to a large and enthusiastic audience of hundreds of Native American students, each of whom was able to bring a non–Native guest. Soon *Look Magazine* was publicizing Oklahomans for Opportunity as "the model for a national effort" (Anderson 130–35).

Behind LaDonna Harris's efforts with Oklahomans for Indian Opportunity lay, on the one hand, the major federal movements of termination and assimilation, and, on the other, preservation of and fidelity to cultural traditions. Sarah Eppler Janda examines the tensions between these seemingly polar opposites, between retaining "traditional culture" and profiting from "mainstream American opportunities," pointing out that Harris denied a contradiction between those choices and insisted that a balance could and should be achieved. The choice for her is tantamount to denying what rhetoricians and logicians sometimes refer to as the "either-or fallacy," the belief that there are only two choices when in reality there may be many choices or at least a combination of the two. Janda states, "Implicit from the very beginning in the goals of OIO were the competing impulses of cultural preservation and integration." Harris, in her life in Washington (where she combined the virtues of a traditional Senate wife with dedication to helping Native Americans improve their lives without renouncing their cultural identity), managed to achieve a balance analogous to the balance that she sought with OIO (35–50).

Along with continuing her work with OIO, LaDonna Harris increasingly was sought out during her Washington years to bring her knowledge and skill to work in a variety of ways. Sargent Shriver, leader of Johnson's War on Poverty, enlisted Harris as an advisor after she spoke with him about the difficulties that Comanches and other tribes had receiving Office of Economic Opportunity funds because they lacked a definite reservation-like land. President Johnson followed by appointing her to the National Council on Indian Opportunity (NCIO), where she was the only nonelected tribal official. She served on the board of the Urban League and helped to create the Urban Coalition. Harris subsequently held hearings in a number of large cities throughout the country (Memoir 80–82, 95–98). All of these endeavors dovetailed well with her OIO goals.

When LaDonna Harris was named chairperson of the National Women's Advisory Council on the War on Poverty in January 1968, she resigned as president of OIO, recognizing that she had much to offer beyond the state level. Combining her commitment to Native Americans with a growing focus on women, in 1971 she helped to create the National Women's Political Caucus (NWPC). This organization brought her into collaboration with some of the most famous pioneers of twentieth-century feminism, among them Bella Abzug, Betty Friedan, and Gloria Steinem. Also involved in creation of the NWPC was Shirley Chisholm, who in 1968 became the first African American woman to be elected to the United States Congress, and who in 1972 would seek the Democratic Party's Presidential nomination, becoming the first African American to seek the Presidential nomination of a major party and the first woman to attempt to become the Democratic Party's nominee. Within a few years, Harris herself would seek elective office as a Vice Presidential candidate. She also would soon create a national version of OIO.

Having devoted much effort to mental health issues in the past, LaDonna Harris was a natural choice to be appointed to the Joint Commission on Mental Health of Children in November 1967. The report on minority children that she would help write concluded, amid much controversy, that racism was the greatest source of harm for minority children (Anderson 144n.53).

One of LaDonna Harris's largest single accomplishments occurred during the Nixon presidency. It involved the Taos Pueblo tribe's loss of Blue Lake in the early twentieth century when it was made part of Carson National Forest in New Mexico. Blue Lake is sacred to the Taos Pueblo people, as they believe that their ancestors originally came from the lake. For over sixty years they had been trying to reclaim the lake and surrounding land including Taos Mountain. A delegation from the Taos Pueblo came to Washington to meet with Fred Harris, who asked LaDonna to join the session. Senator Henry Jackson of Washington, the chair of the Interior Committee, opposed returning the lake and land, largely because Senator Clinton Anderson of New Mexico, a veteran senator with considerable influence, opposed the return. LaDonna and Fred elicited support from civil rights groups and the African American community, raising the matter from an individual state to a national civil rights issue. President Nixon strongly supported greater self-determination for Native Americans, so if the Harrises could get a bill through Congress returning the Blue Lake region to the Taos Pueblo, it would likely be signed into law.

With the assistance of a young Navaho woman and White House Fellow, Bobbie Green, LaDonna prepared a report on Native Americans for the National Council on Indian Opportunity that included a number of recommendations, including the return of Blue Lake to the Taos Pueblo. The report generated considerable public attention, and the return of Blue Lake as mandated in House Resolution 471 gathered increasing political support by a body of senators that ranged from the liberal Ted Kennedy and George McGovern to the conservative Barry Goldwater (Memoir 88–90; Voice 31; Janda 59–63). Anderson was extremely upset with Fred Harris, telling her husband, according to LaDonna, "'Fred, we don't mess with your Indians in Oklahoma and you shouldn't mess with mine.'" She recounts her husband's response: "'They're not yours, senator'" (Voice 31). By this time, however, the issue had been nationalized, removing it from the concept of "home state noninterference" (Gordon-McCutchan 195). LaDonna, according to R.C. Gordon-McCutchan, put in many hours lobbying for passage of H.R. 471 (197). On December 2, 1970, the Senate passed the legislation 70 to 12, and on December 15, President Nixon signed the legislation, returning 48,000 acres, including Blue Lake, to the Taos Pueblo. The signing was highly emotional, even for Nixon; Gordon-McCutchan quotes

LaDonna Harris describing the signing event, noting especially "'the dignity and the reverence'" of the Taos attendees, how Nixon was moved by "'the joy of the occasion,'" and "'the [Taos] people showed that they were so directly affected by the return [of Blue Lake] as to who they were and how they saw themselves continuing that it captured everyone'" (218). An additional 764 acres were returned in 1996. The return of Blue Lake and the surrounding 48,000 acres is described on the Taos Pueblo website as the "single most dramatic event in the recent history of Taos Pueblo land" because of its importance to "the spiritual, cultural and economic health of the Pueblo."

LaDonna Harris (second from left) and her husband, Senator Fred Harris (with crossed arms), join Taos Pueblo and government officials at President Nixon's signing of legislation returning Blue Lake to the Taos Pueblo. President Nixon has completed his introductory address and yielded the microphone to the Taos Pueblo Cacique, or religious leader, Juan de Jesús Romero (courtesy Richard Nixon Presidential Library and Museum).

LaDonna Harris's activism and influence during the Washington years was extraordinary. She was at least partly responsible, as Stephen M. Sachs points out, for adding Native American advisory committees in federal agencies during the Johnson administration, for the addition of "Indian Desks" in agencies that impact Native Americans during the Nixon administration, and, in short, for most of the "structural innovations" that have occurred since 1968 to create better coordination of federal programs that impact Indigenous programs, thereby enhancing tribal self-determination (414).

LaDonna's political activity, meanwhile, involved working on behalf of her husband during his successful reelection campaign for the United States Senate in 1966 and his unsuccessful attempts to gain the 1972 and 1976 Democratic nomination for President. Fred had decided not to run again for the Senate in 1972. Throughout these years, LaDonna had established and led an organization that would endure well beyond her Washington years, beyond her marriage, and into the present: Americans for Indian Opportunity (AIO).

Americans for Indian Opportunity

LaDonna Harris had become increasingly disappointed with the National Council on Indian Opportunity, which, under the direction of Vice President Spiro Agnew, had largely become inactive. Consequently, she declined another term on the council and decided to create a new organization over which she would have more control. Thus was born Americans for Indian Opportunity in the spring of 1970. Modeled on Oklahomans for Indian Opportunity, the new organization would continue Harris's efforts to bring tribal governments and the federal government into close cooperation while enhancing tribal self-determination and strengthening Indigenous culture. AIO was and remains both an educational and advocacy organization, casting a wide net over issues—environmental, political, legal, administrative, health, among others—that impact Native peoples.

The mission statement for AIO, available on its website, states this comprehensive effort: "Americans for Indian Opportunity advances, from an Indigenous worldview, the cultural, political, and economic rights of Indigenous peoples in the United States and around the world." In advancing these broad rights, the AIO has been especially aware of governance issues, which has led to sustained efforts to foster effective leadership. At the same time, AIO has turned in two directions regarding education. Harris has been concerned with educating Native Americans about their rights and benefits available to them. Conversely, she has worked hard to sensitive the federal government and its agencies toward Native American needs and rights. Harris has spoken often about educating presidents and other national, state, and local leaders, teaching them "Indian 101" in her famous phrase (Janda 68).

AIO issued "Red Alerts" (topical newsletters) concerning policies, legislation, and other matters of immediate importance as well as "Red Papers" (position papers) on important issues. AIO helped to create the Native American Legal Defense and Education Fund to assist people in need of legal aid and educational support. AIO also co-operated with Oklahomans for Indian Opportunity in administering American Indian Investment Opportunities, Inc., which helped Native Americans establish their own businesses (Janda 69–71).

LaDonna Harris describes in her memoir the initial fundraising that helped get AIO off the ground. In addition to individual donations from a variety of sources, the Ford Foundation contributed start-up funds. Fundraising, however, was not, according to Harris, one of her particular strengths, nor something she especially liked doing. In fact, she writes, "fund-raising was one of the worst things I have ever done in my life." Meeting Coy Eklund, an Equitable Life Insurance Company executive in New York, however, was a major turning point in establishing AIO as a viable entity. Harris points out that Eklund, as a white Republican executive, might not seem like a likely ally, but Eklund had established a friendship with an elderly Ojibwe woman that his father had known and repeatedly communicated with her, mastered the sounds of her language, and created an Ojibwe dictionary. Eklund therefore was ready to respond positively to Harris's plans and became an enthusiastic supporter. Harris, who had served from the start as AIO's president, put Eklund on its board. After she introduced Eklund to Vernon Jordan, Jordan added him to the Urban League board (100–03).

Harris named other prominent and influential figures to the board of AIO as well, including the ballerina Maria Tallchief, actress Candace Bergen, and film producer Ray Stark. Her focus, however, remained on the people she was trying to help. AIO was constituted according to regions, with local tribal peoples playing important roles in their regions. AIO was a major undertaking for Harris, but she was aided, she notes, by having served on many boards previously (Memoir 103–04). Fred Harris describes how he would introduce his wife during his campaigning for President, only slightly exaggerating: "I used to say that she belonged to the national board of directors of every organization anyone had ever heard of—from Common Cause to the National Organization for Women. I called her a 'nonprofit conglomerate'" (*Does People Do It?* 190).

Over the years, AIO has been involved in numerous projects. Stephen Sachs enumerates a number of them. In collaboration with George Mason University, AIO developed the Indigenous Leadership Interactive System (ILIS) to bring more "community consensus and harmony" into tribal government; through ILIS, AIO offered a forum at the Strengthening Children and Families: Networking Urban Indian Centers in the U.S. conference, which was offered in Seattle in 2003 by the United Nations of All Tribes Foundation. AIO was involved in the Messing with Mother Nature Project to examine environmental problems impacting tribes, including developing a publication of that title to assist tribes in working with the federal government. Similarly, it established To Govern or Be Governed: American Indian Tribes at the Crossroads to help tribal governments interact with federal agencies, including the Environmental Protection Agency (EPA). In addition, AIO created INDIANnet, a computer telecommunications network that became part of Native American Communications, to offer communications capabilities, especially making EPA information more accessible; and AIO helped to launch the Council of Energy Resource Tribes (CERT), the National American Indian Housing Council, the National Tribal Environmental Council, and the National Indian Business Association (416–18).

Perhaps the most enduring project of AIO is its Ambassadors Program, which Harris began in 1993 with the help of a three-million-dollar grant from the W.K. Kellogg Foundation (Memoir 122). According to the AIO website, the mission of the program is to help "early to mid-career Native American professionals strengthen, within an Indigenous cultural context, their ability to improve the well-being and growth of their communities." The Ambassadors Program helps participants maintain traditional cultural values while integrating them into the contemporary world. The program includes both curricular and experiential experiences while offering participants opportunities to interact with individuals charged with decision-making. It also offers its ambassadors opportunities to engage in anti-racism training, develop skills in community organizing, and improve their communications skills.

As the AIO website points out, the Ambassadors Program is organized around four "R's": relationships (a kinship with all people and the world), responsibility (to care for each other and for the earth), reciprocity (understanding that all things are interconnected), and redistribution (the requirement that we share wealth, knowledge, and resources).

The AIO website also states that more than two hundred Native American leaders have been trained through the AIO Ambassadors Program. The national vision that LaDonna Harris brought to the creation of the organization is represented in the widespread engagement of the ambassadors, who have been placed in thirty-six states serving over one hundred tribes. According to Aliyah Chavez, in an article published in *Indian Country Today*, LaDonna Harris, among her many successes, is most proud of Americans for Indian Opportunity. As of 2021, she remains the president of AIO, with one of her daughters, Laura, serving as executive director.

LaDonna Harris, president of Americans for Indian Opportunity, appears resplendent in traditional Comanche attire, looking very much the leader she has long been (courtesy Americans for Indian Opportunity, photograph by Wakeah Vigil).

A Vice Presidential Candidate and Other Activities

LaDonna Harris was actively involved in several campaigns in support of her husband as he sought state and national positions. She proved herself an able campaigner and political partner, but the day came when she found herself on the other side of the campaign, as a candidate—and she started near the top, as a candidate for Vice President of the United States in 1980. By this time, Fred's Senate career had ended, and he had twice unsuccessfully sought the Democratic nomination for President. With his political career seemingly over, the Harrises moved from Washington, D.C., to New Mexico, where Fred embarked on an academic career in the Political Science Department at the University of New Mexico in 1976 and LaDonna continued to lead Americans for Indian Opportunity.

In 1980, LaDonna Harris was invited to attend the Citizens' Party Convention and be nominated for Vice President as a running mate for Presidential candidate Barry Commoner, a highly respected scientist and environmentalist who had become deeply concerned about the impact of atomic testing on people's health and on the environment. After consulting with her family, she agreed. In her memoir, Harris describes her difficulties transitioning from campaigning for someone else to campaigning for herself. She adds that running for Vice President was both one of the best and one of the worst experiences of her life. She felt great pressure as a candidate for national office, and money for the campaign was in short supply. However, she took great pleasure from meeting people and staying in supporters' homes. The campaign did not fare well in terms of votes, but it did increase her recognition throughout the country, which proved beneficial in her work within the AIO and with other endeavors (Memoir 110–12; Voices 34–35).

The following year, the marriage, which had been a deep partnership as well as marriage, came to an end. LaDonna Harris, as she points out, had been moving increasingly into her own world and finding her own voice. The divorce, though, was emotionally difficult, as she had not been by herself before, and the divorce, she acknowledges, contributed to a sense of abandonment that went back to her relationship with her parents. There also was a sense of guilt, as LaDonna felt that perhaps things would have been different if she had just paid more attention to the marriage. Janda quotes journalist Rusty Brown from the *Albuquerque Tribune*: "'Thus comes to an end one of the best husband-wife political teams ever to stump the Oklahoma cornfields or crack the Washington power structure'" (76). After the divorce, LaDonna returned to Washington, where she lived for the next ten years while continuing to lead AIO, before returning to New Mexico in 1990, bringing AIO back with her (Memoir 112–13).

LaDonna and Fred, however, reconstructed a strong and friendly relationship, their respect and fondness for each other apparently never really ending. She credits Fred with providing a generous divorce settlement and writes of reestablishing "a good relationship" with him while speaking well of his new wife (Memoir 114–15). Fred remains, LaDonna says in her *Voices of Oklahoma* interview, "a beautiful friend of mine," adding that "it's just a wonderful relationship now, because it was so good and rich throughout our lives" (37–38). Fred, in *Does People Do It?*, refers to the end of his thirty-three-year marriage to LaDonna, "who had been my great and valuable partner in politics and activism," and adds that they have continued to be friends (203).

It would be almost impossible to list every organization that LaDonna Harris has impacted, as a creator, co-creator, supporter, or board member. In addition to the organizations already discussed, she was a founding member of the National Urban Coalition and Common Cause. She was a member of the Global Tomorrow Coalition, served as the U.S. Representative to the United Nations Educational, Scientific, and Cultural Organization (UNESCO) and the Organization of American States (OAS) Inter-American Indigenous Institute. Harris's most recent board memberships have been on Think New Mexico, the National Committee to Preserve Social Security and Medicare, and the Smithsonian's National Museum of the American Indian. She helped develop Advancement of Global Indigeneity to help Indigenous peoples throughout the world work together. Stephen Sachs includes a long list of boards on which LaDonna Harris has served. A sample, in addition to some mentioned above, are Save the Children, Girl Scouts of the USA, National Organization for Women, National Institute for Women of Color, Pax World Foundation, National Institute for the Environment, and National Organization on Fetal Alcohol Syndrome (446n.18).

Awards also have been many. In 2017, LaDonna Harris received the Changing World Prize from the Woody Guthrie Center, which, as its website says, "is dedicated to spreading Woody's message of diversity, equality and social justice." *Ladies' Home Journal* chose LaDonna Harris as "Woman of the Year and the Decade" in 1979. She had received seven honorary doctorates as of 2019 and was a member of the first class of inductees into the National Native American Hall of Fame in 2018. The LaDonna Harris Institute for Native American Studies at the California University of Pennsylvania continues Harris's lifelong mission to educate people about Indigenous peoples and expand diversity. Her famous "Indian 101" phrase serves as the title of a documentary film made about her life by Julianna Brannum, which was completed in 2014.

LaDonna Harris's commitment to advocacy has continued to guide her actions. On January 21, 2017, for example, during the massive Women's March to protest the election of Donald Trump as President and to advocate for human rights for all, Harris was one of the honorary co-chairs. The broad focus of the Women's March, which incorporates not just women's rights but also policies relating to LGBTQ+ rights, health care, immigration, and racial equality among others, is consistent with LaDonna Harris's growth in advocacy and concern, from Native Americans to African Americans to women, to the world. Stephen Sachs has summed up who, at her core, LaDonna Harris is: "an amazing activist of the heart, demonstrating that traditional inclusive and collaborative ways of relating are especially appropriate in the contemporary world" (418).

Note

1. Throughout this chapter, material from "LaDonna Harris: Social Activist and Politician," an interview conducted for the series *Voices of Oklahoma*, will be documented as *Voices* with accompanying pagination based on the published transcript of the interview; and references to Harris's memoir *LaDonna Harris: A Comanche Life* will be documented as Memoir.

References

Americans for Indian Opportunity (AIO) website. aio.org.

Anderson, Gary C. "LaDonna Harris." *The New Warriors: Native American Leaders Since 1900*. Ed. R. David Edmunds. Lincoln: U of Nebraska P, 2001. 122–44.

Chavez, Aliyah. "LaDonna Harris 'Stumbled' Into a Legacy of Impact." *Indian Country Today* 18 Aug. 2019. indiancountrytoday.com/news/ladonna-harris-stumbled-into-a-legacy-of-impact-UzsfOaQfKk2D0ycrBgZUFg.

Gordon-McCutchan, R.C. *The Taos Indians and the Battle for Blue Lake*. Santa Fe: Red Crane Books, 1991.

Harris, Fred R. *Does People Do It? A Memoir*. Norman: U of Oklahoma P, 2008.

_____. *Potomac Fever*. New York: Norton, 1977.

Harris, LaDonna. *A Comanche Life*. Ed. H. Henrietta Stockel. Lincoln: U of Nebraska P, 2000.

_____. Interview with John Erling. *Voices of Oklahoma*. 21 Sept. 2017. m.voicesofoklahoma.com/interview/harris-ladonna/.

Janda, Sarah Eppler. *Beloved Women: The Political Lives of LaDonna Harris and Wilma Mankiller*. DeKalb: Northern Illinois UP, 2007.

LaDonna Harris: Indian 101. Dir. Julianna Brannum. Women Make Movies, 2014.

Sachs, Stephen M. "Returning to Traditional Leadership in Indian Nations: The Example of LaDonna Harris." *Re-Creating the Circle: The Renewal of American Indian Self-Determination*. Ed. LaDonna Harris. Albuquerque: U of New Mexico P. 410–19.

9

Wilma Mankiller
(1945–2010)

Wilma Mankiller rose from poverty in Adair County, Oklahoma, to become Principal Chief of the Cherokee Nation, serving ten years as the first woman to head a major Native American tribe. Her journey was difficult, as she had to overcome many health problems, including two kidney transplants, as well as opposition by some to a woman assuming tribal leadership. Along the way, she became a major activist for both women and Native Americans, on the national stage as well as locally. Among the many honors that she received was the Presidential Medal of Freedom, presented to her by President Bill Clinton in 1998. She became a household name, an adviser to presidents, and a model of what an individual can accomplish by refusing to yield to hardships, whether societal or personal.

Adair County, Oklahoma

Wilma Pearl Mankiller was born on November 18, 1945, in the W.W. Hastings Indian Hospital, located in Tahlequah, in Cherokee County, Oklahoma. Tahlequah is the capital of the Cherokee Nation and has the distinction of having been named one of the one hundred best small towns in the United States, although with a population of over sixteen thousand, it is not especially small. Her father, Charley Mankiller, born in 1914, was Cherokee. The Mankiller name, according to Wilma Mankiller in her memoir, *Mankiller: A Chief and Her People*, written with Michael Wallis, derived from a tribal position held by a person charged with providing security to his village (xxi). Wilma's mother, Clara Irene Sitton, was born in Adair County, the county between Cherokee County and the state of Arkansas. Of Dutch and Irish ancestry, she went by her middle name, Irene, and married Charley when she was fifteen and he twenty-one. The marriage produced eleven children, with Wilma the sixth oldest. As a child, Wilma was regularly called also by her middle name, Pearl. Mankiller notes in her memoir that her mother had learned Cherokee culture not only from her husband but also by growing up in Cherokee country and attending school with Cherokee students (11–12).[1]

Home for Wilma Mankiller as a child was in Adair County, on Mankiller family land referred to as Mankiller Flats near Rocky Mountain, which is a "census-designated place," meaning that Rocky Mountain includes a population defined as a concentration by the United States Census Bureau. The Charley and Irene Mankiller family moved there in 1948, and Charley built a house on the land. The Mankiller family, like many families in Adair County, was quite poor. Wilma Mankiller describes her youth in detail within her memoir, noting that the house had only four rooms, a tin roof, a wood stove, coal-oil lamps used for lighting, an outhouse, and water carried from a freshwater spring (32–33).

Given the cultural backgrounds of Wilma's parents, it was natural that both Cherokee and English were spoken in the house. Her mother learned to speak "passable conversational Cherokee," but at home the family generally used English. Wilma's clothing was usually handed down from older children and/or made from flour sacks, flour having been sold in cloth bags of varying colors and designs. She attended a small local school and developed a great love for reading, which she attributed to "the traditional Cherokee passion for telling and listening to stories," with storytelling and visiting supplying the family's primary means of entertainment (34–44). Adults in the family also enjoyed playing cards, while Wilma and her siblings participated in such typical children's games as hide-and-go-seek and marbles, occasionally improvising in response to nails driven into the wall by seeing who could throw the most Mason jar rubber sealing rings around the nails (*Every Day Is a Good Day* 46). Religion played a modest role in the Mankiller family. At times, the family attended services at a nearby Baptist church, but Wilma admits late in life, "though I certainly do not consider myself a spiritual person, I have always been attracted to people of faith" (*Every Day Is a Good Day* 16).

Another Removal

Shortly before Wilma's eleventh birthday, in 1956, her life changed. In her memoir, she recalls hiding in her bedroom listening to her parents discuss moving, the result, she states, of the family's poverty (69). In October, the family—parents and eight of the children, with two children not yet born and Frieda remaining behind to finish high school—boarded a train to San Francisco. A move was encouraged by Bureau of Indian Affairs agents, with the Mankiller family choosing San Francisco at least partly because Wilma's maternal grandmother lived in California, where, after being widowed, she had remarried and moved to Riverbank, approximately ninety miles east of San Francisco.

The move west would usher in an unhappy period for Wilma, who referred in her memoir to the move as "our Trail of Tears" (68). The reference, of course, is to the forced movement of most Cherokees, including some of Wilma's ancestors, from the Southeast to present-day Oklahoma in 1838–39, a cruel journey that cost thousands their lives. The forced removal was a culmination of policies instituted by President Andrew Jackson. The Mankiller journey was obviously far less cruel, and certainly infinitely less tragic than the original Trail of Tears, as Wilma observes. "The government methods had softened since the nineteenth century," she writes, "but the end result was the same for native people. Instead of guns and bayonets, the BIA used promotional brochures showing staged photographs of smiling Indians in 'happy homes' in the big cities" (69).

Wilma Mankiller devotes chapters four, six, eight, and ten in her memoir to chronicling policies and actions of the United States that seriously and adversely impacted her people from the eighteenth century into the post–World War II era. In addition to her focus on the Trail of Tears, she also places her family's move within the process of "termination" and "relocation" that reached an apex during the 1950s and '60s.

Termination was a policy of ending any relationship between the federal government and tribes, in effect, also dissolving the existence of tribes themselves, including the concept of tribal government. This was done in the specious name of freeing Indians, who would be assimilated into the general United States population, necessitating as well that Native Americans would have to relocate to where there would be jobs. As Charles Wilkinson, who drafted the bill reversing the termination and restoring the Menominee nation in Wisconsin, states in his *Blood Struggle: The Rise of Modern Indian Nations*, "for Indian people the word 'termination' represents the third rail, shorthand for all that is extreme and confiscatory in federal Indian policy" (57). Termination essentially removed Native Americans from their land and their culture. Wilkinson quotes the Klamath Lynn Schonchin, who puts it more bluntly: termination meant "'you're not Indian any more'" (81–82).

As the movement toward termination picked up speed in the U.S. Congress, so did so-called "voluntary" relocation. Dillon S. Myer, head of the Bureau of Indian Affairs, implemented a relocation program in 1951 to encourage individuals to leave their reservations and relocate in urban centers. Termination, strongly opposed by many Native Americans, would gradually fall out of favor as national policy, and would be formally ended by President Richard Nixon in 1970. Some tribes would successfully restore their recognized status, including the Menominee in Wisconsin and the

Grand Ronde in Oregon, the latter restoration discussed in detail in the chapter on Kathryn Harrison in this book.

The Mankillers were not directly impacted by termination, but they were part of the huge relocation that occurred in the 1950s. Their trip by train took two days and nights. Upon arrival, the family had to stay in an old hotel for two weeks in the Tenderloin District of San Francisco. Mankiller recalls in her memoir the family hearing sirens throughout the night, the first time they had ever heard sirens, an ominous sound that reminded the young Wilma of wolves. Much that the family experienced was new, certainly to the children, including neon lights, elevators, and flush toilets (71–72; *Every Day Is a Good Day* 100).

The Mankillers then moved into a flat in the Potrero Hill District, near the rope factory where Wilma's father and brother Don got jobs. Shortly afterward, another brother, James Ray, was born. One new experience after another followed: telephones, bicycles, roller skates. School, however, proved difficult for Wilma, as she found herself behind most students in mathematics and language arts. To compensate, she would stay up late at night reading aloud with her sister Linda so that they could talk the way most students in school talked (72–73).

Life became a little better when the family was able to move into a house in Daly City, south of San Francisco. It was hardly a spacious home for such a large family with its three bedrooms. Wilma shared a bedroom with her sisters but having their own house did not make her feel much better about being in California, and she still strongly disliked school. As she entered seventh grade, she still felt like an outsider as other students teased her for her Oklahoma accent. She adds in her memoir that although she loved her family, she felt confused and lacking in self-esteem. Several times she ran away to be with her Grandmother Sitton (103–04).

As Wilma was preparing to enter eighth grade, her parents, no doubt trying to find a solution to their daughter's unhappiness, allowed her to go live with her grandmother, who by this time had sold her house and moved in with her son and daughter-in-law on a diary ranch near Escalon, California. Mankiller credits her grandmother with helping her face her difficulties and develop greater self-confidence to the point that Wilma even began to feel better about school. She came to enjoy work on the farm, including helping with the milking, and returned to the farm each summer throughout high school (105–07).

Another person who had a great effect on the young Wilma was Justine Buckskin, a Klamath woman. Referred to in the memoir by the name Gustine Moppin (158), she is cited by Mankiller in *Every Day Is a Good Day* as one of the strongest influences on her, starting when Wilma was eleven years old and Buckskin offered her a babysitting job. Buckskin encouraged

Mankiller to attend college, even accompanying her as she enrolled. They remained close for decades. Mankiller refers to the belief that Earth will remember an individual so long as people utter her name, and she often did just that for her early mentor (2–3).

When Wilma returned to her parents, the family was living in a house at Hunter's Point in San Francisco, which was primarily an African American community. For the first time, she came to know Black children. The experience, Mankiller notes in her memoir, gave her an understanding of other cultures that she otherwise might never have gained (110). By this time, the 1960s had begun, Wilma's father was working as a longshoreman, and Wilma began frequenting the Indian Center in the Mission District. Also, she transferred to a high school that, she says, was calmer than her previous high school and that included many Asian students, adding even more to her appreciation for various cultures (108–11).

The Indian Center became an important locus for Mankiller's political awakening, in part because of her father's frequenting of the Center in his new position as a shop steward and union organizer. Wilma acknowledges her father's great influence on her life. Although Charley Mankiller was a registered Republican who still associated the Democratic Party with that of Andrew Jackson, and Wilma states that she sometimes disagreed with him, she profited greatly from her political discussions with her father. Like so many young people, she became a John Kennedy supporter, and her attendance at the Indian Center brought her into consensus Native American views about the failure of the federal government's relocation program. She writes that she and her family went to the Indian Center for support when Wilma's brother Robert died in 1960 after mistakenly using gasoline rather than kerosene to start a fire in a wood stove (111–13). The Indian Center, she states in *Every Day Is a Good Day*, overall was the center of the family's social life (48).

The teen years were something of a mixed bag for Wilma. Robert died, but another brother, William, was born. Self-described as shy, she found her first serious boyfriend, Ray Billy, from the Pomo tribe, and dated him for a year before he broke up with her for another girl. Her academic accomplishments were also mixed: strong in English and literature but weak in science and mathematics and not inclined to join many school extracurricular activities (114–15). She gave little indication in these years of the extraordinary accomplishments that awaited her.

Joining the Revolution

Upon graduating from high school, Wilma seemingly embarked on a life that reflected the broader American culture more than her Cherokee background. She lived with her sister Frances and went to work for a finance company handling routine clerking duties. Soon she was in love with an Ecuadorian man named Hector Hugo Olaya de Bardi, whom she referred to as Hugo. They married in late 1963. Hugo wanted Wilma to be a traditional wife, and she attempted to fill that role. Even then, however, she was becoming more interested in politics, thanks in part to the presidency of John F. Kennedy. In her memoir, Mankiller writes of how devastating the assassination of President Kennedy was to her, referring to the period as one of her loss of innocence, both for the nation and personally for her (148).

Wilma fell ill with a kidney infection in January of 1964, the beginning of a lifetime of combating illness. She also learned from her doctor that she was pregnant. The combination of pregnancy and the kidney infection forced her to remain largely bedridden for much of her pregnancy (149–50). After their child, Felicia, was born, Wilma, Hugo, and the baby moved into a rented house in San Francisco, after living with Hugo's cousins. In 1966, a second daughter, Gina, was born.

At this time, Wilma was becoming increasingly interested in what was occurring politically in California and throughout the country. Having become acquainted earlier with African Americans, she notes in her memoir that the first political organization that she identified with was the Black Panthers. Soon she was closely following the activities of Cesar Chavez and the National Farm Workers Association, the African American civil rights movement, and opposition to the Vietnam War. She often took her daughters to the Haight-Ashbury area of San Francisco but notes that, although interested, she was still primarily a housewife observing what was happening around her (154–57; *Beloved Women* 83–84).

While questioning what was occurring in the country, Wilma also was questioning her own role in society and her marriage. She recalls that her husband's vision for her was as a wife, mother, housekeeper, and cook. The family had one car, and it was under the control of her husband. Wilma, however, started to push back against these expectations. She wanted to learn more about her Cherokee heritage, started saving money to buy her own car, began traveling to tribal events, and enrolled at Skyline Junior College and later San Francisco State College (157–59; *Every Day Is a Good Day* 48–50). Robert Kennedy's presidential run led to considerable interest on Wilma's part in mainstream politics, and his assassination, following that of his brother, was another traumatic blow to Wilma as it was to millions of Americans (160).

Then came the occupation of Alcatraz, which altered Wilma Mankiller's life forever (163).

The Alcatraz Federal Penitentiary was located on Alcatraz Island off the coast of San Francisco. Commonly referred to as "The Rock," the facility was a maximum-security prison that opened in 1934 after being converted from a federal military prison. Its fame rested largely on its reputation as an escape-proof prison and the famous prisoners that it housed over the years, including Al Capone, Machine Gun Kelly, and Robert Franklin Stroud, the latter more famously known as the Birdman of Alcatraz.

The prison was closed on March 21, 1963, with the island being listed as surplus federal property the following year. Disposition of the island and the closed facility excited considerable interest, with the federal government apparently considering turning the island over to the city of San Francisco. Two Sioux cousins, Belva Cottier and Richard McKenzie, turned to the Treaty of Laramie, enacted in 1868, and concluded that it provided for returning to Native Americans land abandoned by the federal government. About forty people subsequently occupied the island for approximately four hours on March 8, 1964. The brief expedition, along with an offering of a nominal purchase price mocking the minimal amounts historically offered to tribal communities for the land they lived on, and planned legal action, did not result in immediate success (Johnson 16–27). However, it did plant a seed that would flower more fully five years later.

A new, symbolic expedition was planned by Adam Nordwall, a Chippewa later known as Adam Fortunate Eagle, for November 9, 1969. Student activists including Richard Oakes (Mohawk) and LaNada Means (Shoshone-Bannock) carried out what turned into an overnight occupation. The activists, however, were far from through. With negotiations occurring involving oilman Lamar Hunt as a potential buyer for Alcatraz Island and a fire having devastated the American Indian Center on October 28, 1969, there was a strong sense of urgency to take action. On November 20, 1969, eighty-nine Native Americans, including women, men, and children, set out for Alcatraz Island. The Coast Guard stopped most of them from arrival, but fourteen people made it through. The occupation was on and would endure for nineteen months, achieving national and international attention and considerable following. Many others, including white supporters, would arrive. Some people stayed for the duration while others spent no more than a day on the island. Approximately four hundred people were camped out on Alcatraz Island at the height of the occupation. The diversity of representation was evident in the title "Indians of All Tribes" under which the occupation occurred.

Richard Oakes sent a message to the Department of the Interior inviting the United States "to acknowledge the justice of our claim" and to decide whether the federal government would use force against those residing on the island or embark on a new way of "dealing with the American Indian" ("Alcatraz Proclamation and Letter"). Many individuals, among them Justine Buckskin Moppin (Klamath), who served as a teacher's aide, played significant roles during the occupation, as the various duties involved in establishing an organized life were divided among the inhabitants.

By the summer of 1971, the occupation clearly was losing ground due to a variety of factors. Electricity and telephone service had been cut off, and fresh water was difficult to get. Several buildings had burned with the cause uncertain. After nineteen months, the numbers of occupiers had diminished, and public interest in the occupation had declined as well. Finally, only fifteen people remained. At that point, on June 11, 1971, government officers had little trouble removing the remaining few. Nonetheless, many saw the occupation as a success as it had brought considerable attention to the struggle for Native American rights and to the historical injustices perpetrated on Native peoples in the United States. It also demonstrated the power that Native Americans, when organized and committed, could wield (Johnson 217–21).

The occupation was of great importance to Wilma Mankiller for very personal reasons. Four of her siblings joined the occupation, including Richard, who became a member of the Alcatraz Council that organized life on the island, and Linda, who went to the island with her three children and stayed until the final removal of the occupiers in June 1971. Vanessa and James also joined the movement. Wilma traveled to the island with Linda aboard the *Clearwater*, a boat donated by the musical group Credence Clearwater Revival and returned to the island periodically. On her trips to the island, she did not stay overnight but instead returned to the mainland to help at the temporary Indian Center that was used as a replacement for the one that burned and that served as a command post and fund-raising center for the Alcatraz occupation. The occupation, Mankiller states in her memoir, gave her on a daily basis increasing self-respect and pride (193).

During the occupation, Wilma Mankiller suffered a huge loss when her father, Charley, died of polycystic kidney disease, which results in the growth of cysts on the kidneys. He died in February 1971 at the age of fifty-six. The family took him back to Oklahoma for burial in Echota Cemetery, where he was interred near his parents and a child of his that had died as a result of a miscarriage (198–201).

The disease that had caused Charley's death, Wilma learned during her father's illness, she had inherited. The diagnosis explained her many infections, and she was told to expect kidney failure in her thirties (198–99). The disease would continue to impact her health for the rest of her life.

At the same time, Mankiller's marriage continued to be troubled as she sought to establish her own identity and pursue her growing call to social action. From the late 1960s into the 1970s, she became involved in many important social and political activities in addition to the Alcatraz occupation. She served as director of the Native American Youth Center in East

Oakland and began a period of about five years working with the Pit River people in legal action against the Pacific Gas and Electric Company regarding land rights in northern California while also continuing to attend San Francisco State University (202–04).

Wilma decided in 1974 to end her marriage to Hugo. She also resumed using the Mankiller name and moved to Oakland. There she worked as a social worker for the Urban Indian Resource Center (212–13). In *Every Day Is a Good Day*, Mankiller discusses important influences on her, such as her involvement with the Oakland Intertribal Friendship House, her co-founding of California Indians for a Fair Settlement to work for a just settlement of land claims, and attendance at a treaty conference at the Standing Rock Sioux Reservation in South Dakota. The conference was in preparation for the 1977 United Nations Conference on Indigenous Rights in Geneva, Switzerland. Mankiller assisted the preparations by documenting Europeans' historical treatment of Native tribes as independent nations (82–83). What Wilma Mankiller did not yet realize was how much these experiences were helping to prepare her for future leadership of the Cherokee Nation.

First, however, would come Mankiller's return to Oklahoma. After a difficult year-long struggle with Hugo over custody of their daughter Gina (213–14), Mankiller with her two daughters visited Oklahoma in the summer

Wilma Mankiller, former Chief of the Cherokee Nation, receives the Presidential Medal of Freedom from President Clinton on January 15, 1998 (courtesy William J. Clinton Presidential Library).

of 1976. She describes in her memoir how quickly she became involved in ceremonial dances and various social activities, especially activities sponsored by the Four Mothers Society, a social and religious organization begun in the nineteenth century to support communal ownership of tribal lands (214–15). At this time, she began to recognize more clearly the spiritual dimension of her life and that the land where she had spent her childhood defined who she was even though her childhood home had burned. One of her first acts upon returning to Oklahoma was to bathe in the spring near where her family had lived. Wilma, Felicia, and Gina camped out before moving into an empty cabin that a relative told Wilma about. Mother and daughters read, went swimming, listened to music on their portable radio, played Scrabble, and watched the stars. Wilma experienced a strong sense of freedom back home in Oklahoma, and she and her daughters accepted an invitation to join the Four Mothers Society (*Every Day Is a Good Day* 17–21). Although they had to return to California, Mankiller had made her decision. She would bring her daughters back to Oklahoma permanently.

The Return

Wilma Mankiller and her daughters made their permanent return to Oklahoma in the summer of 1977, Wilma driving a U-Haul truck containing their possessions. Mankiller had no job and no car, and her future prospects were unclear, but she was going home. It helped that her mother had already made the return, and most of Wilma's siblings would eventually follow. Mankiller's job experiences along with her social activism in California had prepared her well, and by the fall she had started working for the Cherokee Nation as an economic stimulus coordinator. Her annual salary was, for the time, a livable $11,000, which allowed her to purchase a used station wagon. Her duties involved facilitating the university training of Cherokees in environmental science and health and then helping them to locate and adapt to roles within their communities (216–17).

It was an auspicious time for the Cherokee Nation, one that needed and, indeed, was open to new talent. The Cherokee Nation was, and remains, the second largest Native nation within the United States, second only to the Navajo Nation. Only recently had the Cherokees been allowed to return to choosing their own chief, the tribal leader having been appointed by the President of the United States since Oklahoma became a state in 1907. The Cherokee Nation also had a new constitution ratified in 1976. Times were changing, and Wilma Mankiller would become a large part of that change.

Mankiller had an expanded role by 1979, serving as a program development specialist. A major part of her job was developing grant proposals, a function that allowed her to use the knowledge that she had gained about treaty rights and intergovernmental relations while working with the Pit River people. She also completed her course work for a college degree in social work and began graduate school at the University of Arkansas at Fayetteville (219).

Then Mankiller's future almost ceased to happen. On November 8, 1979, she left home to meet with the personnel director of the Cherokee Nation about the possibility of adding to her work assignment in order to earn more money. About three miles from her home, an oncoming car pulled out to pass two cars and smashed into Mankiller's station wagon. She describes her injuries in her memoir: her face crushed, her neck cut when the hood was pushed back inside the vehicle, her right leg crushed, the left leg and both ankles broken, several ribs broken. Rushed to a hospital in Stilwell and then transported to another in Fort Smith, she was in critical condition and underwent a near-death experience that she describes in her memoir as "beautiful and spiritual" and which included "a tremendous sense of peacefulness and warmth." Only several weeks later, when Mankiller had started on the long road to recovery that would include seventeen operations, casts on her legs, and a period in a wheelchair, did she learn that the person driving the other car was her close friend Sherry Morris. Sherry's husband, Mike, kept the news of his wife's death from Mankiller for several weeks until he thought that she was out of immediate danger, although Mankiller describes in the memoir her shock and extraordinary pain on learning of Sherry's death, all the more shocking because of how she died (222–25; *Every Day Is a Good Day* 148–50).

A positive result of Wilma Mankiller's close encounter with death, as she notes, was that she had eliminated her fear of death (*Every Day Is a Good Day* 149). As she was still recovering from her injuries sustained in the car accident in early 1980, she found herself gradually developing trouble holding items without dropping them. Then she grew progressively weaker, had great trouble walking and even standing, found it difficult to hold her head up, and could not chew food. One day as she attempted to walk to her front door, she fell forward on the sidewalk, breaking her nose. Her "old friend death," as she describes it, seemed very close again (227). On Labor Day in 1980, as she was watching the Jerry Lewis annual muscular dystrophy telethon, she listened to a woman describing symptoms similar to her own. That led her to go to the Muscular Dystrophy Association center in Tulsa, where she was diagnosed with systemic myasthenia gravis, an autoimmune disorder that results in loss of muscular control over eyes, mouth, throat, arms, and legs, and that makes it difficult to swallow or even breathe ("Myasthenia Gravis"). Fortunately, surgery to remove her thymus and a drug program resulted in steady improvement. Within about six weeks, her symptoms had eased considerably, and she was strong enough in January 1981 to resume her work writing grants for the Cherokee Nation (226–29).

Her health improving, Wilma Mankiller threw herself into her work, helping to create and serving as the first director of the Cherokee Nation's Community Development Department. She led the effort to develop rural-development projects and acquire grants to help support those efforts. At the center of much of her work was a small community of about 350 people, most of them Cherokee, located at Bell, Oklahoma, about ten miles from Mankiller Flats. Partnering with the residents themselves, who did much of the hands-on work, the Community Development Department was able to rehabilitate twenty homes and the community center, build twenty-five new, energy-efficient homes (with support from the Cherokee Housing Authority), and create a water system that for the first time gave residents running water in their homes (233–35; Agnew 214).

During the Bell project, Mankiller met Charlie Soap, a Cherokee whom she described in her memoir as "probably the most well-adjusted male I have ever met" (235). Soap became a co-organizer on the Bell project with Mankiller and clearly Mankiller's "strongest love" she had known. They would marry in 1986 (235–38). When Mankiller left her position with the Community Development Department to run for deputy chief, Soap replaced her, although he had to resign his position upon marrying Mankiller because under Cherokee law relatives of elected officials are barred from working for the Cherokee Nation (Janda 97).

Chief Ross Swimmer decided in 1983 to seek reelection. By that time, he had learned a great deal about Wilma Mankiller's talents and dedication to the Cherokee Nation. Despite some political differences (Swimmer, for example, was a Republican, and Mankiller a Democrat), he asked her to join him on his ticket as the candidate for deputy chief. Initially, Mankiller refused, but as she reflected on how she could help her people from that position, she decided to accept Swimmer's offer. The election process featured separate elections for chief and deputy chief, so a vote for Swimmer was not also a vote for Mankiller. The election was challenging for her, not only because she had not run for office before, but also because she felt especially opposed by some due to her gender. Hate mail, threatening telephone messages, and slashed tires on her car did not deter her. If anything, they seemed to strengthen her conviction that in deciding to run she had indeed made the right decision (239–41).

Her opponents for deputy chief were J.B. Dreadfulwater, who was a well-known gospel singer, and Agnes Cowan, who already had served on the Tribal Council, which may have lessened gender bias against her. Having spent many years away from Oklahoma in California likely hurt

Mankiller with some voters. Charlie Soap worked closely with Mankiller during her campaigning for election, as did her mother and siblings. They employed standard campaign tactics: attending events, meeting people, putting up signs, discussing issues and Mankiller's community experiences (*Every Day Is a Good Day* 151). In the general election, Swimmer won, but no one received a majority for deputy chief, necessitating a runoff between Mankiller and Cowan. That the two top vote getters were women would seem to argue against a strong backlash against women candidates, an argument against sexism having been a major factor in the election that Sarah Eppler Janda makes in her *Beloved Women: The Political Lives of LaDonna Harris and Wilma Mankiller* (92–94). The election, though, seemed to cement Mankiller's view of herself as not only an activist on behalf of Cherokees specifically and Native peoples more generally, but also as a feminist advocating for women's rights.

Mankiller received fewer votes than Cowan in same-day voting but won the absentee voting by a wide margin, giving her the election. Cowan and several other losing candidates sued, charging election fraud. The case hung over Mankiller during her time as deputy chief but was dismissed by a judge two years after the election when a U.S. attorney found no evidence of fraud (Agnew 215–16).

Mankiller describes her role as president of the Tribal Council as perhaps her most challenging role as deputy chief. The fifteen-member council on the whole did not support her, at least at first, viewing her as something of an outsider. Opposition from the three women on the council especially surprised her. She has described her sense of powerlessness when she began but managed to keep trying to adjust, as apparently did at least some of the council members. The wide range of tribal programs—health clinics, water projects, educational programs, elderly assistance, to name a few—kept her busy over the two years she served as deputy chief (242–43). Then came a surprise announcement from Chief Swimmer.

Chief of the Cherokee Nation

President Ronald Reagan nominated Ross Swimmer to become head of the Bureau of Indian Affairs in September 1985. Under the Cherokee Constitution, the deputy chief ascends to the position of chief if the current chief resigns or dies. Consequently, Wilma Mankiller became chief of the Cherokee Nation, being sworn in on December 14 after the United States Senate confirmed Swimmer on December 5. As has been widely noted, Mankiller became the first woman to lead a major Native American tribe, although women had previously led smaller tribes, for example

Dora Schexnider of the Sac and Fox in Oklahoma. John A. Ketcher, a member of the Tribal Council, was chosen by the council to serve as deputy chief. Mankiller would successfully seek a full term in 1987 with Ketcher as her deputy chief, an election that again forced Mankiller into a runoff, this time defeating Perry Wheeler. By the time that Mankiller ran again, in 1991, she had achieved considerable local and national acclaim and, with Ketcher continuing as her running mate, secured an easy win, pulling 82.7 percent of the vote.

Illness continued to place serious roadblocks in Mankiller's way during her years leading the Cherokee Nation. In the closing weeks of her campaign in 1987, she was hospitalized for a kidney infection that would cause irreversible damage and lead to additional hospitalizations for kidney and urinary-tract infections. In the spring of 1989, she underwent a surgical procedure at the University of Oregon to have tops of cysts removed from her kidneys. Unfortunately, the procedure did not prove effective. Faced with the prospect of kidney failure, Mankiller realized that she needed a kidney transplant. She was introduced to Dr. Anthony Monaco, a transplant surgeon at the New England Deaconess Hospital and Harvard University, by Gloria Steinem, with whom Mankiller had worked on the *Ms.* Foundation board. Mankiller's brother Don agreed to give his sister one of his kidneys, and the transplant occurred in June 1990. The operation was successful, and Mankiller was back in Oklahoma performing her duties as chief by August (248–54).

Despite her major health battles, Wilma Mankiller achieved an enormous amount during her ten years as chief.[2] Having come from rural poverty herself and having struggled to establish her identity as an independent woman, she brought these experiences to her role as leader of the Cherokees. In addition, her own health issues surely increased her awareness of the need for improved health care for her people. At the same time that Mankiller was beginning to assume her leadership position, the nation was starting to take serious notice. An article in *People* magazine shortly before Mankiller's inauguration announced her arrival as "the first woman ever to head one of the country's largest tribes" (Van Biema). What she would do over the following decade would be done not just within the Cherokee Nation or the state of Oklahoma but under the glare of a national spotlight.

That spotlight grew quickly. Approximately four months after assuming the position of chief, Mankiller was interviewed at a reception in the U.S. Capitol by Malvina Stephenson for the *Tulsa World.* Stephenson, in her article for the newspaper, noted that Mankiller had overcome poverty, disease, and a tradition of male leadership, and will bring "the same kind of individual effort and enterprise" to her leadership of the Cherokee Nation. Also in 1986, the Oklahoma Federation of Indian Women chose her as American Woman of 1986, and she was named to the Oklahoma Women's Hall of Fame by the Governor's Advisory Committee on the Status of Women. The fame that Mankiller achieved would redound to her constituents and to the Cherokee Nation as a whole in concrete ways. As Brad Agnew points out, writing after the conclusion of Mankiller's years of leadership, "the tribe had received more favorable publicity under Mankiller than at any other time since Sequoyah devised his syllabary," a reference to Sequoyah's development of a system of writing for the Cherokee language in the early nineteenth century (219–20). Agnew may be recalling, in his comparison, Mankiller's own discussion of the great Cherokee linguist in her memoir (81–83).

During the two years of Swimmer's term that Mankiller completed, she moved forward on a number of economic and social programs. She converted a motel and restaurant owned by the Cherokee Nation but struggling financially into a job corps center, the Talking Leaves Job Corps, which had been housed at Northeastern State University in Tahlequah, Oklahoma. She later succeeded in having a new center for the program built. She also pushed forward on a number of self-help projects modeled on what she had worked on at Bell.

In a communication to Agnew after her retirement as chief, she listed a number of what she considered especially important accomplishments (Agnew 222). These included an increase in the sales tax in Delaware County to fund a system for solid waste disposal, providing sewer service to residents near Tahlequah, and many construction projects, among them several clinics, a youth shelter, roads, water systems, a warehouse for Cherokee Nation Industries, bingo facilities, and renovated Head Start and daycare facilities. The bingo facilities represented a major change in Mankiller's position on gambling, as she initially opposed relying on gambling for revenue but changed in order to fund improved health care. Also under Mankiller's leadership, the Nation assumed responsibility for a tribal foster care system and developed a process for handling adoptions. One of the health care facilities was built in Stilwell in 1994. In March 2020, groundbreaking occurred for a major expansion of the facility, now known as the Wilma P. Mankiller Health Center. An article in the *Tahlequah Daily Press* announcing the project describes how the expanded center will positively impact the community, "all while honoring such a great Cherokee leader in former Principal Chief Wilma Mankiller" ("Cherokee Nation Breaks Ground on Expansion of Wilma P. Mankiller Health Center").

Mankiller promoted a more effective justice system in Cherokee Nation by encouraging the Tribal Council to reinstate a district court system, fashion the tribal police into the Cherokee Nation Marshal Service with broader responsibilities and allow Mankiller to negotiate interagency agreements with law enforcement bodies in fourteen Oklahoma counties.

Throughout Mankiller's efforts as principal chief of the Cherokees, she cared far more for practical ways to benefit her community than for ideology. That was true regarding her switch on bingo, but also regarding taxes. While many politicians promise no new taxes or lower taxes, Mankiller looked at what taxes would achieve. Mankiller, authorized by the Tribal Council, negotiated with the State of Oklahoma, and with the Choctaws, Chickasaws, and Seminoles, a tax code that allowed collection of sales taxes on businesses operating on Cherokee land and retention of a portion of those taxes. Regarding taxes, the U.S. Supreme Court had ruled that Oklahoma could collect state taxes on tobacco products that tribal members sold to non–Native Americans. Rather than attempting to collect taxes during these sales, which Mankiller considered too hard to differentiate from sales to tribal members, she negotiated an agreement with the state to pay a 25 percent tax on all tobacco that Cherokees purchased for resale. The tax policies had two significant outcomes so far as Mankiller was concerned. They brought in revenue that helped to finance programs to improve life for the Cherokees in health care, education, and other ways; in addition, Cherokee sovereignty was reaffirmed by the fact that the state was negotiating tax policies with the Cherokee Nation (Janda 124).

While Mankiller was still in Boston recuperating from her kidney transplant, she achieved an especially significant agreement with the Bureau of Indian Affairs. On behalf of the Cherokee Nation, one of five tribes chosen for a self-governing pilot project, Mankiller signed the agreement with the federal government. It allowed the Cherokees to assume greater control over their tribal finances and establish spending priorities consistent with goals established by them rather than by the federal government. In addition, the agreement clearly supported the principle of tribal sovereignty. National recognition of the Cherokee Nation and its leader continued on the upswing as Mankiller was among twelve tribal leaders invited to meet with President George H.W. Bush early in 1991 and was designated as one of three spokespeople for the meeting.

Despite the meeting with President Bush, Mankiller endorsed Bill Clinton for President in 1992. After the election, she participated in an economic conference at Little Rock, Arkansas, sponsored by President-Elect Clinton. As Agnew points out, for the rest of her years as leader of the Cherokee Nation "she would have the attention of the president of the United States and would be the most influential Indian leader in the country" (226).

Other accomplishments during Mankiller's tenure as leader of her people included greatly increasing tribal membership from about 68,000 to approximately 170,000 and building tribal revenue, with a budget that rose to $150 million annually (Verhovek), at the same time limiting the ability of individuals and groups falsely to claim Cherokee identity. Mankiller also encouraged education in the Cherokee language. In April 1994, near the end of her second full term and not long after publication of her memoir, Mankiller attended a meeting of 322 tribal leaders with President Clinton in the Rose Garden at the White House. The summit grew out of a discussion between Mankiller and Attorney General Janet Reno. Sitting next to Clinton, Mankiller moderated the summit. Among topics discussed were tribal sovereignty and religious freedom. Afterward, a conference in Albuquerque enabled leaders from various tribes to express their opinions to Reno and Secretary of the Interior Bruce Babbitt. Out of these events came the Office of Tribal Justice within the Justice Department (Agnew 227).

After ten years as principal chief, with a history of serious health issues, and desiring to spend more time with her husband and family, Mankiller decided not to seek another term. Looking back, she would see great progress for her people and for women especially. She states in *Every Day Is a Good Day* that her elections (and certainly her accomplishments and fame) "were a step forward for women and a step into the Cherokee tradition of balance between men and women" (102).

Continuing the Good Fight

The immediate aftermath of Wilma Mankiller's ten years as principal chief was a period of political turmoil. The candidate that Mankiller endorsed as her successor, George Watie Bearpaw, came in first among several candidates, but prior to the runoff election he was declared ineligible to serve as principal chief because of a felony, despite the felony having been ordered expunged from his record. Joe Byrd, who had come in second, became chief when the Judicial Appeals Tribunal chose not to order a new election, thus essentially awarding the victory to Byrd. Considerable hostility was subsequently directed toward Mankiller, including legal action because she had arranged for severance pay for eleven Cherokee Nation employees. Chief Byrd initiated a series of controversial actions that involved firings and tribal reorganization. Ultimately, the firestorm abated, the lawsuit against Mankiller was dropped at the direction of the Tribal Council, political order was restored, and subsequent Cherokee administrations expressed for Mankiller the respect and admiration that she deserved (262–69, 291; *Every Day Is a Good Day* 153–54).

While Mankiller was facing this political storm, she also was undergoing chemotherapy in Boston for lymphoma and trying to move on to the next stages in her life. When Dartmouth College in Hanover, New Hampshire, offered her a Montgomery Fellowship, she accepted, arriving at the college on January 1, 1996. Attracted by the college's respected Native American Studies program, she threw herself into her academic activities, which included seminars, lectures, and meetings with students. With the weather especially cold, Mankiller suffered from the flu, caught cold, and developed what appeared to be pneumonia. At the time, she was still taking immunosuppressants to prevent rejection of her transplanted kidney, which, she believed, was depressing her immune system. Summoned to Boston by her transplant surgeon, Dr. Anthony Monaco, in February, Mankiller underwent a biopsy, which indicated lymphoma. While awaiting word on the biopsy, she had returned to Dartmouth. On February 25, however, she returned to Boston to have additional tests, which confirmed second-stage large-cell lymphoma. After five weeks of hospitalization, she eventually was released but stayed nearby with friends Bill and Suzanne Presley while undergoing chemotherapy treatments. When her temperature spiked, she was hospitalized again. As side effects of her chemotherapy treatments continued to rob Mankiller of her strength and appetite, and as she suffered hair loss, her oncologist suggested that the lymphoma might have spread to her lungs. A CAT scan subsequently revealed spots on her lungs, and a biopsy determined that she was suffering from a lung infection (269–72).

Mankiller was able to return to Oklahoma in September 1996, driving to a hospital in Fort Smith, Arkansas, for radiation treatments. Complicating her recovery was the failure of her transplanted kidney. Dialysis and blood transfusions followed, along with stem-cell treatments in Nassau, the Bahamas. Declared cancer free early in 1998, Mankiller faced the necessity of another kidney transplant. That occurred on July 22, 1998, when she received a kidney from a niece, Virlee Williamson. For the second time, a family member had stepped forward to save Mankiller (272–73).

Undeterred, Wilma Mankiller moved ahead. She co-edited (with Gloria Steinem and three other women) *The Reader's Companion to U.S. Women's History* (1999). Increasingly viewed as a women's rights advocate as well as an advocate for Native Americans, Mankiller edited, and wrote portions of, *Every Day Is a Good Day*, which includes, as the subtitle says, *Reflections by Contemporary Indigenous Women*, with an introduction by Gloria Steinem (2004). She lectured throughout the country, addressed tribal meetings and various civic organizations, worked with the Oklahoma Breast Cancer Summit to encourage women to have breast screenings, and traveled to Brazil and China. When invited in 2006 to contribute a pair of shoes to the Sole Stories: American Indian Footwear exhibit at the Heard Museum in Phoenix, Arizona, she submitted a pair of undistinguished but practical black walking shoes, which represented her commitment, not to fashion or even ideology, but to working hard and getting good things done for others. She noted that the shoes were comfortable and could be used with the leg brace that she had worn since her almost fatal automobile accident (Smokey). To help celebrate Oklahoma's one hundredth anniversary as a state, Mankiller was invited to give the Centennial Lecture on the Humanities in 2007, following which she was presented with the inaugural Oklahoma Humanities Award by the Oklahoma Humanities Council.

The Humanities award is one of many ways in which Wilma Mankiller has been recognized for her contributions to the Cherokee Nation, Native Americans throughout the country, women, the United States, and the State of Oklahoma. She received the John W. Gardner Leadership Award from the Independent Sector, a group of nonprofit organizations. Other awards included the American Association of University Women's Achievement Award (1993), induction into the National Women's Hall of Fame (1993), induction into the Oklahoma Hall of Fame (1994), induction into the National Cowgirl Museum and Hall of Fame in Fort Worth, Texas (1994), the Elizabeth Blackwell Award from Hobart and William Smith Colleges for her service to humanity (1996), and, posthumously, the Drum Award for Lifetime Achievement by the Five Tribes of Oklahoma, consisting of the Cherokee, Choctaw, Muscogee (Creek), Chickasaw, and Seminole (2010). Among still more awards, Mankiller received fourteen honorary doctorates and was among the first group of individuals, in 2018, to be inducted into the National Native American Hall of Fame. Perhaps the award with the most national recognition was the Presidential Medal of Freedom, the highest civilian honor in the United States, which President Bill Clinton bestowed on Mankiller in 1998.

Wilma Mankiller died on April 6, 2010, the result of still another illness, this one pancreatic cancer. Her life ended, where it had begun, in Adair County, Oklahoma. Well over a thousand people attended her memorial service at the Cherokee National Cultural Grounds in Tahlequah on April 10, including Cherokee Principal Chief Chad Smith, Oklahoma Governor Brad Henry, Gloria Steinem, and Native American leaders from throughout the country. In addition to tribal songs, ceremonies, and personal remembrances during the service, which lasted for two and one-half hours, laudatory statements arrived from Bill Clinton and Hillary Clinton, and from President Barack Obama. Chief Smith and Deputy Chief Joe Grayson presented Mankiller's family with the Medal of Patriotism in honor of the former Cherokee chief, an award usually bestowed on military members. In one of the most telling comments, a friend of Mankiller's, Bob Friedman, recalled her reaction just a few days before her death when she heard that the Affordable Care Act, signed into law by President Obama on

March 23, 2010, had passed, ensuring health care for millions (Adcock). To the end, she had not lost her desire to make life better for others. A few days later came a Congressional Resolution from the U.S. House of Representatives honoring her. She was interred in the Echota Cemetery in Stillwell among other family members.

Recognition of Wilma Mankiller's achievements, however, did not end with her death. A feature film, *The Cherokee Word for Water*, was released in 2013 detailing her involvement with the Bell project. In 2017, another film about her appeared, a documentary titled simply *Mankiller*. That subsequent generations would remember Wilma Mankiller is also indicated by the popularity of her story in books for children, a development that surely pleased her. Most recently is Doreen Rappaport's picture book *Wilma's Way Home: The Life of Wilma Mankiller* (2019), which offers an overview of Mankiller's life with quotations from her interspersed with sections of biographical narrative. Earlier juvenile books about Mankiller include Charnan Simon's *Wilma P. Mankiller: Chief of the Cherokee* (1991), Bruce Glassman's accelerated reader *Wilma Mankiller: Chief of the Cherokee Nation* (1992), Melissa Schwarz's biography for middle school students *Wilma Mankiller: Principal Chief of the Cherokees* (1994), and Linda Lowery's accelerated reader *Wilma Mankiller* (1996).

NOTES

1. Throughout the rest of this chapter, references to *Mankiller: A Chief and Her People* will usually be documented by page numbers alone. All other sources will be clearly identified by author and/or title.

2. I am especially indebted to Sarah Eppler Janda's *Beloved Women* 111–34 and Brad Agnew's "Wilma Mankiller" 217–28 for their summaries and analyses of Mankiller's accomplishments during her ten years as principal chief of the Cherokee Nation

REFERENCES

Adcock, Clifton. "More Than 1,000 Attend Memorial Service for Former Cherokee Chief Wilma Mankiller." *Tulsa World*. 10 Apr. 2010. tulsaworld.com/archive/more-than-1000-attend-memorial-service-for-former-cherokee-chief-wilma- mankiller/article_c698b93e-bb0f-5c84–95f9-b8674465006f.html.

Agnew, Brad. "Wilma Mankiller." *The New Warriors: Native American Leaders Since 1900.* Ed. R. David Edmunds. Lincoln: U of Nebraska P, 2001. 210–36.

"Alcatraz Proclamation and Letter." *History Is a Weapon.* www.historyisaweapon.com/defcon1/alcatrazproclamationandletter.html.

"Cherokee Nation Breaks Ground on Expansion of Wilma P. Mankiller Health Center." *Tahlequah Daily Press* 5 Mar. 2020. tahlequahdailypress.com/news/cherokee-nation-breaks-ground-on-expansion-of-wilma-p-mankiller-health-center/article_b9566d83-a2bb-57c8-a2c1–883ace5acf31.html.

Ehle, John. *Trail of Tears: The Rise and Fall of the Cherokee Nation.* New York: Doubleday, 1988.

Glassman, Bruce. *Wilma Mankiller: Chief of the Cherokee Nation.* Library of Famous Women. New York: Blackbirch P, 1992.

Janda, Sarah Eppler. *Beloved Women: The Political Lives of LaDonna Harris and Wilma Mankiller.* DeKalb: Northern Illinois UP, 2007.

Johnson, Troy R. *The American Indian Occupation of Alcatraz Island: Red Power and Self-Determination.* 1996. Lincoln: U of Nebraska P, 2008.

Lowery, Linda. *Wilma Mankiller.* Minneapolis: Carolrhoda Books, 1996.

Mankiller, Wilma. *Every Day Is a Good Day: Reflections by Contemporary Indigenous Women.* Memorial Edition. Golden, CO: Fulcrum, 2011.

_____, and Michael Wallis. *Mankiller: A Chief and Her People.* Rev. Ed. New York: St. Martin's, 2000.

"Myasthenia Gravis." *Johns Hopkins Medicine.* hopkinsmedicine.org/health/conditions-and-diseases/myasthenia-gravis.

Perdue, Theda. *The Cherokee.* New York: Chelsea House, 1989.

Rappaport, Doreen. *Wilma's Way Home: The Life of Wilma Mankiller.* Los Angeles: Disney/Hyperion, 2019.

Schwarz, Melissa. *Wilma Mankiller: Principal Chief of the Cherokees.* North American Indians of Achievement. New York: Chelsea House, 1994.

Simon, Charnan. *Wilma P. Mankiller: Chief of the Cherokee.* Chicago: Children's P, 1991.

Smokey, Sadie Jo. "Storied Shoes: Wilma Pearl Mankiller." Part 2. *The Arizona Republic* 1 Nov. 2006. newspapers.com/clip/22580258/arizona-republic/.

Stephenson, Malvina. "Wilma Mankiller Always Thrived on Challenge." *Tulsa World* 13 Apr. 1986, updated 25 Feb. 2019. tulsaworld.com/archive/wilma-mankiller-always-thrived-on-challenge/article_bcb62834-c648-546c-bfef-c9126eb29cb0.html.

Van Biema, David. "Activist Wilma Mankiller Is Set to Become the First Female Chief of the Cherokee Nation." *People* 2 Dec. 1985: 91–92.

Verhovek, Sam Howe. "Wilma Mankiller, Cherokee Chief and First Woman to Lead Major Tribe, Is Dead at 64." *New York Times* 6 Apr. 2010, updated 7 Apr. nytimes.com/2010/04/07/US/07mankiller.html.

10

Janine Pease
(Janine Pease Pretty-on-Top)
(b. 1949)

As Janine Pease points out in her introduction to *The Spirit of Indian Women*, Thomas Morgan, Commissioner of Indian Affairs (1889–93), stated that "higher education in the sense ordinarily used has no place in the curriculum of Indian schools" (xiii). Morgan, a Union officer in the Civil War, Baptist minister, and educator, had written of "higher education" for Indians, using the term, for example, in his Report of the Commissioner of Indian Affairs for 1889 (8), and suggesting in his Supplemental Report on Indian Education in the same year that an educational system for Indians "should make ample provision for the higher education of the few who are endowed with special capacity or ambition, and are destined to leadership" (95). What Morgan had in mind as "higher education," however, was high school, which becomes clear in David Wallace Adams' survey of Morgan's proposed system (61–64).

Pease, fortunately, did not follow the antiquated and restrictive thinking of Commissioner Morgan and others who did not believe that Native Americans were suited for higher education in the modern sense of college or university education. She not only reached the highest levels of the educational ladder, earning a doctorate and serving as a college president, but also became one of the great educational leaders of the final decades of the twentieth century and the beginning of the twenty-first.

Recognized for her leadership by her students, United States Presidents, and a variety of organizations, among them the John D. and Catherine T. MacArthur Foundation, which awarded her one of its "genius grants," Pease has made fostering educational excellence for Native American students while strengthening their own traditional heritage her life's work.

Going Higher

Janine Pease was born in 1947 on the Colville Reservation in eastern Washington State, the eldest of four children, resulting, as she writes in *The Spirit of Indian Women*, in her being called "little mother" (xvii). Her parents, Ben Pease, a Crow and Hidatsa, and Margery Jordan, a descendant of Cornish miners, were both from Montana. Ben Pease was originally from Lodge Grass on the Crow Reservation, which would become Janine Pease's home for most of her adult life. Both parents were educators: Ben a high school teacher, principal, and basketball coach, and Margery an English and history teacher. The two had met while attending Linfield College, a Baptist institution in McMinnville, Oregon. One might say that Janine was born to be a teacher. She certainly grew up in the home of educators and, not surprisingly, followed her parents into that world, as well as into her father's world of basketball.

Another important role model for Janine was an aunt, Josephine Pease, who in 1937 graduated from Linfield College, where Janine's parents would meet, becoming one of the first three Crow students to earn a college degree. She majored in business, completing her senior project on the Crows' economic status on the reservation, and minored in English. Josephine Pease returned to the Crow Reservation to teach, securing positions at Soap Creek and later at the Crow Agency School. She also served for two years in the Teacher Corps and directed the Head Start program on the reservation ("The Education of Josephine Pease Russell").

Janine Pease attended Dayton High School in Dayton, Washington, where, in addition to excelling in academics, she starred in basketball. Her father was the principal and girls' basketball coach at Dayton, while her mother taught English there. In the summer of 1966, her father accepted the position of Director of the Columbia Basin Job Corps Center in Moses Lake, Washington. The family moved to Moses Lake, and Janine spent her senior year at Moses Lake High School. In the absence of a girls' basketball team at her new school, she played tennis.[1] After graduating in 1967, she enrolled in Central Washington State College (now Central Washington University) in Ellensburg, majoring in sociology and anthropology while also studying Spanish. The three disciplines would remain important to Pease as she developed a lasting commitment to an educational approach rooted in Crow history and culture, including a profound belief in enhancing the role of her people's Native language.

Following graduation from Central Washington in December 1970, Pease was appointed by Governor Dan Evans of Washington to the Governor's Commission on Youth Involvement. As deputy director of the commission, she worked on extending the vote to eighteen-year-olds, an effort that succeeded when the state legislature passed legislation lowering the voting age to eighteen. The issue of voting rights would remain with Pease, resurfacing prominently during her future presidency of Little Big Horn College. She then tutored minority students at Big Bend Community College in Moses Lake, Washington, followed by a semester of counseling women students at the Navajo Community College in Many Farms, Arizona (now located in Tsaile, Arizona, and renamed Diné College).[2] She returned to Big Bend Community College in January 1972 to direct the Upward Bound Program sponsored by the school. She also taught Native American studies, counseled women students, and coached the women's basketball team.

Pease's heart, however, seemed to be with her father's original home on the Crow Reservation, a place to which she had returned often during summers to see relatives. Consequently, she accepted a position as director of the Adult and Continuing Education Program on the reservation in 1975. Her responsibilities included designing an adult education system on three reservations in Montana, ultimately supervising over fifty employees in eleven adult education centers. Her experiences in curricular development and administration would later serve her well as she led the successful development of a new college on the Crow Reservation.

On a personal level, Pease was in a romantic relationship at the time with Sam Windy Boy, a Chippewa-Cree who also was involved with adult education, in his case with the Day Break Star Center in Seattle, Washington. He moved with Pease when she returned to the Crow Reservation. They would have two children during the 1970s: Roses in 1976 and Vernon in 1979. The couple shared a position as director of Vocational Education in 1978 and 1979. In 1979, the family moved to the Chippewa-Cree Rocky Boy's Reservation near Havre, Montana, where Windy Boy worked at a sawmill and plant that made posts. The marriage, however, began to deteriorate, resulting in divorce in 1983, and Pease was forced to try to provide for her children by herself (Nelson and Johnston 284–85).

After a difficult period financially, Pease was able in 1981 to gain employment at Eastern Montana College, since renamed Montana State University, in Billings, where she provided academic and student-life support for students. Meanwhile, the Crow Central Education Commission was creating a new community college at Crow Agency, Montana. The mission of the tribal college was to prepare Crow students to secure jobs in the area, deepen their knowledge of Crow history and culture, and help the Crow nation to grow financially. In 1982, Pease accepted an invitation to return to the reservation to lead the college.

As Pease was serving Crow students in the new Little Big Horn College, she also returned to school herself. She continued her academic work at Montana State University in Bozeman, earning a master's degree in education (1988) and a doctorate in adult and higher education (1994). Her dissertation dealt with the conception and successful enactment into law of the Tribally Controlled Community College Assistance Act of 1978, which provided funds for tribal colleges. In signing the legislation, which called for grants of "$4,000 for each full-time equivalent Indian student in attendance at such college during such academic year," President Jimmy Carter stated:

> This act provides a needed base of stable funding for postsecondary education on our Indian reservations, and provides American Indians with greater educational opportunities near their families, their tribes, and their places of employment [*American Presidency Project*].

The Act promised greater financial stability for tribal colleges and made creation of a new Crow institution of higher learning a promising endeavor, but one that would require sustained leadership by its equally new president.

A College President

The college that Janine Pease assumed leadership of in August 1982 was a fledgling institution chartered by the Crow Tribe in 1980 and located along the Little Big Horn River in the town of Crow Agency. It was housed in an old gymnasium with the grand total of thirty-two students. Douglass Nelson and Jeremy Johnson summarize part of the challenge:

> The roof leaked, the windows were broken, and any pretense at central heating had long been forgotten. [She] recruited volunteers to repair the facility, wire the building for electrical and telephone services, and scavenge and repair enough old, used, or discarded furniture to provide a minimal amount of tables, desks, and chairs. The old basketball court served as the library, a shower room was used as a science laboratory, and a former water-treatment plant housed the chemistry department [286].

Other challenges included acquiring accreditation for Little Big Horn College, securing financial support beyond the minimal tuition of twenty dollars per credit, developing a curriculum that would prepare students for the work force but also for further education, and recruiting a faculty and staff that could provide quality education. Gaining accreditation depended heavily on not only academic offerings but also on financial stability, sufficient facilities, and a college-worthy faculty and support staff.

Accreditation from the Northwest Association of Schools and Colleges did not come easily. Limited facilities, uncertain finances, and lack of an appropriate faculty salary schedule, according to Nelson and Johnson, led to rejection of accreditation in 1984, with a follow-up visit in 1986 also failing to secure the necessary academic stamp of approval (288). Pease states in "Helps the People," an essay on leadership, that insufficient advanced degrees for faculty and staff also was an area that the accrediting agency noted (160). Starting from virtually nowhere had proved perhaps more difficult than the tribal leaders and Pease had anticipated, but gradual improvement finally led to accreditation in 1989.

In an interview published in the *Tribal College Journal of American Indian Higher Education* in 1991, Pease outlined a number of outreach initiatives that she had led during the early years of the college: the Institute for Children and Families that enabled parents to discuss educational issues and that sponsored seminars on such issues as alcohol and drug abuse; faculty and student involvement to encourage voter registration; seminars on economic issues such as oil and gas exploration; and creation of college archives to assist research efforts on Crow history and various matters of concern to the Crow population. As Pease says in the interview, "The nature of a college is information, and information is extremely powerful in solving problems" (Boyer).

Pease describes a number of other attributes of Little Big Horn College in the same interview. She notes the small class sizes and the positive teacher/student ratio, the "balance of scholarship from multicultural backgrounds," and "the respect the tribal colleges pay to these students as individuals and as members of families and the community." The final point is one that she especially associates with tribal colleges. She adds that tribal colleges have been able to take the structure of a community college "and make it something so tailor-made to their communities. It just can't fail" (Boyer). Little Big Horn College, of course, could have failed, and without the leadership of Janine Pease it might have done so.

Ultimately, a school, more than anything else, consists of students studying subjects with the aid of teachers. Pease was definite about what she wanted in a curriculum, as Nelson and Johnston state: traditional academic subjects with Crow studies at the core of the curriculum. The college came to offer nine programs, including Crow studies, science, mathematics, the humanities, and information sciences—a balance among traditional and contemporary, Crow-specific and broadly focused areas of inquiry. The college also included a freshman seminar that would acclimate students, especially first-generation college students, into college life (287–88). "The immediate impact of education was to give power to the learner, or the idea that knowledge is power," she wrote. "The power to live a good and decent life was the power I envisioned with the courses we offered at the tribal colleges" ("Helps the People" 165).

Little Big Horn College continued to grow under Pease's leadership. The number of students increased to three hundred from thirty-two. The faculty, staff, and administration also increased, with a fixed salary schedule introduced for faculty. Library holdings grew, a process that Pease began, as she writes in "Helps the People," when she "retained a Georgetown University graduate student to select books from the Library of Congress seconds stack each week on our behalf" (165). Improved facilities were constructed, including classrooms, offices, and science and computer labs. Grants became more plentiful to help stabilize revenue, and financial aid was normalized. As a result, Little Big Horn College was successfully reaccredited in 2000.

As of this writing, Little Big Horn College offers eight associate degrees and seven one-year certificate programs, according to the College Catalog. It also offers both classroom-based and on-line instruction. The Mission Statement, which is available on the college website and in its catalog, strongly reflects the vision of its early president:

> The College is dedicated to the professional, vocational and personal development of individual students for their advancement in higher education or the workplace and inspiring Crow and American Indian scholarship. The College is committed to the preservation, perpetuation and protection of Crow culture and language, and respects the distinct bilingual and bicultural aspects of the Crow Indian community.

President Pease wasted no time in connecting the college to the surrounding community. Faced with reports of efforts to prevent Crows from voting in county elections, and recognizing that Crows, despite constituting 46 percent of the population of Big Horn County ("Helps the People" 163), were systematically shut out of representation in local and county government, Pease and other tribal leaders brought legal action against Big Horn County in August 1983, with Pease as lead plaintiff. Testimony in the case, *Windy Boy* [her married name at the time] *v. Big Horn County*, occurred during November 1985, and in June 1986, Federal District Judge Edward Rafeedie ruled that the county at-large election system should be abolished and replaced with voting districts. The result was that Native American voters, who were the majority in some districts but a minority in the county at large, became a stronger voting bloc with improved opportunities to elect Native representatives in county and school board elections. "By 1988," Pease reports, "there was a county commissioner and two school board members elected from the newly formed district- and zone-based elections" ("Helps the People" 164).

Janine Pease, who had been divorced from her first husband during her early days as president, married again in 1991. Her husband, John Pretty-on-Top, was prominent in the Crow Sun Dance. The Sun Dance also is important to Pease, who contributed several personal reflections in the section "Conversations with Native Elders" in *Native Spirit: The Sun Dance Way*, which presents Thomas Yellowtail's insights into the nature and rituals of the Sun Dance. Pease also, as she mentions at the beginning of "Helps the People," participates annually in the Crow Dance of the Seasons (154).

National Recognition

Janine Pease's impact on the Crow Reservation and Little Big Horn College was immense, but her influence extended well beyond the campus and reserva- tion. Increasingly, she was recognized as a national leader in education, espe- cially regarding tribal col-

Janine Pease, educator, advocate for Crow lan- guage studies, and former president of Little Big Horn College (courtesy Dr. Janine Pease, photograph by Adam Singsintimber).

leges and universities. In 1983, shortly after assuming the presidency of Little Big Horn College, she was named president of the American Indian Higher Education Consortium, an organization that originated in 1973 with six tribal colleges in order to foster collaboration in research, to advo- cate for improved education for Native Americans, and to lobby regarding U.S. government legislation and policies. The organization has grown today to include thirty-seven institutions of higher learning. Janine Pease served at a time when the AIHEC was growing and focusing especially on helping students to afford a college education. A major initiative that started with Pease's help was the American Indian College Fund.

Development of the fund started in 1985. As Tod Bedrosian points out in an article in the *Tribal College Journal of American Indian Higher Education*, Senator James McClure of Idaho spoke at an AIHEC dinner in Washington, D.C., in 1985, urging the attendees to solicit support from businesses. The AIHEC continued over the next few years to create marketing materials, pursue grants, and solicit partners in the enterprise. Outreach to Congress continued, with such figures as Representative Morris Udall and Senator Daniel Inouye serving as featured speakers at AIHEC dinners. Senator Inouye of Hawaii was Chairman of the Select Committee on Indian Affairs at the time. By 1989, the American Indian College Fund was a functioning reality, and it continues to assist students at tribal colleges. Pease meanwhile continued to provide important leadership to the AIHEC as president, serving two terms (1983–85 and 1999–2000), in between her presidential terms serving as treasurer of the organization (1986–94), as well as being a founding member of the Board of Directors of the American Indian College Fund (Bedrosian).

President George H.W. Bush, recognizing the inadequate education that too often was available for Native Americans, along with other challenges facing their communities, among them erosion of Native culture, the loss of tribal lands, and limited economic opportunities, established in 1989 The Indian Nations at Risk Task Force charged with "specifically addressing the educational needs of Native America" and devising strategies for improving "academic performance of Native students" (*Indian Nations at Risk* report). President Bush's Secretary of Education, Lauro Cavazos, appointed Janine Pease to the fourteen-member committee co-chaired by William Demmert, Jr., a Tlingit/Sioux and visiting professor at Stanford University who had served as Commissioner of Education in Alaska, and Terrel H. Bell, former U.S. Secretary of Education. Pease, then known as Janine Pease-Windy Boy, was one of two college presidents (along with Bob G. Martin, a Cherokee and president of Haskell Indian Junior College). Other task force members, most of them Native Americans, came from diverse backgrounds, including professional organizations, academic institutions, state government, and tribal leadership.

The final report of The Indian Nations at Risk Task Force, presented in October 1991 to the Secretary of Education, at that time Lamar Alexander, enumerated ten education goals "to guide the improvement of all federal, tribal, private, and public schools that serve American Indians and Alaska Natives and their communities" (i). These goals included access to "early childhood education programs," offering students "the opportunity to maintain and develop their tribal languages," competency in English language skills, mastery of core academic areas, graduation from high school with necessary life skills for successful citizenship, doubling the number of "Native educators," safe alcohol- and drug-free schools, lifelong learning opportunities, effectively restructured schools, and partnerships among schools, parents, tribes, and the community. All of these goals were to be achieved by the year 2000 (i). While recognizing the necessity of mastering

English, the task force recognized the importance of students also maintaining their traditional cultures, including their tribal languages. The task force understood the relationship between cultural identity and academic success, stating, "Bilingual or multilingual children have a greater opportunity to develop their analytical and conceptual skills than monolingual children" (14), a position that Janine Pease would embrace and foster throughout her life.

Janine Pease's successful leadership and influence both locally and nationally were not going unnoticed. In 1990, the National Indian Education Association, which had been established on August 21, 1970, in Minneapolis, Minnesota, as a means by which schools could be better prepared to offer effective education to Native American students, named her Educator of the Year. Three years later, the American Civil Liberties Union recognized Pease with their Jeannette Rankin Award, named after the first woman to serve in the United States Congress. Rankin was elected to the House of Representatives from Montana in 1916. A pacifist, she voted against the declaration of war in 1917 and was not re-elected. However, she did return to the House of Representatives in 1941 for a second and final term, her vote against declaring war on Japan ensuring the end of her Congressional career. Rankin strongly supported civil rights and equality for women throughout her life, and Pease's efforts to expand voting rights for Native Americans clearly coincided with ACLU goals.

Then the John D. and Catherine T. MacArthur Foundation came calling, making Janine Pease in 1994 a MacArthur Fellow, or recipient of what are often referred to as the Genius Awards. The program attempts to encourage people of great talent and potential to develop their talents, attempt new challenges if they wish, or even change careers. The stipend of $625,000, paid over five years, is intended to offer recipients the freedom to do that. The Janine Pease page on the MacArthur Foundation website recognizes her as "a champion of political empowerment for Native Americans." Pease, not surprisingly, spent her five years doing what she had been doing: applying her creativity and dedication to helping Little Big Horn College and its students.

By this time, when national and state leaders wanted talented, experienced, and effective representatives, Janine Pease was one of the individuals that they often turned to. President Bill Clinton, therefore, when considering appointments to the Board of Advisors on Tribal Colleges and Universities that would help implement Executive Order 13021 that he had signed in 1996, selected Janine Pease. She was tasked, along with the other board members, with advising on enabling tribal institutions of higher learning to make effective use of a wide range of federal programs as called for in the executive order. President George W. Bush would later revoke and replace that order with his own Executive Order 13270, which from a practical standpoint continued the initiative begun with 13021. Pease also was a founding member of the Smithsonian's Museum of the American Indian and served in the 1990s for four years as a Trustee during the early fund-raising and planning period of the museum.

At the state level, Janine Pease was not only named to the Montana Districting and Apportionment Commission, charged under the State Constitution with establishing legislative and congressional districts based on the next federal census, which in this case was to occur in 2000, but was named to serve as the presiding officer of the commission. Four members appointed by the majority and minority leaders of the Montana Senate and House were to select a fifth member and presiding officer, presumably someone who would be bipartisan. The four original appointees, however, were unable to agree on a choice, and the Montana Supreme Court consequently appointed Pease to the leadership position on August 3, 1999. Under Pease's leadership, the Montana Districting and Apportionment Commission completed its challenging work and forwarded its plan to the Montana Secretary of State on February 3, 2003.

Given Pease's achievements on every level from the Crow Reservation to the state of Montana to the federal government, it should have come as no surprise that she was named as one of the one hundred most influential Montanans of the century, a recognition bestowed on her by the *Missoulian* daily newspaper in Missoula, Montana, in 1999.

Departure and Return

While Janine Pease was building a national reputation, on the Crow Reservation opposition was growing to her presidency of Little Big Horn College, not, apparently, among those who should matter most at a school—students and faculty—but among some members of the Board of Trustees, and that opposition put accreditation for the college in considerable jeopardy. *The Chronicle of Higher Education* followed the events closely and reported on them in several articles.[3]

Six members of the Board of Trustees wrote to President Pease on November 21, 2000, demanding her resignation. Not surprisingly, Pease rejected the demand. Subsequently, about seventy-five students marched to Crow tribal headquarters in support of the president. They also expressed their concern that firing Pease might endanger the college's accreditation, which would seriously undermine the quality of their degree if not the actual survival of the college. Losing accreditation was not by any means a stretch, as Sandra Elman, the executive director of the accrediting agency for colleges and universities in the region, the Northwest Association of Schools and Colleges, had notified Dillard Bird in Ground, Sr., the acting chairman of the Board of Trustees, that the attempted firing might negatively impact continuing accreditation. Reasons for the action remain somewhat unclear, although members of the Board charged financial mismanagement, inadequate day-to-day management of the college, acting without approval of the trustees, and failure to hire enough Crow employees. The president rejected the accusations and cited support from students, faculty, and staff. She also stated that some newly elected tribal leaders wanted to reclaim a grant of three million dollars that had been given to the college toward building new facilities. Supporters alleged that some of the trustees were former employees or relatives of former employees seeking revenge for perceived mistreatment by Pease. In "Helps the People," Pease goes into detail regarding a specific accusation that she was inappropriately disbursing grant money from the Crow Nation and the American Indian College Fund intended for new campus construction, effectively shutting out Crow contractors from performing the work. Pease points out that the American Indian College Fund required contractors to be bonded, which the Crow contractors were not (167–68).

The situation became increasingly unstable over the next few months. Trustees named an interim president, Henry Real Bird, who then rejected the position, but later accepted it. Unsuccessful efforts were made within the Board to expel some trustees, plans to engage a mediator were on and then off, and at a board meeting some one hundred fifty supporters of the president surrounded her, some of them crying and many praying aloud. Tribal police allowed Pease to enter the main campus building the day after the meeting but prevented Real Bird and some trustees from doing so.

Finally, Pease's position as president was terminated on Saturday, January 13, 2001, by the Tribal Council at a council meeting. Henry Real Bird was named interim president. According to the *Chronicle*, two faculty members resigned in protest and approximately forty students, almost one-sixth of the student body, withdrew from the college. The *Missoulian* on January 15 quoted Pease as saying, "It hurts to look at 18 years of really good work and see it stomped in the face." The Commission on Colleges and Universities of the Northwest Association of Schools and Colleges informed Real Bird that accreditation would be ended on June 15 unless Little Big Horn College could satisfy the commission's concerns. A major part of these concerns was over the governance structure of the college, specifically the process for firing a president. At issue was whether the College Board of Trustees made decisions without undue influence being exerted by tribal leaders. The *Chronicle* quotes Sandra Elman as stating, "The commission's unambiguous requirement that the college's governing board be

solely responsible for the selection, evaluation, and termination of the president has been violated" (5 February 2001). The association required an interim report by February 15 that was to include, among other matters, an assurance that student supporters of Pease had not been penalized in any way. A fuller report was demanded by April.

In response to the college reports, the Northwest Association removed the June show-cause order, although it did place Little Big Horn College on probation until the spring of 2002. Among actions taken was a binding resolution passed by the Tribal Council to establish the authority of the Board of Trustees over the college. Ultimately, the probation was lifted, and Little Big Horn College today is fully accredited. Nor would the break between Janine Pease and the college be permanent, as she would return as an important member of the college community.

Between her departure and return, Janine Pease continued her educational mission in a variety of ways. Initially, she established a consulting business to share her expertise in Native American higher education. She coordinated a distance learning consortium on behalf of Fort Peck Community College, later working on a Developing Institutions grant for Fort Peck. Fort Berthold Community College and Iowa State University also employed her for major projects, as did the Kellogg Foundation, Sinte Gleska University in South Dakota, and the Institute of American Indian Arts ("Helps the People" 170–71).

In 2003, Pease accepted the position of Vice President for American Indian Affairs and Planning at Rocky Mountain College in Billings, Montana, a position that she held until 2008. Rocky Mountain, according to its website, has long been related to three religions: the United Church of Christ, the United Methodist Church, and the Presbyterian Church. Although not a tribal college, Rocky Mountain made a concerted effort to increase the number of Native American students, especially transfer students from tribal colleges that offered only two-year degrees. Adding Janine Pease fit well with this effort. She describes her roles at Rocky Mountain in an email-conducted interview:

> At Rocky Mountain College I was the Vice President for American Indian Affairs and Planning. In this role I was the administrator for all programs and grants that served American Indian students, including a consortium with the tribal colleges in Montana. I also instructed two Native American Studies courses per semester. RMC had a grant for the development of bachelor's degrees among twenty students located at four reservations: Crow at LBHC, Assiniboine & Sioux at Fort Peck Community College, Northern Cheyenne at Chief Dull Knife College and Assiniboine and Gros Ventre at Fort Belknap College. These On-line in real time courses were provided over a two-year period in Environmental Resource Management, supported by an NSF grant. We developed and administered an Americorps program to have American Indian

college student mentors meet with at-risk American Indian high school students at Senior High School in Billings. We also had several Department of Energy grants to support the consortium schools in information technology and the development of certified personnel in the MS certificates program. I became the institutional planner in the third year at RMC, so I assumed a central role in the strategic planning process for the college [Interview].

Pease's next move was to Fort Peck Community College in Poplar, Montana, an Assiniboine-Sioux institution, in 2008. She remained there as Vice President for Academic and Vocational Programs until 2010. In the same interview referenced above, she summarizes her work at Fort Peck:

At Fort Peck Community College, I served as Vice President for Academic and Vocational Programs. I held a traditional vice president's role in hiring, supervising and evaluating full- and part-time faculty members, and in reviewing all programs of study, including many one-year and two-year vocational certificate programs. While at FPCC I authored and/or coordinated three major programs: the NSF grant for science and math curriculum alignment among the FP community college and the high schools on the FP Reservation (Poplar, Wolf Point, Brockton and Frazier); the Vocational Education Project that supported five vocational training fields at the colleges, with labs upgrading and expansion AND the Carl Perkins Vocational Education grants for FPCC that supported materials and supplies for the vocational fields; and finally, I authored and administered a National Endowment for the Humanities grant for the development of several chapters in a Fort Peck history book, a speaker series on the FP history, a monthly book club at the college and a community summit on the Assiniboine and Dakota languages. Finally, I served as the accreditation liaison officer for the college. The college was under a mandate to improve program learning outcomes, and had two one-visitor site visits and reports on this issue while I was there. We improved over the two years. I also instructed SS 101 Intro to Sociology in person and at distance, every semester. I supervised Admissions, Registration and the Library [Interview].

During Pease's tenure at Rocky Mountain and Fort Peck, she obviously drew upon her considerable experience as president of Little Big Horn College in order to carry out the multiple roles that she assumed. Her expertise and experience, however, were not confined to academic institutions, as she also was tabbed for public service by the state of Montana. Governor Judy Martz appointed her to the Montana Human Rights Commission in 2003, a position that she held until 2006. In this role, she was one of five commissioners whose responsibility was to judge complaints of alleged discrimination at the highest level, that is, to decide on appeals to negative decisions of the Human Rights Bureau and appeals from final decisions by the Hearings Bureau. At the conclusion of her service on the Human Rights Commission, she was appointed by Governor Brian Schweitzer to the Board of Regents of the Montana University System, where she served for the next five years. It is indicative of the widespread respect that Pease enjoys in Montana that both a Republican governor (Martz) and a Democratic one (Schweitzer) chose her for important and prestigious positions of public trust. As a regent, she was able to encourage students to move from two-year tribal colleges into the university system in order to continue their education.

Whatever hard feelings persisted regarding Janine Pease's forced departure from Little Big Horn College seemed to have lessened considerably during the decade since her departure, for as her service on the University Board of Regents was coming to an end, she was offered and accepted the position of Cabinet Head for Education for the Crow Nation, an office within the Crow Tribal Executive Branch. She writes of her swearing-in, which occurred in February 2011:

> As I repeated after the Speaker the oath of office, I had an instantaneous revisit of the 2001 tumultuous termination scene in the Crow Tribal Council meeting in January 2001. I read the oath and the swearing-in was completed. The assembly gave a standing ovation with applause. To some degree, this vote gave vindication for the harsh struggle of 2001 ["Helps the People" 172].

A major accomplishment during her two years as the Education Head was the awarding of a three-year Native American Language Preservation and Maintenance grant totaling approximately $877,000 from the Administration for Native Americans of the U.S. Department of Health and Human Services. The grant funded a preschool language immersion project at the Crow Head Start and the Songbird Daycare Center. The funded project also required parents to attend Crow language and culture seminars with the goals of Crow language use within the family and increased fluency among families, especially focused on young children in order to reverse declining use of the Crow language among the young. The grant coincided well with a longtime passion of Janine Pease's: encouraging learning of the Crow language, especially through a language immersion approach. She earlier had engaged in extensive pedagogical research as a project of the American Indian College Fund supported by the W.K. Kellogg Foundation of Battle Creek, Michigan, that resulted in a lengthy report by Pease titled *Native American Language Immersion: Innovative Native Education for Children and Families* (October 2003).

The *Native American Language Immersion* report includes extensive reporting on and analysis of language immersion projects, both within and beyond the school setting. The report is heavily pedagogical, with attention to both theory and practice. Throughout, Pease recognizes, as she had long done, connections among Native language, tribal culture, and academic success. As Richard Littlebear, president of Chief Dull Knife College in Lame Deer, Montana, writes in the introduction to the report:

This study is for people who want Native American languages to not only survive, but also prosper and be so strengthened that they remain relevant and conversationally useful indefinitely. Saving and further strengthening our Native languages is the very same as saving our own core cultural beings while helping instill a long-neglected sense of pride and self-worth in our peoples [5].

He continues, noting the relevance of Native language study to effective learning as he lists some of the benefits of retaining Native languages: "increased self-esteem, higher Native student retention and educational attainment, and even the preservation of Native worldviews that are urgently needed as rudders in many of today's complex social situations" (5).

In the conclusion to her report, Janine Pease reiterates the value of Native language study and its connections to broader goals. She has been discussing throughout the report "language learning experiences that are unprecedented in their positive impact on education, individual and family strengthening, intergenerational partnerships and tribal health and wellbeing" (81). A few paragraphs later, focusing on a language immersion approach to language learning, she writes, "Native language immersion is education, culture, language, community, family, leadership" (81). Her concluding paragraph restates the major benefits of language immersion:

Most intriguing about the Native and Indigenous language immersion models is the clear and positive connection between Native and Indigenous language and culture with educational achievement.... Native American Language Immersion is a source of hope for Native America; it is innovative education for Native children and families [82].

Giving people, especially students, hope through education, Native language study, an embracing of Native culture, and by exercising the rights of citizenship, such as the right to vote, has essentially been the life of Janine Pease. She continues to do this, and the results continue to demonstrate her success. In an article in the *Billings Gazette* of June 25, 2017, "Crow Women Gather to Practice Language, Saying 'Our Language Is Our Identity,'" the importance of learning among adult language learners is illustrated by the Crow Language Club of Crow women living in Billings who are determined, as the article states, "to keep their language alive." The same article notes the challenge, since most of those fluent in Crow are fifty years of age or older, but it also reports on the progress: While 35.9 percent of the students attending Crow Head Start or Songbird Daycare in 2011 were not able to speak the Crow language at all, "through a three-year language immersion program, 90 percent of the preschool students became either fluent or were able to understand the Crow language by 2015." Among those cited as instrumental in integrating the study of the Crow language into the preschools is Janine Pease (Webb).

Janine Pease's completion of the circle of departure and return in relationship to Little Big Horn College was completed in January 2014, when she rejoined the college as a faculty member teaching sociology, humanities, and communication arts courses. Among the courses that she has taught are American Indian Representation in Film, Introduction to Native American Studies, Introduction to World Religions, Introduction to Sociology, and developmental courses in reading and writing. Always the educator!

However, Janine Pease has never been one-dimensional, and she continued at Little Big Horn College to fulfill other important roles along with her teaching. One of those was as the Accreditation Liaison and Institutional Planning Officer. Focusing especially on assessment and learning outcomes, she led the college through its seven-year evaluation by the regional accrediting agency, the Northwest Commission on Colleges and Universities. Among her responsibilities was coordinating all of the accreditation reports (Interview).

In addition to her engagement with teaching, accreditation, and planning, Janine Pease has continued her commitment to the Crow language. She is heavily involved with Little Big Horn College's partnership with The Language Conservancy (on whose Board of Directors she sits) in order to offer summer institutes for teachers who are helping children learn to speak the Crow language. By the end of the summer of 2017, teachers from fourteen schools, both public and private, had attended three Crow-language institutes. The Conservancy is also responsible for developing language immersion materials and a Crow language dictionary (Interview).

Pease also serves as Board Chair for the Crow Language Consortium, a nonprofit corporation that she helped to develop and that also is involved in preparing Crow language instructional materials. She has served as director and coordinator for grant projects that include the Crow Dictionary Project. In addition, she is director of the Natural World Book Series with a grant from the Institute for Native American Development. Teachers in pre-kindergarten through second grade in reservation schools are members of the Crow Language Consortium, with half-days devoted to Crow language immersion. The consortium sponsors a summer institute annually to assist teachers in preparing for language-immersion instruction (Interview).

Another involvement for Janine Pease with Crow language learning was the Chickadee Lodge Language Immersion School. Pease served as principal of the school for three years until it closed in June 2020. The school operated within the Crow Agency Public School and included students in kindergarten and first and second grades (Interview)

During the past four years (as of this writing), Pease has worked with

Crow and Crow-related historians to write "a people's history" with special emphases on women and children. She serves as coordinator and editor. A "version of this writing," Please notes, was published by the University of Chicago for a Field Museum exhibit titled "Apsáalooke Women and Warriors," *Apsáalooke* being an autonym for *Crow* (Interview).

Janine Pease retired from her full-time position with Little Big Horn College on June 30, 2020. In October 2020, she received a Lifetime Achievement Award from the Association of Tribal Archives, Libraries and Museums. Her work on behalf of the Crow language and her efforts to foster a strong educational experience that keeps alive Crow culture and history, however, are likely to continue for some time, while the fruit of those efforts will surely be harvested far into the future.

Notes

1. The information about Janine Pease's high school years comes from an email interview with her dated 15 September 2017.

2. For much of the biographical information on Janine Pease's early life, I am indebted to Douglas Nelson and Jeremy Johnson's essay "Janine Pease Pretty-on-Top."

3. Much of the information presented here regarding the events surrounding the termination of President Pease is drawn from several *Chronicle* articles published from December 8, 2000, to August 1, 2003, that are available online on the website for *The Chronicle of Higher Education* (http://www.chronicle.com/article).

References

Adams, David Wallace. *Education for Extinction: American Indians and the Boarding School Experience 1875–1928.* Lawrence: UP of Kansas, 1995.

Bedrosian, Tod. "Planning for the Future: A History of the American Indian College Fund." *Tribal College Journal of American Indian Higher Education* 1.1 (1989). 15 May 1989. tribalcollegejournal.org/planning-future-history-american-Indian-college-fund/.

Boyer, Paul. "We Just Can't Fail: Little Big Horn College President Janine Pease-Windy Boy Talks about Teaching and Tribal Development." *Tribal College Journal of American Indian Higher Education* 2.4 (1991). 15 Feb. 1991. tribalcollegejournal.org/fail-big-horn-college-president-janine-pease-windy-boy-talks-teaching-tribal-development/.

The Chronicle of Higher Education. chronicle.com/article/Students-at-Indian-College/1765; chronicle.com/article/Battle-at-Little-Big-Horn-Puts/22675; chronicle.com/article/Tribal-Council-Ousts-President/108654; chronicle.com/article/President-Is-Forced-Out-at/8492; chronicle.com/article/Little-Big-Horn-College-Could/108376; chronicle.com/article/Accreditation-at-Risk-for/10469; chronicle.com/article/Regional-Accreditors-Remove-3/20920.

"The Education of Josephine Pease Russell." *Women's History Matters* 22 July 2014. montanawomenshistory.org/the-education-of-josephine-pease-russell/.

"Janine Pease." "MacArthur Fellows Program." *MacArthur Foundation* July 2015. macfound.org/fellows/498/.

Morgan, Thomas Jefferson. *Annual Report of the Commissioner of Indian Affairs, for the Year 1889; Supplemental Report on Indian Education.* digital.library.wisc.edu/1711.d/History.AnnRep89.

Nelson, Douglas, and Jeremy Johnston. "Janine Pease Pretty-on-Top." *The New Warriors: Native American Leaders Since 1900.* Ed. R. David Edmunds. Lincoln: U of Nebraska P, 2001. 281–97.

Pease, Janine. "Conversations with Elders." *Native Spirit: The Sun Dance Way.* By Thomas Yellowtail. Ed. Michael Oren Fitzgerald. Bloomington: World Wisdom, 2007. 85–97.

_____. Email interview. 15 Sept. 2017; updated 13 Jan. 2021.

_____. "Helps the People: The Dance of the Seasons (Ak bi li kkux she': Ash he'e lee taa li ssua): A Retrospective on Leadership." *American Indian Stories of Success: New Visions of Leadership in Indian Country.* Ed. Gerald E. Gipp, Linda Sue Warner, Janine Pease, and James Shanley. Santa Barbara: Praeger, 2015. 153–76.

_____. Introduction. *The Spirit of Indian Women.* Ed. Judith Fitzgerald and Michael Oren Fitzgerald. Bloomington: World Wisdom, 2005. xi–xviii.

"S. 1215 (95th): Tribally Controlled Community College Assistance Act." govtrack.us/congress/bills/95/s1215/text.

"Tribal College President Fired." *Missoulian* 15 Jan. 2001. missoulian.com/tribal-college-president-fired/article_fce5fd6e-7ff0-5341-8b9f-f2d883827ceb-html.

"Tribally Controlled Community College Assistance Act of 1978 Statement on signing S. 1215 Into Law." *The American Presidency Project.* presidency.ucsb.edu/ws/?pid=29997.

Webb, Jaci. "Crow Women Gather to Practice Language, Saving 'Our Language Is Our Identity.'" *Billings Gazette* 25 June 2017. billingsgazette.com/news/local/crow-women-gather-to-practice-language-saying-our-language-is/article_0237b1c2-25a5-5f0b-b81b-e64b31f1a60a.html.

11

Joy Harjo (b. 1951)

Joy Harjo is a prominent and highly acclaimed poet, musician, and political and cultural activist. The recipient of many awards for her poetry, Joy Harjo has taught at several universities, performed widely as a musician, released CDs of her music, and spoken out on important issues of the day. She is especially committed to exploring her Muscogee/Creek culture and opposing violence against women. She possesses one of the most eloquent and important voices reflecting Indigenous values in the twenty-first century. In June 2019, Joy Harjo was named Poet Laureate of the United States, the twenty-third individual to be named to this post, but the first Native American to be so honored.

Youth

Joy Harjo was born on May 9, 1951, in Tulsa, Oklahoma, to a Mvskoke (Muscogee/Creek) father, Allen Foster, whose ancestors included a half–African Baptist minister, and a mother, Wynema Baker Foster, whose multicultural background included Cherokee, Irish, French, and German. Three younger siblings would follow: Allen (1952), Margaret (1955), and Boyd (1957).

Joy Foster's childhood was not easy, beginning with a difficult birth that, according to her memoir, *Crazy Brave*, almost killed her mother and necessitated the infant being placed on a ventilator (30). At the age of four, Joy suffered polio symptoms during a polio epidemic. An extremely painful spinal tap returned the good news, however, that she had not contracted polio. Greater problems would arrive through her parents' difficult marriage. Her father, an airline mechanic, according to Harjo drank heavily and at times was physically abusive to Joy's mother. To Joy, however, he was often loving and tender. As she writes in *Crazy Brave*, "I adored my father and I feared him" (32). The daughter's future engagement with her cultural background was likely seeded in those early years. An ancestor of her father's, Monahwee, was a Creek leader in the Red Stick War of 1813–14 against General Andrew Jackson. Defeat would result, after enactment of the Indian Removal Act in 1830, in the removal of Native American nations from the South along what is widely referred to as "the Trail of Tears." After the Creeks were resettled in Indian Territory, which later became part of Oklahoma, another ancestor, Samuel Checotah, served as principal chief of the Creeks and also became a Methodist minister.

One of Joy's greatest childhood pleasures was listening to her mother singing, something that she was quite talented at; her mother also introduced Joy to poetry with a copy of Louis Untermeyer's *Golden Books Family Treasury of Poetry*. At the age of eight, she experienced her parents' divorce, and as difficult as home life was on occasion, it would grow even more challenging.

Wynema remarried a much older man, and the family moved into his house, separating Joy from her friends and schoolmates. Harjo writes that the stepfather quickly proved abusive, not only to Wynema, but also to the children. Joy recalls seeing him holding her sister in the air by one of her legs. He then removed his belt and beat her with it, threatening Joy as well if she misbehaved. Joy's mother confided in her that he had threatened to kill mother and children if she ever divorced him (*Crazy Brave* 57–58).

The house, according to Joy, was now empty of her mother's beautiful singing. Wynema once had even recorded a song, "Weeping Willow," that she had written. Shortly after her remarriage, she was invited by Leon McAuliffe to perform one of her songs with his group, the Cimarron Boys, at a community picnic. Listening to her mother sing, Joy notes, "I heard the mother who held my hands and sang and danced in the kitchen with her plants all around. I felt her spirit reach up and touch the sun when she sang" (*Crazy Brave* 62). On the way home, the stepfather belittled his wife, putting an end to her singing. "I imagine this place in the story," Joy Harjo writes, "as a long silence" (*Crazy Brave* 63).

Joy's refuge was in school, where she did well, earning high grades, along with extensive reading, listening to music, sketching, and, until her stepfather found her diary and ordered her not to sing anymore in the house, writing and singing. She acted in plays in elementary school and looked forward to participating in high school. Again, her stepfather intervened. According to Harjo, when she returned home from a theater meeting at school, he beat her, grounded her for a month, and ordered her not to try out for the play (*Crazy Brave* 75). Much that would become so important in her later life was now denied her.

Finding Her Way

As Joy Harjo points out in *Crazy Brave*, she told her mother that she wanted to attend a school where she would be with other Indian students.

With the help of the Bureau of Indian Affairs, she decided to apply for admission to the Institute of American Indian Arts (IAIA) in Santa Fe, New Mexico, a school that attracted students from throughout the country. IAIA was established as a high school in 1962. Its website notes that the institution became a two-year college in 1975 and a Congressionally chartered college in 1986. It moved to a permanent campus in 2000 and in later years added baccalaureate degrees in several areas, including Indigenous Liberal Studies, and, in 2013, its first graduate program, in Creative Writing. Her successful application included a portfolio of her art. The school's current website, under the heading "Creativity Is Our Tradition," lists Joy Harjo among the illustrious alumni of the Institute.

At the Institute, Joy benefited from having Louis Ballard as her adviser, mentor, and lifelong friend. Ballard, a prominent Quapaw-Cherokee composer and educator, would serve as National Curriculum Specialist for the Bureau of Indian Affairs from 1968 until 1979; publish *American Indian Music for the Classroom* (1973), *Music of North American Indians—Music 7 and 9* (1975), and *Native American Indian Songs* (2004)—pedagogical works that included CDs and guidance for teachers; and be named to the Oklahoma Music Hall of Fame (2004) along with receiving many other awards.

Yet despite Ballard's influence, Joy refrained from any formal study of music, reflecting the continuing effect of her traumatic life with her stepfather. As she notes in her memoir, "Music is direct communication with the sacred" (*Crazy Brave* 85). An eventual return to music would become an important part of her self-realization and spiritual growth. It was at the Institute of American Indian Arts, she writes,

> that my spirit found a place to heal. I thrived with others who carried family and personal stories similar to my own. I belonged. Mine was no longer a solitary journey [*Crazy Brave* 86].

That healing, however, did not come easily. Feelings "of rage and destruction" led her to cut herself, not an unusual adolescent act, but she did not repeat it, opting instead "to slash art onto canvas, pencil marks onto paper," along with writing stories (91). Theater also helped, although her primary academic area had become art, with a focus on courses in drawing and painting. Joy became a production assistant on the school production of Shelagh Delaney's *A Taste of Honey*. Soon she turned to acting, with a major role in *Mowitch*, a play written by Monica Charles, who was a post-graduate student at the school. The student production was scheduled for a tour through the Northwest, which required permission from the participants' parents. Not surprisingly, Joy's stepfather refused, but her mother, exercising considerable courage in disagreeing with her husband, granted permission. The tour, which included performances in Washington State and Oregon, Joy remembered years later as one of the highlights of her life (*Crazy Brave* 115).

Harjo, in an interview conducted by Priscilla Page and published in *Wings of Night Sky, Wings of Morning Light: A Play by Joy Harjo and a Circle of Responses*, recalls how her drama teacher at the Institute of American Indian Arts, Rolland Meinholtz, was one of her most important mentors ever. She knew that Meinholtz believed in her, and under his guidance she learned to overcome the extreme stage fright that had afflicted her. Through drama, she developed more self-confidence and a clearer sense of who she was (99).

One of the performers in *Mowitch*, a talented dancer named Phil Wilmon, who was an older Cherokee student, was Joy's boyfriend. At the conclusion of the tour, Joy, pregnant with Phil's child and having completed her course of study at the Institute, returned to her mother and stepfather's home. Now seventeen years old, Joy expected to marry Phil and anticipated receiving a bus ticket from him so she could join him in Tahlequah, Oklahoma, the capital of the Cherokee tribes in the state. When no ticket arrived, her brother, Allen, loaned her the money to make the trip.

Initially, Joy roomed with Phil's friends and then his grandmother before joining Phil, who lived with his mother, sister, and daughter. At the W.W. Hastings Indian Hospital, Joy gave birth to their son, Phil Dayn. While her son was still an infant, she, her husband, and the two children moved to Tulsa, Oklahoma. Phil's mother and her daughter soon joined them in Tulsa, living next door to Joy and her family.

Life was not easy in Tulsa, as money was scarce and Joy's relationship with her mother-in-law was trying. Finding that moving to Tulsa had been a mistake, Joy and her family returned to Santa Fe where they had friends from their school days. Joy worked at a gas station, then left that job to train as a nursing assistant at a hospital. As she points out in her memoir, she found herself paying half of her modest earnings to her son's babysitter, only to discover that her husband was having a relationship with the babysitter (136–37). That ended Joy's marriage, and she decided to embark on a premed program at the University of New Mexico in Albuquerque. Joy moved with her son, soon to be joined by her thirteen-year-old brother, Boyd, who was forced by the stepfather to leave home.

At the university, Joy switched from premed to studio art. She also finalized her divorce from Phil. She soon met an Acoma Pueblo man she had seen at a National Indian Youth Council press conference. A poet, he helped Joy realize, she wrote, that "poetry did not have to be from England or of an English that was always lonesome for its homeland in Europe" (*Crazy Brave* 141). They began living together, but the relationship, as Harjo points out in *Crazy Brave*, involved periods of great difficulty, and Joy eventually ended it (142–58). However, the relationship produced a daughter, Rainy Dawn, Joy's second child. In the memoir, Harjo chooses not to identify the poet.

At this point, Joy Harjo was close to finding her way into the future, a future that would also include the past. When she painted, she would feel close to her grandmother Naomi Harjo Foster. Although Naomi had died before Joy was born, Joy often examined the grandmother's painting of two horses in a storm that was hanging in her house. Deeply affected by the painting, Joy took her grandmother's name "Harjo" as her own surname when she enrolled in the Muskogee tribe at the age of nineteen (Pettit 8). In addition to inspiring Joy regarding her Native heritage, including a plan to create a series of sketches of contemporary warriors for an art class (*Crazy Brave* 150), the image of horses would provide both visual and thematic inspiration to Joy as she turned more fully toward poetry.

That turn would come soon. Harjo, continuing with her studies, changed her focus to creative writing and contributed poems to the university's student magazine. She writes in her memoir of a recurring nightmare of being chased. One night she found herself in her dream cornered by her adversary, a monster that for the first time she saw in the nightmare. Then her fear vanished, and the monster also disappeared, leaving her with a great feeling of freedom. The poem that she wrote in the aftermath of this final rendition of the nightmare appears in her memoir (161–63).

Harjo writes that it "was the spirit of poetry" that found her. "I had come this far without the elegance of speech," she writes, noting that although she obviously could speak "everyday language," she lacked "the intricate and metaphorical language" of her ancestors. She notes various ways of visualizing this spirit, including as "a hundred horses running the land in a soft mist," and concludes with the simple statement: "I followed poetry" (163–64).

Poetry, Music, and Cultural Activism

After graduating from the University of New Mexico in 1976, Harjo was accepted into the prestigious Iowa Writers' Workshop at the University of Iowa in Iowa City. The experience involved a serious cultural shock for the young mother of two. She states in an interview conducted by Pam Kingsbury in 2003 and published in *Soul Talk, Song Language: Conversations with Joy Harjo*, "We knew no one, and there was no visible Indian community. I was torn away from the familiar and in a vulnerable position so I'm sure that set my lens" (39–40). She speaks of the program respectfully, but it is clear that the experience was challenging and often not enjoyable. "It became immediately obvious," Harjo continues in the interview, "that I spoke a very different language, arrived in Iowa from a sensibility that was tribal, western, female, and intuitive, a sensibility different than most of the other workshop participants" (40).

Feeling like an outsider, Harjo, as she says in the Kingsbury interview, joined a few other students, including the poet Sandra Cisneros, in a Third World Writing Workshop. Although she felt that her background, next to that of most workshop participants, was limited, envying "their excellent educations, their long study of poetry, their confidence in their knowledge, their art" (40), she obviously was more successful in the workshop program than at times she felt. During the final semester of her two-year experience, for example, Harjo was one of four participants selected to read some of their work for potential financial benefactors of the Writers' Workshop. She adds that when asked about her experience in the Writers' Workshop, "I always tell them that the workshop was a useful technical school, probably the best. I had to nourish my soul otherwise" (41).

After completing her M.F.A. at Iowa, Joy Harjo embarked on what would prove to be a long teaching career at several institutions while also seeking publication of her poetry. She initially taught at her alma mater, the Institute of American Indian Arts, before moving to Arizona State University, back to the IAIA, and then at the University of Colorado, the University of Arizona, the University of New Mexico, and UCLA. In January 2013, Harjo became a member of the American Indian Studies faculty at the University of Illinois at Urbana-Champaign. She moved to the University of Tennessee at Knoxville in 2016 to assume the John C. Hodges Chair of Excellence in English.

While teaching, Joy Harjo also strove to achieve publishing success with her poetry. Her chapbook *The Last Song* appeared in 1975 while she was still a student at the University of New Mexico. *What Moon Drove Me to This?* (1979) and *She Had Some Horses* (1983) were issued by literary presses. Harjo makes clear in the Kingsbury interview that she was very conscious of the reputation of the publishers with which she worked (42–43). She attempted to interest Norton in *She Had Some Horses*, but the publisher declined to publish the book, as it did with Harjo's *In Mad Love and War*, the latter subsequently published by Wesleyan University Press in 1990. In between, the University of Arizona Press released her *Secrets from the Center of the World* in 1989. Both university presses were certainly quality presses but generally would not have had the marketing reach that Norton enjoyed.

Harjo broke through with Norton when she offered them a third collection, *The Woman Who Fell from the Sky* (1994). The relationship with Norton would continue, through subsequent poetry collections—*A Map* to the Next World: Poems and Tales (2000), How We Became Human: New and Selected Poems: 1975–2001 (2004), Conflict Resolution for Holy Beings: Poems (2015), An American Sunrise (2019)—plus her memoir, Crazy Brave, Reinventing the Enemy's Language: Contemporary Native Women's Writing of North America (1997), which she co-edited, and When the Light of the World Was Subdued, Our Songs Came Through: A Norton Anthology of Native Nations Poetry (2020), for which she was the principal editor. Norton also reissued She Had Some Horses in 2008.

Harjo's publications include the children's picture books The Good Luck Cat (2000) and For a Girl Becoming (2009). The first of the children's books followed the birth of Harjo's first grandchild. She notes in an interview with Loriene Roy, published in Soul Talk, Song Language, "It was with her birth that the need to tell stories was released in me. I wanted her to know about my beloved Aunt Lois Harjo, and the stories she told me" (61). Those stories that Joy had received from her aunt involved cats and how they bring good luck. The second book also was connected to a grandchild, as Harjo wrote it as a poem "for a coming of age event honoring a grandchild," although she adds that she intends the book for all of her grandchildren (Roy interview 61).

She Had Some Horses marked Harjo's arrival as an important American poet. It was written with the financial support of the poet's first Literature Fellowship from the National Endowment for the Arts. Harjo is quoted in an article for the NEA Arts as attesting to the importance of that fellowship. With it, she says, "I was able to buy childcare, pay rent and utilities, and my car payment while I wrote what would be most of my second book of poetry, She Had Some Horses, the collection that actually started my career. The grant began the momentum that carried me through the years" (Perry). In referring to the book as her second, she appears not to be counting the chapbook The Last Song, the poems in that collection having been included in What Moon Drove Me to This? Although Harjo has said that her best poems are not in She Had Some Horses (interview with Susan Thornton Hobby published in Soul Talk, Soul Language 80), the collection remains perhaps Harjo's best known and most widely read collection.

Organizing the contents of She Had Some Horses was a challenge for Harjo. She states in an interview conducted by Joseph Bruchac and published in his Survival This Way: Interviews with American Indian Poets:

> I had a hard time with this book for a long time. I could not put it together right. So a friend of mine, Brenda Peterson, who is a fine novelist and a very good editor, volunteered. She did an excellent job, and what I like about it is that the first poem in the first section is called "Call It Fear." It was an older poem. And the last section which is only one poem is called "I Give You Back," which has to do with giving back that fear [99].

"I Give You Back" is the poem that Harjo also published near the end of her memoir, *Crazy Brave*, the poem that she describes having written after she finally manages to banish a recurring nightmare, and which she associates with acquiring "the spirit of poetry" and "the elegance of speech" (161–64).

Horses appear throughout the poems in *She Had Some Horses* with a great variety of visual images and concepts associated with them. Horses at times are actual horses; at other times they are symbolic, shadowy, identified with people, prehistoric as well as current, spiritual, within the individual, in the sky, a statue, multi-colored, neighing and singing, the poet herself, volcanic and ice. Like most poets, Harjo is reluctant to try to state what her poems mean, asserting in the introduction to the volume, "Like most poets, I don't really know what my poems or the stuff of my poetry means *exactly*" (ix). She does, however, offer a range of associations for the horses. Sometimes quite literally the "horses are horses" (ix). She also notes the historical importance of horses for her people, refers to a cousin who could speak with horses, describes a somewhat mystical appearance of a horse during a drive through New Mexico, recalls a specific horse named Casey, and offers a range of transformations that a horse might undergo ("a streak of sunrise, a body of sand, a moment of ecstasy"). "Or a herd of horses galloping from one song to the next could become a book of poetry" (ix–x).

Already, Joy Harjo in this collection has established a framework for her subsequent poetry as well as for other dimensions of her creativity. Her poetry is rooted in both the present and the past, with time flexible and nonlinear rather than strictly chronological. It is fact-filled but also mythological in the sense of narratives that, although not always literally factual, convey fundamental truths. Harjo defines myth as "root stories, or rather, the shifting, dynamic template of spirit from which a people or peoples emerge ... not some imagined past, rather, the dream works of the communal self" (interview with Harbour Winn, Elaine Smokewood, and John McBryde in 2009, in *Soul Talk, Song Language* 74). Her poetry thus reflects her own shared cultural background, although it also can be highly individualized and personal. A criticism of the Iowa Workshop approach that she offers in the Kingsbury interview presents a continuing explanation of her work: "[A]t the Iowa Workshop the prevailing rule was that to embellish a poem or poetry with emotive expression was to tarnish the expression of it, to get in the way of the words. This has metamorphosed into the text-without-human-connection mode of thinking about poetry, about the making of literature. It must be a lonely world, that world" (44).

Even before beginning school, Harjo was approaching the world in a manner prophetic of how she would later create her very expansive poetry. She notes in another interview, conducted by Simmons Buntin in 2006 and also published in *Soul Talk, Song Language*, "Before I went to school my world was vast because I lived for the most part in my imagination. It was a live thing, with as much texture and viability as what is called 'real.' My spirit traveled all over the world" (37).

Nor does Harjo isolate poetry from other forms of artistic expression. In addition to her interest and background in the visual arts, she has long been engaged in the world of music. She states in the introduction to *She Had Some Horses* that in writing poetry she is "aware of stepping into a force field or dream field of language, of sound," and likens each poem to a journey that changes with each poem, "as the ocean or the sky is never the same from one day to another. I am engaged," she says, "by the music, by the deep" (ix).

Joy Harjo demonstrates her poetic and musical accomplishments at her induction as Poet Laureate of the United States (courtesy Joy Harjo, photograph by Shawn Miller).

This synthesis of poetry and music for Harjo is both explicitly stated and concretely practiced, with both modes of expression intimately connected to who and what Harjo is. "Music was and is my body," she says in the first interview that appears in *Soul Talk, Song Language*. "I don't think I ever felt a separation between music and my body. Words make bridges but music penetrates" (Interview with *Triplopi* 5). In another of the interviews, with Rebecca Seiferle, Harjo identifies poetry, music, and dance as having originated together and asserts that without them she "would not be alive" (28–29). She has written songs as well as poems without drawing a hard and fast division between the two. In the Buntin interview, she explains that she has "written some songs as lyrics," and has "transformed some poems to lyrics" (33). In yet another interview, with Tanaya Winder, in speaking of her public performances Harjo notes, "The interweaving of stories, poetry, and music emerged organically as I traveled about to read" (57); she then adds another form of expression, dancing, to the mix. "I am a dancer at heart," she says. "I find images or sounds by moving them, and moving with them. Images may also be at the heart of a song." Turning to another genre that she has worked in, she adds, "A play is more like writing a symphony and telling a story, at the same time, especially a play with music" (58).

The growing fusion of poetry and song is especially obvious in one of her more recent books of poetry, *Conflict Resolution for Holy Beings*. Following the poem "We Were There When Jazz was Invented," Harjo includes the first of several poems ("Reality Show") that she identifies within parentheses after the title as a song. With some poems, she uses a more specific term to identify the poem, for example, "Beautiful Baby, Beautiful Child" as a lullaby, "One Day There Will Be Horses" as a traveling song, and "Everybody Has a Heartache" as blues. Other poems—"Fall Song," "Sunrise Healing Song," and "Indian School Night Song Blues," among others—are identified as specific types of songs within their titles.

Short compositions, most of them prose pieces, occur between poems in *Conflict Resolution for Holy Beings*. Many of these testify to the important qualities and powers that music exhibits. Singing is the primal creative act (16). Music also is highly personal to Harjo, who speaks of depending on love to play her saxophone (27). She notes that we can lose ourselves and find ourselves again through music (33). In another passage, she chronicles the hours from midnight into morning through the passage from drum to guitar, bass, and the singer, with 5:00 a.m. the time for birds (41). Additional comments continue to clarify how important music is to Joy Harjo, including the ideal song that she senses but cannot yet actually hear, and which inspires her to continue, almost transforming her saxophone into a human being (95).

A saxophonist and flautist, in addition to a singer and composer, Harjo released her first music CD, *Letter from the End of the Twentieth Century*, in 2003. Since then, she has released several more CDs, including *Red Dreams, Trail Beyond Tears* (2010), which on her website she describes as "a traditional flute album"; and *Indian Rezervation: Blues and More*, a three-CD collection of three hours of music, thirty minutes of video, and accompanying printed material. Among her CDs is *She Had Some Horses* (2006), which primarily consists of the poet reading a selection of the poems from the printed volume, but with some bonus music tracks included. Her most recent CD is *I Pray for My Enemies* (2021).

Harjo also has formed and performed with her own bands, most recently the Arrow Dynamics. In the Kingsbury interview, referring to her earlier band, Poetic Justice, she describes the nature of her performance, which consists of a synthesis of poetry and music: "Sometimes we'd work the music around the poems. Other times I'd bend the poems around the music, rewrite, add choruses, or a bridge. Since then I've written poems to go with particular vamps or melodies" (44).

In addition, Harjo has performed in a one-woman show, *Wings of Night Sky, Wings of Morning Light*. The combination of narrative and song is a play in which Harjo appears as a Mvskoke woman named Redbird, accompanied by a guitar player, the Guardian Musician.

Wings of Night Sky, Wings of Morning Light

Wings of Night Sky, Wings of Morning Light may be the single composition that gives the most thorough picture of who and what Joy Harjo is. The Public Theater presented the play as a workshop and staged reading during the Public Theater Native Theater Festival in New York City in December 2007. The first full presentation of the play occurred in March 2009 at the Autry in Los Angeles in the series of Native Voices at the Autry, a program created by Randy Reinholz and Jean Bruce Scott. Reinholz, a Choctaw and director of the School of Theatre, Television, and Film at San Diego State University, directed the play. *Wings* has been staged in a variety of locations since then and was published with related materials by Wesleyan University Press in 2019.

Through song, poetry, and narrative, *Wings* presents what is both personal and expansive. There is much of Harjo's life in the material. Anyone who has read her *Crazy Brave* will recognize references to her youth, her mother, her stepfather, and a variety of autobiographical incidents. She even adapts a song written by her mother, "A Long Time Ago," for inclusion in scene 3. Yet this is far more than a memoir. Redbird, the protagonist, as Priscilla Page states in "Reflections on Joy Harjo, Indigenous Feminism, and Experiments in Creative Expression," which follows the published play, is "an everywoman of sorts" (48). The description of Redbird in the dramatis personae as "somewhere in her later twenties, thirties, forties, or fifties" (14) makes it clear that she represents more than just one woman at one point in the woman's life. Harjo explains in an interview conducted by Priscilla Page and also included in the *Wings* volume: "I didn't want to be bound by my very personal story; rather, I wanted the freedom to move, so I fictionalized the story" (100).

The play occurs around a kitchen table, the most universal and connecting of all domestic foci. As Harjo writes in the introduction to *Reinventing the Enemy's Language: Contemporary Native Women's Writings of North America*, which she and Gloria Bird edited, "the kitchen table is ever present in its place at the center of being" (19). She recalls that "*Reinventing the Enemy's Language* was conceived during a lively discussion of native women meeting around a kitchen table" (19). Priscilla Page, in the essay mentioned above, notes that not only is the table where people eat and learn life's lessons but also, quoting Joy Harjo, adds "'We have given birth on this table, and have prepared our parents for burial here'"; also, at the kitchen table, "'we sing with joy, with sorrow. We pray of suffering and remorse. We give thanks'" (44).

Redbird announces upon entering that she is welcoming the audience to a ceremony. Throughout the ceremony, Redbird sings, dances, speaks, plays the saxophone (and occasionally the flute, drum, and rattle), and assumes several roles, including the Spirit Helper, Mother, a Navajo drag queen named Marty, and a tree that had been Redbird's partner's lover and that Redbird pulls out of the ground to free her. Priscilla Page explicates the importance of the tree incident allegorically, showing Harjo's commitment to "Indigenous feminism" (52):

> Harjo depicts a bond between the women who free themselves from Sonny. She writes this woman, who is Sonny's lover, as a tree who is saddened to be bound by her roots. Redbird, at first jealous of the tree and resentful of Sonny's affections toward the tree, becomes attracted to her songs…. The two women are able to leave when Redbird pulls the tree out by her roots. It is the women's bond to each other that allows them to literally seize their freedom together [*Wings* 49].

At the end of the play, Redbird carries a basket of food and other items onstage and distributes them to members of the audience, a traditional "giveaway" that is often part of important Native ceremonies. The play then concludes with the song "Goin' Home," as Harjo reemphasizes the importance of family and community. As Mary Kathryn Nagle writes in an introduction to the play, "Harjo's heroine takes her audience on a journey through generations of trauma and survival in a musical revelry that celebrates American Indian resistance" (*Wings* 2). Nagle perceptively notes that "Joy Harjo is not Redbird. But Harjo and Redbird are constructed from the same fabric, the same experience, the same survival" (8). One might add that Redbird includes Harjo but also much more.

As of the writing of this chapter, Joy Harjo was working on another musical, *We Were There When Jazz Was Invented*. Harjo has taken issue with how Native Americans' contributions to jazz have largely been ignored (*Wings* 56), and her musical would help to right the wrong.

The Enemy's Language

Writers speak of finding their voice, which usually means their distinctive combination of style and substance. In the case of Joy Harjo, her voice ironically includes as its medium the language used by those who took the Native Americans' land, culture, and language. Although there has been a resurgence in efforts by various tribal organizations to expand knowledge and use of Native languages, English remains the primary language for most Native peoples.

According to Harjo, "When our lands were colonized the language of the colonizer was forced on us. We had to use it for commerce in the new world, a world that evolved through the creation and use of language." However, she notes that "when we began to create with this new language that we nam*ed it ours, made it usefully tough and beautiful*" (*Reinventing the Enemy's Language* 23–24). She claims, in using English, that a great transformation has been effected:

> But to speak, at whatever the cost, is to become empowered rather than victimized by destruction. In our tribal cultures the power of language to heal, to regenerate, and to create is understood. These colonizers' languages, which often usurped our own tribal languages or diminished them, now hand back emblems of our cultures, our own designs: beadwork, quills if you will. We've transformed these enemy languages [21–22].

That transformation serves a bedrock need: survival. Survival for Harjo personally and for all Native peoples. Harjo says in an interview conducted by Laura Coltelli that she does not believe she "would be alive today if it hadn't been for writing." She adds, "Writing helped me give voice to turn around a terrible silence that was killing me." That survival, she realizes, far exceeded her personal life: "And on a larger level, if we, as Indian people, Indian women, keep silent, then we will disappear, at least in this level of reality" (*Winged Words* 58). She acknowledges in the same interview that when she writes, "there is an old Creek within me that often participates," a collective self that provides cultural memory, but a memory, Harjo says, that is "not just associated with past history, past events, past stories, but nonlinear, as in future and ongoing history, events, and stories" (57).

For Harjo, writing (and singing) in English is not merely accepting the language as it is and using it for good ends, but actually changing the language. In the Coltelli interview, she points out that she is consciously altering English, creating "a land-based language," which recognizes "the spirit of place" (63). Joni Adamson perceptively explicates what Harjo has in mind when she refers to a "land-based language":

[W]hen Harjo observes that she is struggling to transform English into a land-based language, she is speaking of her search to find ways to speak of a world in which nature and culture, event and place are not separate. She is seeking to infuse her primary language—English—with the moral force of American Indian oral traditions, to speak not just of places but of the ancient and historical events that occurred in those places [122].

"In a sense," Adamson writes, "Harjo's search for a land-based language is the search for a middle place where deadly silences give way to voices that speak of the values by which individuals and communities organize and regulate their lives in relation to each other and to the places they inhabit" (126).

Recognition

Joy Harjo has been steadily gaining recognition as a poet and social activist since the publication of *She Had Some Horses*. She rightly has received acclaim for her efforts on behalf of Native American culture and the rights of not only Indigenous women but all women. In January 2019, Harjo was named to the Board of Chancellors of the Academy of American Poets, becoming the first Native American named to the board, which has been in existence since 1946. Among her responsibilities is consulting on the recipients of the Wallace Stevens Award, which she received in 2015. Consistent with Harjo's desire to aid others, she will provide leadership to the Poets Emergency Fund, which assist poets who are undergoing special hardships.

The selection of Harjo as a Chancellor of the Academy of American Poets was another in a long list of honors. Her memoir *Crazy Brave* received an American Book Award in 2013 as well as a 2013 PEN Literary Award. She has received a Guggenheim fellowship, the Griffin Poetry Prize in 2016 for her *Conflict Resolution for Holy Beings*, the Poetry Foundation's Lilly Prize in 2017, the Jackson Poetry Prize (2019) from *Poets & Writers*, a Native American Music Award (NAMMY) as Best Female Artist of the Year in 2009 for her CD *Winding Through the Milky Way*, the William Carlos Williams Award from the Poetry Society of America in 1991, an American Book Award for *In Mad Love and War* in 1991, a lifetime achievement award from the Native Writers Circle of the Americas in 1995, and many other awards. Although Joy Harjo has stepped down as Hodges Chair of Excellence at the University of Tennessee, Knoxville, she remains busy. A second memoir, *Poet Warrior*, is forthcoming.

As of the writing of this chapter, both Joy Harjo's accomplishments and the recognition of those accomplishments continue without any indication of slowing down. Proof of that occurred in June of 2019 when Librarian of Congress Carla Hayden announced Harjo's selection as Poet Laureate of the United States, the first Native American to serve in this position. The official title is Poet Laureate Consultant in Poetry to the Library of Congress. The Poet Laureate's official duties typically include presentation of a reading and lecture as well as the introduction of other poets in a poetry series at the Library of Congress. Her laureate project, "Living Nations, Living Words," includes an online map showing the location of Native American poets in the United States and recordings of the poets reading their poetry. In November 2020, Harjo was reappointed for a third term, only the second person (along with Robert Pinsky) to serve three terms as Poet Laureate. From this vantage point of national leadership, Joy Harjo inspires and enriches the world of American poetry.

References

Adamson, Joni. *American Indian Literature, Environmental Justice, and Ecocriticism: The Middle Place*. Tucson: U of Arizona P, 2001.

Allen, Paula Gunn. *The Sacred Hoop: Recovering the Feminine in American Indian Traditions*. Boston: Beacon Press, 1986.

Bruchac, Joseph. *Survival This Way: Interviews with American Indian Poets*. Tucson: Sun Tracks and U of Arizona P, 1987.

Coltelli, Laura. *Winged Words: American Indian Writers Speak*. 1990. Lincoln: U of Nebraska P, 1992.

Harjo, Joy. *Conflict Resolution for Holy Beings: Poems*. New York: Norton, 2015.

_____. *Crazy Brave: A Memoir*. New York: Norton, 2012.

_____. *She Had Some Horses*. 1983. New York: Norton, 2008.

_____, and Gloria Bird, eds. *Reinventing the Enemy's Language: Contemporary Native Women's Writings of North America*. New York: Norton, 1997.

_____, with Priscilla Page. *Wings of Night Sky, Wings of Morning Light: A Play by Joy Harjo and a Circle of Responses*. Middletown, CT: Wesleyan UP, 2019.

_____, and Tanaya Winder. *Soul Talk, Song Language: Conversations with Joy Harjo*. Middletown, CT: Wesleyan UP, 2011.

Perry, Emily. "Joy Harjo: An Unstoppable Force." *NEA Arts Magazine* (2015). arts.gov/stories/blog/2016/archives-joy-harjo-unstoppable-force.

Pettit, Rhonda. *Joy Harjo*. Boise State University Western Writers Series, Number 133. Boise: Boise State U, 1998.

Swann, Brian, and Arnold Krupat, eds. *I Tell You Now: Autobiographical Essays by Native American Writers*. Lincoln: U of Nebraska P, 1987.

Wald, Catherine, ed. *The Resilient Writer: Tales of Rejection and Triumph from 23 Top Authors*. New York: Persea Books, 2005.

12

Debra Anne Haaland
(b. 1960)

On January 3, 2019, the first session of the 116th Congress convened. The list of firsts for women in the United States Congress was extensive, a list catalogued in *The New York Times* publication *The Women of the 116th Congress: Portraits of Power* (182–83). Among the firsts were the first Native American women to be elected to Congress: Sharice Davids, a member of the Ho-Chunk (Winnebago) nation, elected to represent Kansas's Third Congressional District; and Debra Haaland, a Laguna Pueblo chosen in New Mexico's First Congressional District. Both women came to Washington with a great deal of relevant experience and quickly became important members of a Congress that not only engaged with a wide range of policy issues but also faced the impeachment of the President of the United States.

Representative Haaland's accumulation of "firsts," however, was not finished. After serving a second term as a member of the House of Representatives, and after another Presidential election, the new President, Joe Biden, named Haaland Secretary of the Interior. After approval by the Senate, Haaland was sworn in on March 16, 2021, becoming the first Native American to serve in a President's Cabinet. The importance of that "first" was magnified by the reality that after so much Native American unhappiness over the years with varied aspects of the Bureau of Indian Affairs, Debra Haaland, as Secretary of the Interior, also would be in charge over the BIA. Haaland's new role has been widely acclaimed by a wide range of Indigenous people and carries with it, given the fraught history of the BIA, a sense of justice.

Professional and Political Background

Debra Anne Haaland was born on December 2, 1960, in Winslow, Arizona, to Mary Toya and J.D. "Dutch" Haaland. An enrolled member of the

199

Laguna Pueblo people, Debra Haaland, who usually goes by "Deb," traces her ancestry back though her Native American mother, as she stated in an interview with *The Guardian*, to when her "ancestors migrated to what is now New Mexico, where the Pueblo Indians live, back in the late 1200s" (Tobias). She states in the same interview: "No one else can claim that they have been there any longer than our people, than the Pueblo people. I feel like perhaps my voice is important right now to testify to our longstanding care for the land."

Both Haaland's mother and father, the latter a Norwegian-American, served in the United States Armed Forces. Mary Toya is a Navy veteran who, according to Haaland's biography posted on the House of Representatives site, later worked for twenty-five years as a federal employee involved in Native American education. J.D. "Dutch" Haaland served thirty years in the Marines, receiving the Silver Star during the Vietnam War for heroic actions that saved the lives of fellow Marines in 1967 at Con Thien, a Marine combat base near the Demilitarized Zone in Quang Tri Province, where heavy combat occurred during 1967 and 1968. He also received two Purple Hearts, a medal given to soldiers wounded or killed in battle, among the fifteen medals that he was awarded during his long career (Obituary). Mary and Dutch met while they were both stationed at Naval Station Treasure Island, a former Naval station on Treasure Island in San Francisco Bay. Dutch died on February 26, 2005, and was interred at Arlington National Cemetery.

Debra Haaland, as the child of military parents, moved often during her early years. She has two sisters, Denise and Zoe, and a brother, Judd. Denise lives on a ranch in New Mexico, Zoe is a registered nurse, and Judd owns a construction company and participates in one-hundred-mile ultra-marathons. Debra has served on her brother's racing crew on occasion.

Debra Haaland learned as a child what a military family is like, including its effect on the rest of the family, as she moved often. According to the biographical sketch on the House of Representatives website, she attended thirteen schools as she was growing up. That experience likely impacted her determination to ensure a strong educational base for her daughter, Somah. Haaland volunteered at her child's pre-school, which enabled the future Congresswoman to afford pre-schooling her daughter. The biography referenced above also points out Haaland's paycheck-to-paycheck existence for a good part of her life, a pattern that many of her former constituents experience.

Despite her financial challenges, Haaland was able successfully to conclude her own formal education, earning a degree as an English major from the University of New Mexico at Albuquerque in 1994, the same institution that her daughter graduated from, and also completing a law degree at the University of New Mexico School of Law in 2006. As a law student, she worked on the *Tribal Law Journal*; was active in the Native American

Law Students Association; participated in moot court, which involves sim-ulated court or arbitration proceedings; and participated in the first jury trial at the Laguna Tribal Court under the auspices of the Southwest Indian Law Clinic, which offers law students the opportunity to represent Native clients in court proceedings and agency hearings (press release, 29 March 2019). Her background also includes business experience, as she oper-ated a salsa business, Pueblo Salsa, producing and canning the salsa. As an engaged Laguna Pueblo member, Haaland later served as chairwoman of the Laguna Development Corporation Board of Directors and adminis-tered an organization that aided adults with developmental disabilities.

Increasingly interested in politics, Debra Haaland attended a lead-ership training program, Emerge New Mexico, completing the program in 2007. The goal of Emerge New Mexico was to increase the number of Democratic women in political office. She previously had shown her polit-ical activism, supporting a bill in the New Mexico Legislature in 2005 that broadened the opportunity for members of New Mexico tribes to qualify for in-state tuition at New Mexico institutions of higher learning.

Haaland subsequently became heavily involved in politics. She was a full-time volunteer for Barack Obama's successful 2008 campaign for the presidency. In 2010, she was the Native American Vote Manager for Diane Denish's gubernatorial effort. She served in a similar role two years later for the New Mexico branch of Organizing for America, a project of the Dem-ocratic National Committee that was established after President Obama's election to advance the President's agenda, especially health care reform. Increasingly prominent in both New Mexico Democratic and Native Amer-ican circles, Haaland served in 2012–13 as Native American Caucus Chair for the State Democratic Party.

Haaland was her party's nominee for Lieutenant Governor of New Mexico in 2014, running with gubernatorial candidate Gary King, although the King-Haaland ticket lost to Republicans Susana Martinez and John Sanchez. In 2015, Debra Haaland was elected to a two-year term as chair-person of the State Democratic Party, in which role she helped Democrats retake control of the New Mexico Legislature. Haaland helped to score another important victory in 2017 when she worked with New Mexico LGBTQ+ civil rights activists to persuade the state legislature to ban con-version therapy. The ban was signed into law by Governor Martinez.

On to Washington

Given Debra Haaland's experience with New Mexico politics, decid-ing to run for the United States House of Representatives to represent New

Mexico's First District was a logical progression. She faced several opponents in the June 5, 2018, Democratic primary but won by a substantial margin over her next closest competitor, gaining 40.6 percent of the primary vote to Damon Martinez's 25.8 percent. Antoinette Sedillo Lopez received 20.6 percent of the votes, while three other challengers gained fewer than 6 percent each. Haaland's extensive work on behalf of the New Mexico Democratic Party and Native Americans earned her endorsements from such political heavyweights as former Senator Harry Reid (D–Nev.) and Representative James Clyburn (D–S.C.), as well as from the Congressional Black Caucus and a number of major organizations, among them Equality New Mexico, the National Organization for Women's Political Action Committee, the Planned Parenthood Action Fund, the National Education Association of New Mexico, and the American Federation of Teachers New Mexico. The To'hajiilee Chapter of the Navajo Nation and the Tribal Alliance of Sovereign Indian Nations also endorsed Haaland (*Ballotpedia*).

The general election was even more decisive. Haaland received 59.1 percent of the vote to Republican Janice Arnold-Jones' 36.3 percent and Independent Lloyd Princeton's 4.5 percent (*Ballotpedia*). Her triumph on November 6, 2018, meant that she would be one of the first two Native American women (along with Sharice Davids) to become members of the House of Representatives. Haaland's campaign website in the general election featured, among other issues, her commitment to "universal public healthcare," "a woman's right to choose," "full access to contraception," the need "to act fast to counteract climate change and keep fossil fuels in the ground," and "100% renewable energy" (*Ballotpedia*). These would be only some of the issues that Debra Haaland would engage on once she entered the House of Representatives on January 3, 2019.

Joining the House

Debra Haaland, having entered the House of Representatives with an impressive background that included leadership within her state's Democratic Party and a reputation for being able to get things done, not surprisingly received a number of important assignments within both the House committee system and the Democratic Caucus. Among those committee assignments were Vice Chair of the Committee on Natural Resources; Chair of its Subcommittee on National Parks, Forests, and Public Lands; membership on its Subcommittee for Indigenous Peoples of the United States; and membership on the House Armed Services Committee and its subcommittees on Readiness and Military Personnel. She also was named the Freshman Class Representative to the House Democratic Steering and

Policy Committee and House Democratic Region VI Whip (an area that includes New Mexico, Texas, and Arizona). In December 2019, the Congresswoman was added to the House Committee on Oversight and Reform, the primary investigative committee in the House. The following January she was named to the Oversight and Reform Committee's Civil Rights and Civil Liberties Subcommittee, an appointment that she planned to use in order to ensure that every New Mexico resident would be counted in the 2020 census and to defend their voting rights (press release, 24 January 2020).

Haaland was named Co-Chair of the Native American Caucus, Vice Chair of the Equality Caucus, Vice Chair on Families and Children Living in Poverty for the Majority Leader Task Force on Poverty and Opportunity, Vice Chair for the Democratic Women's Working Group, and Deputy Whip for the Congressional Progressive Caucus. Among the many other caucuses and groups that she was named a member of were the Air Force Caucus, the Bipartisan Task Force to End Sexual Violence, the Congressional Human Trafficking Caucus, and the Safe Climate Caucus. (For a complete list, see Haaland's entry on the government website.)

Legislating for the People

Debra Haaland brought to the House a number of legislative concerns, especially relating to Native Americans, the environment, military veterans, members of the LGBTQ+ community, and immigration. The range of her interests included the type of focus on the environment that made her choice for Secretary of the Interior, in the minds of many observers, an obvious one. At the same time, her progressive stance on protecting the environment and on other issues would lead to most Republicans opposing her confirmation, which succeeded on a 50–41 vote with just four Republicans voting to approve her. Above all, however, she brought with her a serious commitment to represent members of her Congressional district, and more broadly, the people of New Mexico, a commitment that she displayed early and often. As she noted upon taking the oath of office, "I can't wait to bring New Mexico values to Congress. As the representative for the families in the state's first Congressional district, I will be an advocate for renewable energy jobs to protect our land, air and water, a fighter to expand opportunities for our kids, and a champion for equity" (press release, 3 January 2019).

Faced early in the year with a government shutdown, Haaland couched her concerns within a particular focus on residents of her state, stating, "The real national emergency right now is thousands of New Mexicans not being able to put food on the table or pay rent, because of the government shutdown" (press release, 8 January 2019). In response to the practical impact of the shutdown, she cosigned a letter to Secretary of Agriculture Sonny Perdue demanding information on how the government would address the lack of funding for the Supplemental Nutrition Assistance Program (SNAP), known more commonly as the food-stamp program. In a press release announcing the letter, Haaland turned, as she would do many times, to her own personal experiences: "Like many New Mexicans, I know what it's like to rely on food assistance to feed my family, and it's important that we get a full understanding of the effects this government shutdown will have on those benefits" (9 January 2019). Haaland followed up her statements by returning to New Mexico to meet with Transportation Security Administration workers at the Albuquerque International Airport on January 11. The next day she met with federal workers, small business owners, and local business leaders at Central New Mexico Community College in Albuquerque to discuss the effect of the government shutdown on a wide range of workers. Such meetings with groups of her constituents would become standard procedure for Haaland in order for her to remain in touch with those who had sent her to Congress.

Throughout the remainder of the year, then Representative Haaland conducted a great many listening and discussion sessions with constituents regarding a wide range of issues, such as shutdown-impacted workers, Native Americans' health care, hunger, sacred sites, and national monuments. She also instituted a pattern of supplying staff by means of a "mobile office" to help residents deal with federal agencies concerning such matters as Social Security, veterans' benefits, Medicare, Medicaid, and passports.

Given Haaland's lifelong connections to the military, it should not be surprising that her trips home have included visiting New Mexico's national laboratories: the Los Alamos National Laboratory, Sandia National Laboratories, White Sands Missile Range (where anti-missile systems are tested), and Trinity Test Site (the location of the first atomic bomb detonation). Supporting these sites would remain a high priority for her.

These constituent trips would often trigger personal responses. For example, invited to speak at the opening of the El Voto Feminino Exhibit at the National Hispanic Cultural Center in Albuquerque, an exhibit that featured *Pan American Unity*, a woodblock mural by the local artist Julianna Kirwin picturing a number of important American women, among them the late Supreme Court Justice Ruth Bader Ginsberg, the poet Joy Harjo, and Haaland herself, Haaand, as she often does, personalized the experience. She noted the responsibility that her positions within Congress and the mural place on her: "As a single mom, I remember focusing on ensuring my daughter had access to education, role models, and experiences that would expand the limits of her imagination, so that she could do whatever she wanted to do in life. And now that I'm in Congress, it's my goal to be a role model for young girls, so that they see someone like them in this position. We're here to leave the ladder down for those coming behind us—the work never stops" (press release, 24 January 2020).

Young people, especially in their role as students, have received considerable attention from Haaland. For example, on April 18 she was the commencement speaker at Southwestern Indian Polytechnic Institute, a member of the American Indian Higher Education Consortium. In a government class at Del Norte High School, she answered students' questions that ranged, as the Congresswoman's press release notes, from climate change and the border wall to the ban on transgender individuals serving in the military and the high cost of attending college (18 April 2019). Her return on May 3 included visits with fifth-grade classes at the San Antonito STEM Magnet Elementary School at Sandia Park, New Mexico; and with students at the Sandia Preparatory School in Albuquerque.

During a whirlwind round of appearances on May 11 and 12, Haaland honored students across a wide range of ages. On May 11, she gave the commencement address at her alma mater, the University of New Mexico School of Law. The address marked a return by Haaland to the law school where, on March 29, she had given the keynote address at a celebration of the twentieth anniversary of the *Tribal Law Journal*, the journal on which she had worked as a law student at the university. On May 12, she attended a reception honoring the high school winners of the Congressional Art Competition. Haaland and Chair Raul Grijalva of the House Committee on Natural Resources Committee hosted high school students from New Mexico for a mock hearing on June 24. The hearing was part of the curriculum for the Santa Fe Indian School Leadership Institute offered at Princeton University's Woodrow Wilson School of Public and International Affairs. Younger children were her primary audience on July 6, when she appeared on KUNM's *The Children's Hour* for a radio broadcast from the Central and Unser Library in Albuquerque. Later that month, she spoke at the Pre-Law Summer Institute at the American Indian Law Center at the University of New Mexico School of Law.

Consistent with her interest in education, the Congresswoman voted on January 16, 2020, to reverse the "Borrower Defense" rule that Secretary of Education Betsy DeVos had implemented, a change that limited the amount of relief a student can receive after being defrauded by a predatory college and that increased the difficulty of seeking relief. According to the press release from Haaland's office on January 16, at the close of 2019 almost one thousand New Mexico students were still awaiting Secretary DeVos' decision regarding their appeals for relief. A few days later, on January 21,

Haaland shifted her focus to high school students, announcing the Bosque High School winners of her Congressional App Competition.

Not surprisingly, many of the policies and legislative actions that Representative Haaland has supported relate directly to her view of what would benefit her constituents. Within approximately the first year of her entry into Congress, those efforts included attempts to raise the minimum wage; establish a Medicare for All health care program; increase access to voting by establishing same-day registration during early and election-day voting throughout the country; create a national budget that supports national parks, national labs, military installations, solar and wind energy, education, job creation, and Native American tribes; install wireless internet service on school buses to assist students who lack internet access in their homes; oppose the Trump administration's attempts to end the Affordable Care Act, especially its attempt to eliminate protections for people with pre-existing conditions; prohibit "lunch shaming" in schools, that is, any action that would embarrass students who cannot afford to pay for their school lunches; authorize an Energy Technology Maturation Program at the Department of Energy to facilitate national laboratories working in partnership with the private sector; and enact the Comprehensive Addiction Resources Emergency (CARE) Act, which would provide $100 billion nationally over ten years, including $10.4 million annually for New Mexico to combat drug addiction.

Additional Congressional efforts by Haaland that had a local, regional, or tribal focus included the Family First Transition and Support Act of 2019 to support state and tribal child welfare systems; the Mamas First Act to increase access to midwives and doulas under Medicaid; urging the Postal Service to improve its facilities in Albuquerque; the Universal Child Care and Early Learning Act to enable low-income families to secure free child care and early learning opportunities for their children; opposing storage of high-level nuclear waste in New Mexico; legislation to support increased research and treatment for Cavernous Cerebral Malformations (CCM), a disease affecting the brain and spinal cord primarily found in Hispanics in southwestern states; expanded compensation for people exposed to radiation from uranium mines or nuclear weapon sites; opposing the Trump administration's withdrawal of $125 million from construction projects at New Mexico military bases to use for construction of a wall at the Mexican border; an appeal to the Federal Emergency Management Agency to reimburse New Mexico locations and agencies for providing humanitarian assistance to asylum seekers; opposing the Trump administration's plan to reduce food stamp availability while pointing out that she herself had "relied on food stamps to feed my daughter and me when I was going to school as a single mom" (press release, 12 December 2019); and affirmation of a farmer's bill of rights.

Haaland's policy and legislative positions in the main represented majority positions in the Democratic-led House of Representatives to which she was elected. In the Republican-majority Senate, however, many of the legislative initiatives that she and the House supported met a brick wall either because of policy differences or because the Senate majority leader wanted to focus as much as possible on approving President Trump's judicial nominees.

Native Americans

Jennifer Steinhauer points out in her book *The Firsts: The Inside Story of The Women Reshaping Congress* that Deborah Haaland, as did Sharice Davids, ran for Congress openly as a Native American rather than seek

Debra Haaland, one of the first two Native American women elected to Congress, became, as Secretary of the Interior, the first Native American to be named to a Presidential Cabinet position (courtesy then–Representative Haaland's Congressional Office).

to submerge her cultural identity in favor of some sort of generic identity. Faced with pushback from some that she was playing identity politics, Haaland explained to Steinhauer: "It made me feel like, if you've always been represented in this country, then, yeah, I understand what you're saying. But if you've never been represented, if you've never seen yourself, it's hard to call it 'identity politics'" (191–92). Steinhauer writes that "Haaland is fully aware of the importance of her role to tribe members. 'They don't have to explain things to me. They can just come in and talk about their issue,' she told me, knowing that they have 'a congressperson who understands…'" (195).

While Haaland fully recognized that she represented everyone in the First Congressional District of New Mexico and, more broadly, had a responsibility to aid her entire state and the nation, she took her tribal responsibility seriously. It was, as a survey of her Congressional activities during her first year in Congress demonstrates, one of her highest priorities. Within her first month, she was participating in a hearing regarding how the government shutdown was affecting Native American tribes and listening to individuals from Indian Country testifying on its impact on their communities and on public lands (January 15, 2019). A few days later, on January 18, she was one of the speakers at the Indigenous People's March at the Lincoln Memorial and announcing that the march "is a national platform to raise the issues that negatively impact our communities the most— voter suppression, the border wall, the missing and murdered, human trafficking and lack of resources—just to name a few.... As one of the first Native American women in Congress, I see it as my responsibility to educate my colleagues about the federal government's trust responsibility and provide a voice to advocate for those who have historically not had a seat at the table to make a long-awaited change" (press release, 18 January 2019).

Haaland was named near the end of January as co-chair, along with Congressman Tom Cole, a Chickasaw and Republican from Oklahoma, of the bipartisan Native American Caucus. Accepting her role, Haaland promised to "be a strong advocate for Native communities in New Mexico and across the country to improve education opportunities, protect and increase access to quality healthcare, expand broadband services, address the silent crisis of missing and murdered Indigenous people, and ensure that tribal sovereignty is respected" (press release, 30 January 2019).

Among the many issues that Haaland has pursued relative to Native Americans, none have appeared to engage her personally more than Indigenous women who have been murdered and/or remain missing, along with related issues such as domestic abuse and suicide. When she delivered the formal response to National Congress of American Indians President Jefferson Keel's presentation on the State of Indian Nations, she both highlighted these concerns and foreshadowed her continuing efforts regarding them, affirming that the "crisis of missing and murdered Indigenous and violence against women cannot be overlooked any longer." She presented some of the sobering statistics regarding Native women, including that they are "10x more likely to be murdered and 4x more likely to be sexually assaulted when compared to the national average," and that "in 2016, it was reported that 8 in 10 Native women had survived serious violence during their lifetimes; 50% have suffered sexual violence; and 90% of these cases have involved a non–Native perpetrator." Haaland also pointed out legislation that she was supporting, such as "Savanna's Act and VAWA [the Violence Against Women Act] to provide our women with programmatic resources that will expand to urban areas where many Native Americans are frequently overlooked in this silent crisis" (press release, 11 February 2019).

The Violence Against Women Act became law in 1994. The act expired during the government shutdown of 2018–19 but was temporarily reinstated in January 2019. On February 15, 2019, the Violence Against Women Act expired again. Although the act was reauthorized by the House of Representatives in April 2019, with thirty-three Republicans joining Democrats in support, the Republican-controlled Senate refused to consider it. As summarized in a press release on May 5, 2019, Haaland introduced during her first year in Congress several bills or amendments in order to address issues related to Native American women who were victims of violence and/or had gone missing.

Haaland's efforts to move Congress to respond to the tragic realities that the leading cause of death in the United States for Indigenous women between the ages of ten and twenty-four is murder, that the murder rates for American Indian and Alaska Native women are ten times the national average, and that 84.3 percent of American Indian and Alaska Native women (press release, 14 March 2019) have suffered violence have taken many forms. On March 14, 2019, for example, she arranged for a hearing before the Subcommittee for Indigenous Peoples of the United States, the first hearing in the history of the House of Representatives on missing and murdered Indigenous women (press release, 13 March 2019). Several women representing Native tribes testified at the hearing.

On April 19, Haaland welcomed the Gathering of Nations to her Congressional district, which brought together Indigenous nations from around the world. The Miss Indian World competition occurred simultaneously. Together, the Congresswoman and both organizations announced their intention to "bring attention to missing and murdered Indigenous women as a call to action" (press release, 19 April 2019). Haaland continued to focus on this issue in her article "Women are Disappearing and Dying in Indian Country. We Must Act," published in *The Guardian* on May 2, 2019, to coincide with the forthcoming National Day of Awareness for Missing and Murdered Native Women and Girls (May 5). In her article, Haaland urges action: "We must commit as a country to the principle that every person deserves justice—every person deserves the same attention when they go missing, regardless of whether they are located in rural or urban areas, Native or an immigrant, rich or poor." She challenges "law enforcement around the country to commit to that effort," and personalizes this tragedy rather than rely solely on statistics: "When your community is at risk—when it could be your daughter, your sister or your mom—the issue demands urgency. The attention this issue has received wouldn't have been possible without the women in Indian country saying, 'enough is enough, we deserve to feel safe too.'"

As the twenty-fifth anniversary of the Violence Against Women Act approached, Debra Haaland and Tom Cole joined tribal leaders from throughout the country on September 11, 2019, to honor Native women survivors of violence. The event included a traditional shawl ceremony, with the red shawl symbolizing protection and, with its color, love for all.

Close to two years later, Secretary Haaland was vowing in her Senate confirmation hearings to give the issues of violence against Native American women and Native women who have gone missing high priority. In the Congress, reauthorization and updating of the Violence Against Women Act seemed more possible. On March 8, 2021, a bill to accomplish this was introduced in the House of Representatives.

Many other issues impacting Native Americans also have occupied Debra Haaland's time and concern. To name a few: protecting food stamp eligibility; ensuring accurate census counting on tribal lands; improving housing conditions in Indian Country; correcting Native maternal health disparities, chronic kidney disease, and diabetes among Native Americans; and addressing nutritional deficiencies and obesity among children, cycles of poverty in Indian Country, and health care and other challenges facing Native American veterans. She also is committed to strengthening Native culture (including access to wildlife and rebuilding the buffalo population), increasing funding for Native libraries, supporting tribal sovereignty, safeguarding tribal cultural and religious items, encouraging economic development, securing and extending Native Americans' right to vote, and encouraging Native language programs.

In some cases, efforts by Haaland and others resulted in substantial financial support, for example, $114 million from the Indian Health Service to construct three New Mexico facilities and $2.5 million for research into causes of kidney disease among Native Americans. A rare piece of legislation that made its way into becoming law during Haaland's first session of Congress was the Esther Martinez Native American Languages Programs Reauthorization Act, named after a revered traditional storyteller from the Ohkay Owingeh Pueblo. The bill, as summarized in Haaland's press release of July 9, 2019, reauthorized two federal Native American language programs until 2024 and expanded eligibility for participation to "smaller-sized Tribal language programs."

Haaland's guest Isleta Pueblo Chief Judge Verna Teller on November 13, 2019, became the first Native American to offer the opening prayer in the House of Representatives. Haaland herself on March 7 had become the first Native American to preside over House debate from the Speaker's chair. In November, she led a bipartisan group recognizing November as National Native American Heritage Month, a designation that had been signed into law by President George H.W. Bush in 1990. She also cosponsored a bill to change Columbus Day into Indigenous Peoples' Day, a change that already had occurred in New Mexico. Another "first" that drew Haaland's attention was the selection of Joy Harjo as poet laureate: "Joy Harjo's voice has been so important to the stories that need to be told, and now she's making history as the 1st Native American United States Poet Laureate" (press release, 19 June 2019).

Public Lands and the Environment

Debra Haaland's efforts to achieve greater justice and a better life for Native Americans and her commitment to protecting the environment are complementary, as the Antiquities Act, which she co-sponsored in February 2019, demonstrates. The full title of the bill is The America's Natural Treasures of Immeasurable Quality Unite, Inspire, and Together Improve the Economies of States Act of 2019. Many of the nation's public lands include sites sacred to Native Americans. In introducing this bill, the first piece of legislation that Haaland introduced in Congress, she noted: "As my first piece of legislation this bill expands on my efforts to fight climate change by protecting land from extraction, honor our sacred sites, and ensure our beautiful places are here for future generations. Our public lands are not for sale" (press release, 7 February 2019).

The same press release states that the act "comes in response to President Trump's attempt to eliminate 2 million acres of protections for Utah's Bears Ears and Grand Staircase-Escalante national monuments." On December 4, 2017, President Trump had reduced Bears Ears acreage by approximately 85 percent and Grand Staircase Escalante by about 47 percent. The act would express support for the fifty-two national monuments that presidents had established from 1996 to 2018, reinforce the law that requires an act of Congress to reduce a national monument created by presidential proclamation, protect Bears Ears National Monument, and create additional public lands in New Mexico and Nevada (press release, 7 February 2019).

Although the Antiquities Act did not become law, portions of it were included in the Public Lands Package, which did pass Congress and was signed into law by President Trump on March 12, 2019. Among other provisions, the Public Lands Package created 273,000 wilderness acres, authorized millions of dollars for public lands and recreational sites through the Land and Water Conservation Fund, and supported New Mexico's outdoor-based economy.

One of the public land areas that has especially drawn the Congresswoman's attention and commitment is the Bears Ears National Monument.

She supported reintroduction of the Bears Ears Expansion and Respect for Sovereignty Act on January 30, 2019, legislation that would expand the monument to 1.9 million acres, include additional land identified by tribes as home to "sacred artifacts and cultural resources," and restore tribal consultation in managing the Native American archeological and sacred sites at Bears Ears, which number over 100,000 (press release, 30 January 2019).

It is certain that as Secretary of the Interior, Haaland's commitment to Bears Ears as well as to other sacred sites and public monuments remains strong. An article in *National Catholic Reporter* after Haaland's confirmation includes supportive and optimistic statements from a number of Indigenous and environmental individuals and organizations concerning Haaland's role as Secretary. The executive director of New Mexico Interfaith Power & Light, Sr. Joan Brown, specifically references Bears Ears National Monument and her hope that Haaland will restore Bears Ears to what it was previously (Roewe 5).

Another specific site that Representative Haaland has exerted great effort to protect is the Chaco Culture National Historical Park located in northwestern New Mexico. The park is an important pre–Columbian historical site and includes extensive ancient ruins. She, along with several colleagues, reintroduced the Chaco Cultural Heritage Area Protection Act to prevent drilling or mining for minerals within a ten-mile radius of the park. Haaland noted that Chaco Canyon "is a sacred place that should be valued the same way we value other sacred places" and that "public lands must be protected" (press release, 9 April 2019).

Haaland's efforts were likely at least partly responsible for New Mexico Land Commissioner Stephanie Garcia Richard's executive order on April 30, 2019, declaring a moratorium on new oil and gas development on state land around Chaco. In May, the Tenth Circuit Court of Appeals "ruled that the Bureau of Land Management had illegally approved dozens of oil and gas drilling permits when the agency failed to account for the cumulative impacts of hydraulic fracturing near Chaco Canyon and Chaco Culture National Historical Park" (press release, 29 May 2019). On May 29, Haaland, as Chair of the House Subcommittee on National Parks, Forests, and Public Lands, announced in a press release that Secretary of the Interior David Bernhardt had agreed to place "a year-long hold on leasing within a ten-mile perimeter around Chaco Canyon." However, as the Trump Administration approached what would be its end, plans had resumed for extensive oil and gas extraction around Chaco.

For Haaland, the natural environment should be enjoyed, but nature must be preserved in order to be enjoyed, and its continued existence in anything like its present condition, Haaland recognizes, is in serious jeopardy because of climate change and those human actions, including oil and gas development projects, that have the potential to alter the climate with great harm to individual locales and the planet as a whole. Accordingly, Haaland strongly supported the Climate Action Now Act, which called for the United States remaining in the Paris Agreement. The bill did not become law, but in 2021 President Biden resumed membership in the Paris Agreement.

Haaland's efforts regarding the environment are not the result of a recent conversion. Tom Solomon, co-coordinator of 350 New Mexico, a climate organization, stated of her earlier work that she "has been a pretty fierce climate advocate for a long time" and described her important role in establishing alliances among environmentalists and Indigenous communities that helped lead to the Energy Transition Act, mandating that public utilities in New Mexico achieve "clean and renewable energy standards by 2045," which became law in New Mexico in March 2019 (press release, 15 May 2019).

The major threats to clean air and water, unpolluted land, protection of sacred sites, and general public health, in Haaland's estimation, include oil and gas development projects. She has supported legislation that would compel companies to finance cleanup efforts from mining on public lands, protect the residents of Sandoval Country in New Mexico from damage to their environment and their health from a proposed gravel mine, and reduce toxic emissions from oil and gas drilling. Haaland states in a press release of May 14, 2019, that "when I toured drilling sites near Chaco Canyon, it was clear that many people in New Mexico are breathing in air poisoned by methane emissions released by oil and gas companies."

She has alerted citizens and lawmakers to problems with PFAS contamination (perfluoroalkyl and polyfluoroalkyl substances used in many products, including firefighting foam) of groundwater near Air Force bases in New Mexico and throughout the country. Although the PFAS Damages Act did not become law, some of its provisions were included in the National Defense Authorization Act of 2020. In October 2019, Haaland, along with other members of the New Mexico Congressional delegation, introduced the Western Water Security Act to improve water management and address the effects of extended drying conditions in the West caused by climate change. Looking farther into the future, Haaland on February 7 co-sponsored the Thirty by Thirty Resolution to Save Nature, which set goals of conserving at least 30 percent of ocean water and land by 2030 (press release, 7 February 2020).

On these and other environmental issues, Debra Haaland, as Secretary of the Interior, has the opportunity to have a much larger impact than she did as a member of the House. Certainly, a great many individuals and organizations are counting on that.

Honoring Those Who Serve

As the child of military parents, Debra Haaland became acquainted with military life as a child and has retained her identification with the rewards and challenges of military life. Upon entering the House of Representatives, Haaland wasted no time in moving to support the military, including the welfare of individual military members and their families and also retired veterans, along with the broader military establishment, including important military installations in New Mexico. On being named to the House Armed Services Committee and its Readiness and Military Personnel Subcommittees, she said, "As someone who grew up in a military family, I know that our service members are at their best when their families receive top-notch support while they are busy training for critical missions. These subcommittees will allow me to work for our district and state by ensuring the folks who serve at Kirtland Air Force Base, the Air Force Research labs, and Sandia National Labs have support to execute their missions, and that these installations can continue to create jobs that contribute to our economy" (press release, 23 January 2019).

Haaland's concern for the welfare of service members has especially focused on housing, recognizing that substandard housing not only affects military families when they are together at home but poses an additional worry for individuals away from the base who are concerned about the family members they left behind. In a press release dated March 13, 2019, Rear Admiral Titley is quoted stating at a subcommittee hearing of the Readiness Subcommittee of the House Armed Services Committee that "while they are forward deployed, there's nothing more distracting than when you think your family is not safe."

In order to gain firsthand knowledge of military housing conditions, Haaland has met with many military families, including through town halls at which she and Kirtland commanders discussed housing issues with Kirtland residents. In April 2019, Haaland and Senator Elizabeth Warren introduced the Military Housing Oversight and Service Member Protection Act in response to reports of "unsafe and unsanitary conditions in privatized, on-base housing for military personnel and their families" (press release, 26 April 2019). The same press release includes Haaland's listing of problems with the housing, including "mold, infestation, and structural problems." The bill, among other provisions, would enhance military families' rights to ensure that their homes are safe and clean, along with providing for compensation and medical treatment for family members who developed medical problems because of the housing. However, as with much legislation during Haaland's first term, this bill did not become law.

Debra Haaland, however, played an important role in getting provisions into the National Defense Authorization Act for 2020 that included housing protections, among them a tenant bill of rights for military families, a mechanism for tracking housing complaints, and efforts to remove mold from housing units. Her concerns regarding the quality of military housing were further substantiated by a report on privatized military housing released by the U.S. Army Inspector General in September 2019. Increased funding for military family housing and research and development possibilities for Kirtland were among provisions that she helped incorporate into the 2021 National Defense Authorization Act.

In addition to housing, Haaland has expressed great concern for the health of military personnel, their families, and veterans. She has visited the Veterans Benefits Administration office in Albuquerque to discuss how better to reach veterans who live in rural New Mexico. She noted at the time that she is the child of military parents and that her mother continues to receive benefits through the Veterans Administration (press release, 29 August 2019). As a member of the Women's Veteran Taskforce, she supported good health care for the growing number of women veterans, including in such areas as gynecology and obstetrics. With suicide a significant problem afflicting the military as well as the rest of the country (in recent years more than 6,000 veterans annually having ended their lives by suicide), Haaland also became involved in addressing this issue. During September of 2019, for example, she co-hosted with Congressman Steven Horsford of Nevada a veterans' panel to hear from individuals who have worked with veterans considering suicide.

On Memorial Day in 2019, Haaland met with Gold Star Mothers in Albuquerque and then addressed the audience at a ceremony honoring those who have died for their country. Speaking very personally about her childhood in a military family, she recalled how when her father, Major Dutch Haaland, had gone to Vietnam when she was six years old, Haaland's mother, Mary Toya, had Debra and her siblings write letters to their father every night. After his death in 2005, his family discovered those letters in his footlocker. This daughter of two military veterans said, "When I assumed my role on the House Armed Services Committee, I made it my core mission to ensure we provide every support we can to the brave women and men who carry on the traditions of service that we honor today" (press release, 27 May 2019). Symbolizing the Congresswoman's commitment, she invited Brigadier General Michele LaMontagne, Commander of the Air National Guard at Kirtland, to be her guest at President Trump's State of the Union address on February 4, 2020. As the Congresswoman's press release of February 3 notes, "General LaMontagne is the second woman and the first openly LGBTQ+ person to serve in this leadership position at the New Mexico Air National Guard."

Supporting Inclusiveness

Very early in Debra Haaland's tenure in the House of Representatives, she spoke out in response to the Supreme Court's ruling in support of President Trump's ban on transgender individuals serving in the military: "Preventing people from devoting their lives to their country simply due to their gender identity is a cruel affront on American values.... This irrational ban distracts from service, does nothing to promote military readiness, and directly opposes the American belief in coming together to support our country regardless of background" (press release, 22 January 2019). The ban struck at multiple points of congruence for Haaland: her own experiences as a member of a military family, her commitment to aid current and past members of the military, and her strong belief in the rights and dignity of members of the LGBTQ+ community. On February 27, Haaland met with transgender members of the military who were about to testify before the House Armed Services Committee, pointing out that transgender service members "come from families in which service is a tradition, they go through the same training and abide by the same requirements, and they are actively serving overseas. They deserve fairness and respect" (press release, 27 February 2019).

A few days later, Haaland celebrated her membership on the Equality Caucus, which "serves as a resource for Members of Congress, their staff, and the public on LGBT issues at the federal level," with Bunnie Benton Cruse, Chair of the New Mexico Transgender Resource Center Board of Directors at the Congresswoman's office in Washington. Haaland put the transgender flag up outside her office as a symbol of her resolve to help transgender individuals. Adrian N. Carver, Executive Director of Equality New Mexico, recognized that resolve, declaring that "Congresswoman Haaland has long been a champion of the LGBTQ+ community in New Mexico—she has always sought ways to create opportunity for our community" (press release, 30 January 2019). Another important leader in the transgender community, Mara Keisling, Executive Director of the National Center for Transgender Equality, was Representative Haaland's guest at the State of the Union on February 5, 2019.

Representative Haaland's concern for equal rights and equal justice is directed toward not just transgender individuals but rather the entire LGBTQ+ community. Some examples include her introduction of the Elder Pride Act in April 2019, which would create an office of Inclusivity and

Sexual Health in Health and Human Services and offer grants to organizations that serve LGBTQ+ seniors; her reception of the National Center for Lesbian Rights Vanguard Award for using her Congressional platform to advance equality for members of the LGBTQ+ community; writing to the Trump Administration to oppose its interpretation of the Immigration and Nationality Act, which denies citizenship to children born outside of the United States through "assisted reproductive practices" (press release, 6 June 2019); and commemorating the fiftieth anniversary of the Stonewall Uprising, which was in response to a violent raid by police conducted on June 28, 1969, on the Stonewall Inn, a New York City bar frequented by gays and lesbians.

Significant change on one LGBTQ+ issue important to Secretary Haaland occurred when President Biden withdrew the ban on transgender individuals serving in the military.

Immigration and a New Role

Immigration is another subject that enjoyed Debra Haaland's attention during her time in Congress. Her principled positions and compassion regarding immigrants have not gone unnoticed. On February 16, 2019, she was honored with the William C. Velasquez Trailblazer award from the U.S. Hispanic Leadership Institute. In presenting the award, Cindy Nava, Chief Administrative Officer of the Institute, said of the Congresswoman: "Deb's track record working to represent communities of color in New Mexico is proof of her passion and willingness to create platforms for unheard communities to rise" (press release, 20 February 2019). In co-sponsoring legislation to create the National Museum of the American Latino, Haaland stated, in explaining her involvement, "Although Latinos represent the largest ethnic group in the nation, their innumerable contributions to American culture and history are often ignored by our history books" (press release, 18 October 2019). A directive approving the museum was included in the large Consolidated Appropriations Act enacted in December 2020 that also included $900 billion in stimulus relief in response to the coronavirus pandemic.

The compassion and commitment that Haaland has demonstrated toward Native Americans and members of the military, as well as toward others, is very much in evidence in her Congressional statements and actions where immigrants and refugees are concerned. In October 2019, she and other members of the New Mexico delegation succeeded in gaining $30 million in grants through the National Board for the Emergency Food and Shelter Program to reimburse local civic and church-related entities for the expenses that they incurred in assisting asylum seekers. In the same month, Haaland, along with Representative Pramila Jayapal of Washington State, introduced the Health Equity and Access under the Law for Immigrant Women and Families Act. The legislation would remove barriers to Medicaid and health care insurance under the Affordable Care Act that currently exist for immigrants. She also opposed President Trump's plan to reduce sharply the number of refugee admissions per year, stating that "refugees are an essential part of our communities—they pay taxes, build businesses, their children have friends at school, and they deserve to be safe and create better lives for their families" (press release, 23 October 2019).

Haaland's support for immigrants led her to vote against the Fiscal Year 2020 budget minibus (a minibus being a bill that includes only a few appropriations rather than a more comprehensive omnibus appropriations bill), even though the bill included some features that she supported, because the bill retained a large number of ICE (U.S. Immigration and Customs Enforcement) detention beds and supported the administration's efforts to build a border wall while, in her words, "forcing immigrant parents to make heartbreaking decisions because of a senseless *remain in Mexico* policy" (press release, 17 December 2019).

Haaland has also opposed the rising prevalence of hateful rhetoric and hate crimes against immigrants. She has consistently opposed such policies and actions regarding immigrants at the Southern border as separation of families and requiring asylum seekers to remain in Mexico while awaiting processing. The separation of children from their parents is something, Haaland notes, that Native Americans historically have been well aware of (press release, 10 May 2019). She wrote to Federal Bureau of Investigation Director Christopher Wray in April 2019 requesting an investigation of militia groups patrolling the Southwest border to inhibit asylum seekers attempting to enter the United States. Another demand for an investigation occurred in early November, this time calling on Homeland Security to examine ICE actions regarding the death of Roxana Hernandez, a Honduran transgender woman, who died in ICE detention.

The Dreamers and others with similar status have received Haaland's support as well. In March 2019, she co-sponsored the Dream and Promise Act "to protect our Dreamers [those who came to this country as children and are protected under the Deferred Action for Childhood Arrivals (DACA) program established by President Obama], Temporary Protected Status (TPS) and Deferred Enforced Departure (DED) holders, allowing them to contribute fully to New Mexico's communities and the country while providing a pathway to citizenship" (press release, 18 March 2019). In June, she supported a similar bill, the Dream and Promise Act, which passed the House of Representatives.

At a roundtable discussion with Hispanic leaders during Hispanic Heritage Month, October 2019, the Congresswoman and other participants expressed concern regarding what the Supreme Court might decide in response to the administration's attempt to invalidate DACA. Haaland signed an amicus brief in support of the program. As of this writing, the Court has ruled that the position argued by the Trump administration was inadequate, granting temporary relief to the hundreds of thousands of Dreamers.

Throughout her term in Congress, Haaland remained focused on these and other issues that impact the welfare of Americans in New Mexico and throughout the country. Although elected to a second term, she agreed to accept appointment as Secretary of the Interior rather than continue in Congress. Some of the issues discussed above do not directly relate to this new position, but Haaland will have an opportunity to continue her advocacy for her policy positions in Cabinet sessions as she carries out her primary duties in her history-making role as Secretary of the Interior.

REFERENES

Agoyo, Acee. "Native Women Make History with Seats in New Congress." *Indianz.com* 4 Jan. 2019. indianz.com/News/2019/01/04/native-women-make-history-congress.asp.

"Congresswoman Deb Haaland Representing the 1st District of New Mexico." Press Releases. Congressional website. haaland.house.gov/media/press-releases; also About.haaland.house.gov/about.

"Debra Haaland." *Ballotpedia.* ballotpedia.org/Debra_Haaland.

Haaland, Debra Anne. "Women are Disappearing and Dying in Indian Country. We Must Act." *The Guardian* 2 May 2019. theguardian.com/commentisfree/2019/may/02/missing-murdered-indigenous-women-deb-haaland.

Manning, Sarah Sunshine. "Two Native American Women Are Headed to Congress. This Is Why It Matters." *The Washington Post* 8 Nov. 2018. washingtonpost.com/outlook/2018/11/08/two-native-american-women-are-headed-congress-this-is-why-it-matters/?noredirect=on.

Moscatello, Caitlin. *See Jane Win: The Inspiring Story of the Women Changing American Politics.* New York: Dutton, 2019.

New York Times. The Women of the 116th Congress. Foreword by Roxane Gay. New York: Abrams Image, 2019.

"Obituaries: Haaland." *Albuquerque Journal* 4 Mar. 2005. obits.abqjounral.com/obits/show/15 1921.

Roewe, Brian. "Indigenous, Environmental Groups Celebrate Confirmation." *National Catholic Reporter* 2–15 Apr. 2021: 5.

Steinhauer, Jennifer. *The Firsts: The Inside Story of the Women Reshaping Congress.* Chapel Hill: Algonquin Books of Chapel Hill, 2020.

Tobias, Jimmy. "'It's My Homeland': The Trailblazing Native Lawmaker Fighting Fossil Fuels." *The Guardian* 15 May 2019. theguardian.com/environment/2019/may/15/deb-haaland-public-lands-fighting-trump-drilling.

13

Sharice Lynnette Davids
(b. 1980)

On January 3, 2019, the first session of the 116th Congress convened. The list of firsts for women in the United States Congress was extensive, a list catalogued in *The New York Times* publication *The Women of the 116th Congress: Portraits of Power* (182–83). Among the firsts were the first Native American women to be elected to Congress: Sharice Davids, a member of the Ho-Chunk (Winnebago) nation, elected to represent Kansas's Third Congressional District; and Debra Haaland, a Laguna Pueblo chosen in New Mexico's First Congressional District. Davids established still other firsts by becoming the initial openly gay individual elected to Congress from Kansas as well as the first Native American member of the LGBTQ+ community to be elected. Like Debra Haaland, Sharice Davids came to Washington with a great deal of relevant experience and quickly became an important member of a Congress that not only engaged with a wide range of policy issues but also faced the impeachment of the President of the United States.

Youth

Sharice Lynnette Davids was born on May 22, 1980, in Shawnee, Kansas, in the Kansas City area near the Missouri border. Her maternal grandfather, Frederick J. Davids, an army veteran, was born into the Stockbridge-Munsee band of the Mohican Nation in Oneida, Wisconsin. Over almost thirty years, he served during three wars: World War II, the Korean War, and the Vietnam War. Davids' daughter, Crystal Herriage, followed her father into the military, serving over twenty years before working for the U.S. Postal Service and, following her daughter's lead, earning a college degree from the University of Missouri–Kansas City. Crystal, a member of the Ho-Chunk Nation (formerly known as the Wisconsin

Winnebago Tribe), reared Sharice as a single mother, inspiring her daughter to achieve considerable success both academically and professionally while also developing a strong commitment to helping military veterans that she would take with her to Congress.

Sharice Davids attended Leavenworth High School, the Haskell Indian Nations University, the University of Kansas, Johnson County Community College (where she earned an associate degree in liberal arts in 2003), and the University of Missouri–Kansas City. She graduated from UMKC in 2007 with a B.A. in Business Administration, focusing especially on small business and accounting, emphases that corresponded to some of her job experiences, which included serving as an assistant manager at the Sonic Drive-In, driving for the Corkscrew Wine Company, working as a barista at The Coffee Break, and assisting with operations for the Downtown Kansas City Marriott as an executive meetings coordinator. Following graduation, Davids attended Cornell Law School, earning her law degree in 2010. She was admitted to the Missouri Bar later that year after passing the Missouri Bar Examination in July. While a law student, she served as a summer associate in the Corporate Practice Group for Sonnenschein Nath & Rosenthall LLP, an international law firm that in 2010 merged with Denton Wilde Sapte of London, forming SNR Denton (biographical information from Davids' *LinkedIn* profile and *Ballotpedia*).

Professional Background

After being admitted to the Missouri and South Dakota bars in September 2010, Sharice Davids worked for SNR Denton for almost two years in the firm's Corporate and Indian Law & Tribal Representation Practice Groups. This was not the first time that Davids had taken a position that allowed her to assist Native Americans. During the summer of 2008, she had worked as a teaching assistant in the American Indian Law Center, helping students improve their research and legal writing skills.

Davids left SNR Denton in August 2012 to become Director of Economic Development for the Red Cloud Indian School on the Pine Ridge Indian Reservation in South Dakota. According to Davids' *LinkedIn* profile, she "[d]eveloped a full entrepreneurial program at Red Cloud Indian School, including high school coursework and an after-school program and created a small business incubator for alumni and community members." The school, according to its website, is "administered by the Jesuits and the Lakota people"; the website offers a detailed description of its Economic Development Initiative, which "gives Red Cloud students the knowledge, tools, and support necessary to develop their own business plans or even launch their own start-up companies." The program includes, in addition to the business curriculum, the 7 Gen Business Center, which offers "one-on-one business development mentoring right on campus" and start-up support that can include "a limited amount of funding to cover startup costs." Davids' interest in aiding with small-business development would continue to be evident in her subsequent pre–Congressional experiences as well as in her efforts as a U.S. Representative.

Coinciding with, but also extending beyond, Davids' years at Red Cloud Indian School was her work with Ceiba Legal, LLP, which provides legal representation to individual Native Americans, tribal governments, and businesses that wish to establish partnerships with tribes. In November 2014, Davids accepted a new position on the Pine Ridge Indian Reservation as a member of the leadership team, serving as Deputy Director of the Thunder Valley Community Development Corporation. She managed, according to her LinkedIn profile, "a variety of projects and activities, including creating organizational infrastructure to accommodate personnel and budget growth, legal needs, community development project management." Among the initiatives implemented during Davids' tenure on the leadership team (November 2014–August 2016) were a program to help young adults develop home construction skills and a concerted effort to encourage locally grown food.

During the final fifteen months that Davids was with the Thunder Valley Community Development Corporation, she also served on the Board of Directors of Twelve Clans, Inc., and for a time as its chairperson. Twelve Clans, according to the mission statement on its website, is "the sovereign wealth fund of the Ho-Chunk Nations" and "provides diversified business and investment resources for the future development of the Nation." In August 2016, she left her positions with the Development Corporation and Twelve Clans to go to Washington, D.C.

Mixed Martial Arts Athlete, Small Business Advocate, and White House Fellow

Sharice Davids would take a fascinating array of experiences and talents into her first political race. No shrinking violet in facing opponents, she entered the world of mixed martial arts in 2006, winning five of six amateur contests. In 2013, she briefly stepped up to professional status, splitting two contests. Politics may not be a contact sport, but it certainly can demand courage, strength, and moral, if not physical, stamina, qualities honed in her athletic endeavors as well as in her ongoing role as an activist for the rights of Native Americans, LGBTQ+ individuals, the poor, and those trying to make a better life for themselves by entering the business world.

Davids was the guiding force behind the creation of Starty Pants, which, as the organization states, was created "to contribute to the celebration of people who are breaking the mold of what an entrepreneur or start up founder looks like. We primarily highlight women, people of color and LGBTQ entrepreneurs." Videos present interviews with such people as the African American Whitney Manney, the creator and designer of a new fashion label featuring ready-to-wear fashionable clothing, interviewed by Sharice Davids. The name is an obvious play on "smarty pants," which typically denotes someone who seems to step out of his or her assigned role with comments and/or actions considered socially improper. The individuals highlighted by Davids clearly are crossing the stereotyped boundaries established by much of society but are doing so not only appropriately but with considerable success.

This desire to help people become what they can be was surely reinforced for Sharice Davids by her tenure as a White House Fellow in Washington, D.C. She was one of sixteen people selected to spend 2016–17 in the White House Fellowship program. There she worked in the Department of Transportation during the conclusion of President Barack Obama's second term as President. Davids' announcement of her candidacy for United States Representative highlighted the catalytic impact of her time as a White House Fellow: "After completing a year as a White House Fellow in Washington during the Obama-Trump transition," she stated, " I know that now is the time to take action for our community and for our nation."

On to Washington

Winning election to the House of Representatives from the 3rd Congressional District in Kansas was not going to be easy. Seeking reelection to his fifth term was Republican Kevin Yoder. In addition, Sharice Davids had several primary opponents seeking the Democratic nomination. Brent Welder gave Davids a hotly contested race, with Davids finishing first with 37.3 percent of the primary votes to Welder's 33.8 percent, according to final results published by *Ballotpedia*. Tom Niermann took 14.3 percent of the votes, with the rest going to Mike McCamon (7.0 percent), Sylvia Williams (4.7 percent), and Jay Sidie (2.9 percent).

Meanwhile, Yoder was easily renominated, 68.1 percent to Trevor Keegan's 18.7 percent and Joe Myers' 13.2 percent. In the general election, Davids emphasized several themes. In *Ballotpedia*'s survey on July 9, 2018, Davids listed as her top priorities:

Safe communities
Easy access to quality affordable healthcare
Excellent education no matter your zip code

In the same survey, she also highlighted as issues that she was passionate about "Increasing transparency and participation" and "Addressing systemic and structural barriers that prevent equality."

Davids' campaign website emphasized opposition to the Republican tax bill as "a corporate giveaway and a handout to the wealthiest 1 percent of Americans," the "financial burden" that it would impose on subsequent generations, and that small businesses "are the lifeblood of America and need to be front of mind when creating economic policy." She promised to work for a middle-class tax cut and support small businesses. Attempting to establish a personal connection with her potential constituents, she labeled a campaign ad released on October 24, 2018, as "Working for You" (*Ballotpedia*). Other issues that she raised included gun violence and the need for expanded Medicaid coverage. Her campaign materials also illustrated her mixed martial arts expertise, emphasizing her willingness to fight for the people she would represent.

Many voters were motivated by the desire to see an Indigenous woman who also was a member of the LGBTQ+ community achieve political influence. LGBTQ+ rights had become an important issue for a great many Kansas people, especially after the Kansas Legislature, a few months before the election, passed legislation allowing faith-based adoption agencies that rejected same-sex couples to retain state funding. About a month prior to the election, Davids visited Q-Space, an organization of LGBTQ+ young people. She spoke with them, hugged each one, and clearly empathized with their concerns, demonstrating her commitment to a population marginalized by the state political establishment (Lowry and Bergen).

When the final results were in, Davids had won with 53.6 percent of the vote. Yoder, who earlier in the year had become chairperson of the Homeland Security Budget Committee and was thus responsible for funding President Trump's wall along the southern border, had 43.9 percent, with the remaining 2.5 percent going to the Libertarian candidate, Chris Clemmons (*Ballotpedia*).

Joining the House

Sharice Davids was sworn in as a member of the 116th Congress on January 3, 2019. On November 29, 2018, the Democratic caucus had elected her, along with Representative Jesus "Chuy" Garcia of Illinois, as co-whip for Region 4, which includes the Democratic representatives from

Illinois, Indiana, Kansas, Missouri, and Oklahoma. Her responsibilities as a co-whip, according to a press release of November 30, would include "lining up support for policy positions, tracking votes, and ensuring Members are present on the House floor for close votes." Her selection for this position illustrated the important roles being given to new House members even as the Democratic caucus was selecting former Speaker Nancy Pelosi to serve again as the leader of the House of Representatives.

The House committees and subcommittees to which Sharice Davids was appointed generally coincided with the priorities that she especially cared about and for which she ran for election to the House of Representatives. For example, Davids was appointed to the House Transportation and Infrastructure Committee. Although the committee may not sound especially engaging, in fact it can have considerable influence on people's everyday lives. As Davids notes in a press release of January 17, 2019, the committee "has jurisdiction over areas that touch every aspect of our lives—especially so in the Kansas City Metro area with its strategic position in our country's heartland as a major transportation hub," adding that she looks forward to advocating "for much needed economic development and investment in our roadways, airport, railways, transit network, and local water infrastructure." The press release points out that during her tenure as a White House Fellow, Davids had worked under Secretary Anthony Foxx in the Department of Transportation and emphasizes the experience that gave her in "economic and community development ... bringing infrastructure to communities that lacked it."

Davids' appointment, announced in a press release a few days later (25 January 2019), to the House Small Business Committee meshed well with the earlier appointment regarding policy areas. Davids states in the press release:

> Entrepreneurship is baked into the DNA of the Kansas Third District and I appreciate the opportunity to bring that voice and vision to the Small Business Committee.... I look forward to supporting our small businesses and helping make sure they have the tools they need to take care of their employees, grow their companies, and contribute to our economy.

The release adds that Davids intends to help "small businesses through increasing access to capital, advocating for fair taxation, and reducing hurdles to success." The same press release announces her membership on three subcommittees of the Transportation and Infrastructure Committee: Highways and Transit, Economic Development, and Aviation.

Representative Davids moved quickly to highlight her local constituents, discussing local entrepreneurs and businesses at hearings of the Transportation and Infrastructure Committee and the Small Business Subcommittee on Economic Growth, Tax, and Capital Access on February 7. In the former, she pointed out the importance of the Highway Trust Fund to her district, focusing especially on the U.S. 69 Corridor expansion project through Overland Park and the North Loop project, which affected Wyandotte County. She also discussed concerns that employees at the Kansas City Air Route Traffic Control Center in Olathe had shared with her during a recent "Sharice's Shift," a job shadowing program that Davids had originated in order to ascertain challenges facing businesses in the Third District. In the latter hearing, she explored, according to the press release, "the challenges faced by minority-owned, women-owned, and veteran-owned" businesses, three categories of individuals whom Davids would continue to support, and how the owners have managed to overcome those challenges.

In early March, Davids was tabbed by her party to be a member of the New Democrat Coalition's Healthcare and Technology task forces. The Healthcare Task Force, according to the press release announcing her

appointment (4 March 2019), focuses "on ways to stabilize the individual markets and protect and expand on the ACA [the Affordable Care Act, or Obamacare] to work toward universal affordable health care." Effective and affordable health care would continue to be an important focus for Davids during the Congressional session. The Technology Task Force, which Davids was selected to co-chair, is concerned with such issues as "emerging technology, global competitiveness, innovation, data privacy and artificial intelligence."

April brought yet another role for Representative Davids: Vice Chair of the Subcommittee on Aviation within the Committee on Transportation and Infrastructure. Congressman Peter De Fazio of Oregon, chair of

Sharice Davids joined Debra Haaland in 2018 as the first Native American women elected to Congress. She also became the first openly gay individual to represent Kansas in Congress (courtesy Representative Davids' Congressional Office).

the committee, in a press release (9 April 2019), praised Davids' contributions to the committee, adding, "As Vice Chair, Congresswoman Davids will play a key role as the Committee not only continues its work to ensure the safety of our Nation's airspace, but also as we work to improve our critical airport infrastructure, create good-paying aviation jobs across the country, and integrate new users and technologies that will shape the future of U.S. aviation." He further noted that Representative Davids "represents the hardworking women and men at the FAA Kansas City Air Route Traffic Control Center."

Legislating for the People

Sharice Davids lost no time in attempting to connect with her constituents. On the day when she was sworn in as the Third District Representative, she announced that she would locate a District Office in Overland Park, Kansas, at 7325 West 79th Street, the location of her predecessor's office. She retained the same phone number that Congressman Yoder had used, making it as easy as possible for her constituents to connect with her. Retaining the same location and phone number also implied an appealing bipartisan attitude on her part. She announced a second office in Wyandotte County in Kansas City, to be located in the Brotherhood Building at 7th and Minnesota, the first Third District Congressional office in Wyandotte County in years. The county office opened on March 21, preceded the day before by an open house to welcome county residents. As she stated in a press release (23 January 2019), "It's important that I'm hearing from people from all corners of this district and I hope people from WyCo will visit us often and consider us a resource." The press release of January 3 highlighted some of the many areas in which her offices would be ready to assist constituents: "backlogged veterans' benefits, Social Security and Medicare issues, stalled tax refunds, passport issues"; while also noting some of the federal agencies that her office staff would work with: "the Internal Revenue Service (IRS), the Small Business Administration (SBA), the Department of Defense (DOD), and the Department of Housing and Urban Development (HUD)."

In order to maximize accessibility for constituents needing help, Davids decided to add pop-up offices to her permanent ones. The first occurred on February 27 at Spring Hill City Hall and would be followed by twenty-six more pop-up events during her first year in Congress. Constituents were invited to walk in or call ahead to guarantee a one-on-one meeting with a staff member. In addition, she instituted town hall meetings where constituents would be able to ask questions and give Davids feedback. The first was held on May 24, with people who could not be present encouraged to participate online.

Further contributing to Sharice Davids' ability to interact with constituents and learn their concerns was the outreach program mentioned earlier, "Sharice's Shifts." She initiated the job-shadowing program on January 18 at a coffee shop, Espresso Yourself, in Shawnee. She served coffee, bused tables, chatted with customers and employees, and discussed with co-owners Amy Becker and Jessica Montes their experiences. Along with Davids' interest in encouraging small business innovation, this particular "Shift" related as well to her commitment to assist LGBTQ+ individuals and members of other minorities, as both co-owners are members of the LGBTQ+ community. Davids states in a press release describing this meeting: "You can't represent the Kansas Third District from behind a desk in Washington D.C." (18 January 2019).

Supporting Small Businesses and Economic Success

Sharice Davids' recent experience as a student certainly contributed to her understanding that student loan debt is a huge impediment to economic success in the future. After holding a round-table session at Overland Park on the difficult effect of student-loan debt on her constituents, Davids co-sponsored two bills that she believed would help address the problem. The Relief for Defrauded Students Act would help students gain relief for federal loans taken out to attend colleges that had defrauded students. One such institution that was alleged to have taken advantage of students in this way was Wright Career College, located in Overland Park, which had gone out of business (press release, 11 July 2019). The second bill, the Fee Free Student Loan Act, would remove hidden administrative fees from federal student loans. Davids asserts in the press release, "We should be encouraging—not penalizing—folks who want to pursue higher education … by eliminating these unnecessary and costly fees, reducing the burden of student loans up front, so that all our students can succeed." As of this writing, like so many bills introduced into the House during the 116th Congress, these had not been enacted into law as they ran up against a Republican-led Senate where the emphasis was more on confirming judges than on passing Democratic-sponsored legislation.

Representative Davids announced in a press release of July 18 that she had proudly voted to raise the federal minimum wage "to help hard-working Kansans and their families." She also noted an amendment that she had co-sponsored to examine the effects of the bill halfway through its implementation and expressed regret that a tax credit for small businesses to help cover the cost of wage increases had not been adopted. She stated that she would continue to work within the Small Business

Committee "to champion Kansas small businesses and set them up for success." Raising the federal minimum wage, however, had no chance in the Senate at the time, although a number of states either had already raised their state minimum wage or were in the process of doing so.

On October 21, 2019, the House passed the Women's Business Center Improvement Act, which Davids had co-sponsored with Representative Jim Hagedorn, a Minnesota Republican. The legislation increased funding for the Women's Business Center Program, which includes centers throughout the country, including Kansas. The centers offer small business training, primarily to women-owned businesses. The increased funding, raised to $31.5 million annually from $18 million, passed the House unanimously. One such center is located in Fairway, Kansas, in the Kansas City metro area. The press release for October 21 states that the Kansas City Women's Business Center "serves over 600 clients annually in the Kansas City Metro and across the state of Kansas through business trainings, workshops, counseling, and access to capital programs." The legislation was referred to the Senate, which, however, did not act on it.

As the year approached its end, Davids expressed her support for the United States-Mexico-Canada Agreement (USMCA), a trade agreement replacing the North American Free Trade Agreement (NAFTA), which had been signed into law by President Bill Clinton and went into effect on January 1, 1994. As usual, she addressed the issue with a sharp focus on residents of Kansas and especially of the Third District:

> The Third District is a major trade hub and our community, along with the entire state of Kansas, benefits most when our country has a strong, fair trade policy. I'm pleased that we've reached a bipartisan compromise on the USMCA that will bolster Kansas' economy. This improvement on our previous trade agreement will support workers, protect the environment, and increase access to affordable prescription drugs [press release, 10 December 2019].

The House passed the USMCA on December 20 with Davids voting for it and stating in a press release of that day that she had "worked diligently alongside our labor community to ensure that the priorities of our community were reflected in the USMCA." The trade agreement also passed the Senate and subsequently was signed by President Trump. It was finally ratified by Canada in March 2020.

Native Americans

Sharice Davids has made it clear that she is representing all of the people in her Third District, but she cannot ignore the reality of being one of the first two Native American women to be elected to Congress and that this accomplishment poses the obvious expectation on the part of Native Americans that Davids is there also to advocate and legislate on their behalf. Davids clearly has taken that role and her identity seriously. On March 6, 2019, she and Representative Debra Haaland, along with nineteen other co-sponsors, introduced a resolution recognizing Native American women during Women's History month. As the press release issued that day reports, "It is the first time a resolution recognizing Native American women has been introduced in the U.S. House." Davids is quoted in the release:

> Every March, we come together to celebrate women who have shaped our nation's history, and those who continue to pave the way for future generations. Native American women are not always thought of in that celebration, so I'm proud to partner with Rep. Haaland to make sure we remember all that Native American women have contributed to our society, to advocate for Native women, and to work on the issues impacting our communities.

On May 15, Davids voted to pass the Mashpee Wampanoag Tribe Reservation Reaffirmation Act, reaffirming the tribe's reservation as trust land and, as the May 15 press release states, also voted for a bill that reaffirms "the authority of the Secretary of the Interior to take land into trust for Indian tribes." Trust land is land held by the United States government in trust for tribal peoples with the requirements that the federal government protect that property, including its natural resources, and recognize and accept self-government on the land. The Indian Reorganization Act of 1934 allows the federal government to place additional land in trust. The House passed the Mashpee Wampanoag Tribe Reservation Reaffirmation Act on May 15, 2019. In addition, Davids co-sponsored reintroduction of Savanna's Act, "which aims to help law enforcement better respond to the crisis of missing and murdered Indigenous women by increasing coordination and data sharing" (press release, 15 May 2019). Savanna's Act would potentially help reduce the serious problem of Native American women and girls suffering violence, which occurs at a rate higher than for any other female group in the United States, a crisis, Davids says, "that has devastated our communities and has been neglected for too long" (press release, 15 May 2019).

Representative Davids brought to the House Transportation and Infrastructure Committee and the Highways and Transit Subcommittee in September 2019 her plea for "greater inclusion of tribal voices in federal policy" (press release, 17 September 2019). In a letter to Committee Chair Peter De Fazio and Subcommittee Chair Eleanor Holmes Norton, published in the September 17 press release, Davids made her argument for such inclusion in passionate detail. She wrote:

For far too long, the Native American voice has been woefully underrepresented in Congress. Issues that have relevance to the tribal community have routinely been minimized and ignored. It is my hope that our committee can serve as a proving ground for the greater inclusion of tribal voices in federal policy this congress and that tribes can be regularly consulted on national infrastructure issues.

Davids then outlined "starting points for how the committee can pursue this inclusion." Her recommendations included "inviting tribal witnesses to hearings," revising the formula used in distributing Tribal Transportation Program (TTP) funds, setting aside a portion of U.S. Department of Transportation grants "for planning and construction in order to address the inherent disparity between tribal lands and their city/county counterparts," and by establishing improved oversight of the distribution of funds to disadvantaged business enterprises in order to eliminate funds going to business enterprises that do not deserve the disadvantaged designation. Davids' detailed knowledge of local conditions is represented by such specific problems she cites as the necessity of Cheyenne River Sioux bus drivers having to offload students while "navigating particularly hazardous hills and roads" and then have the students get back on the bus after the bus had reached a safer stretch of road. This is the sort of information that tribal witnesses could provide regarding transportation and infrastructure inequities.

The LGBTQ+ Community

As the first Native American member of the LGBTQ+ community to be elected to Congress, and the first openly gay individual to represent Kansas in Congress, Sharice Davids was determined to help protect the rights of LGBTQ+ persons. She spoke out against President Trump's ban on transgender individuals serving in the military, arguing, in support of House Resolution 124 opposing the ban, that "Americans should be allowed to serve our country regardless of how they identify." In the same press release (11 November 2019), she states that the "ban on transgender individuals serving in the military demeans the service of thousands of brave transgender service members, hurts our military readiness, and doesn't reflect our values as a nation."

In November, in opposition to an effort to allow foster care and adoption agencies receiving federal funds to deny on religious grounds LGBTQ+ parents' right to adopt children, Representative Davids took action. She expressed her views in a press release on November 5, 2019, asserting that no child should be denied "a stable, safe and loving home" simply because "a parent is a member of the LGBTQ community." At the same time, Davids criticized a similar policy that the Kansas legislature had passed and that became law, "further limiting the number of safe and loving homes available to these children" at a time when "the Kansas foster care system [is] already being overwhelmed with children."

Davids further states in the same press release her support for the Every Child Deserves a Family Act introduced by Congressman John Lewis and the Equality Act, which was passed by the House in May but was not taken up by the Senate. The latter legislation would formalize freedom from discrimination for LGBTQ+ individuals. The Lewis-introduced bill offered the following goal:

> To prohibit discrimination on the basis of religion, sex (including sexual orientation and gender identity), and marital status in the administration and provision of child welfare services; to improve safety, well-being, and permanency for lesbian, gay, bisexual, transgender, and queer/questioning foster youth; and for other purposes.

Health Care

One of the most basic rights, the right to good health care, is another of Representative Davids' major concerns, a priority that she punctuated by hosting at the State of the Union address on February 5, 2019, Laura Robeson, a Kansas health care advocate and mother of a then seven-year-old son suffering from cerebral palsy, cortical vision impairment, and epilepsy. In a press release announcing Davids' invitation to Robeson (30 January 2019), she emphasized her support for President Obama's Affordable Care Act and decried efforts to destroy the health care act, which would remove protections for people with preexisting conditions, such as those affecting Laura Robeson's son.

In that same release, Davids asserted that she is "working to make sure more Kansans—not fewer—are able to get healthcare." Consistent with that goal, Representative Davids expressed her appreciation for a bipartisan agreement between Democratic Governor Laura Kelly of Kansas and the Kansas Senate Majority Leader, Republican Jim Denning, announced on January 9, 2020, to expand Medicaid in the state. About ten months earlier, Davids had quoted Governor Kelly as naming Medicaid expansion as her priority and added her own voice to the effort asserting, "It's essential that Kansas joins the 36 states that have already expanded Medicaid to lower healthcare costs, increase access to quality healthcare coverage, and protect those with pre-existing conditions in our own communities" (press release, 14 March 2019).

Other health care issues also drew Davids' attention. She released a report on the high cost of diabetes medication, especially for seniors in her Third District, noting that "17,000 seniors and disabled Medicare beneficiaries" in her district have been diagnosed with diabetes. Her report included statistics on how the cost of diabetes medicines in the Third District is several times higher than in Australia, Canada, and the United Kingdom. Also, she noted that 66,000 of her constituents were uninsured (press release, 14 August 2019).

Representative Davids helped secure $650,000 for Vibrant Health, a Wyandotte County health center that "provides medical, dental, mental health and women's health services to underserved and uninsured children and adults in Wyandotte County." The center was one of seventy-seven throughout the United States that received New Access Points grants and "full designation as a Federally Qualified Health Center from the U.S. Department of Health and Human Services out of an estimated 700 applicants." The grant for Vibrant Health was especially useful, given that, according to Vibrant Health CEO Patrick Sallee, "Wyandotte County has historically ranked 99 out of 103 counties in Kansas when it comes to health outcomes" (press release, 12 September 2019).

On November 18, Davids introduced the Insurance Accountability and Transparency Act, which would require insurance companies to update their directories every six months to prevent billing surprises for individuals unintentionally receiving care from out-of-network providers (press release, 18 November 2019). On December 5, Representative Davids announced the winners of her district's App Challenge, "a nation-wide competition hosted by the U.S. House of Representatives to encourage middle and high school students to learn to code and pursue careers in computer science and other STEM related fields." Four students from the Blue Valley Center for Advanced Professional Studies developed their app, "SafeSpace," as a compilation of texting and hotline resources "for those who are suffering from depression, anxiety, sexual assault, drug abuse, or other forms of mental illness" (press release, 5 December 2019). The Blue Valley Center is a high school initiative that offers magnet programs within the Blue Valley School District in Overland Park, Kansas. Later in December, Davids voted for the Lower Drug Costs Now Act to allow Medicare to negotiate with pharmaceutical companies to decrease drug prices. The bill would make the lower cost available also to individuals with private insurance, establish a maximum out-of-pocket limit of $2,000 for Medicare recipients, and offer dental, hearing, and vision benefits through Medicare. Renamed the Elijah E. Cummings Lower Drug Costs Now Act after the iconic civil rights activist and longtime member of the House who passed away on October 17, 2019, the bill passed the House but like so many House-passed bills did not receive Senate action.

Honoring Veterans

Representative Davids' mother served approximately two decades in the military, so it is no wonder that the daughter developed a strong commitment to military veterans, a commitment that she followed through on early in her service in the House of Representatives. In a press release on March 4, 2019, Davids announced her intention to offer a two-year paid fellowship to a wounded or disabled veteran. The fellowship was offered within the Wounded Warrior Fellowship Program and would involve working in Davids' Overland Park office. The individual would be engaged in assisting veterans and acting "as a facilitator between constituents and federal, state, and local agencies." She stated in the press release:

> As the proud daughter of an Army veteran, I know the sacrifices made by the brave men and women who serve our country, and the importance of giving back to those who serve when they return. I'm honored to have the opportunity to have a Wounded Warrior Fellow in our district office to ensure the veterans and service members of Kansas' third district receive the care and services they deserve.

Through this program, Davids was successful in adding a veteran to her Congressional staff.

Davids introduced The Successful Entrepreneurship for Reservists and Veterans Act (SERV Act) with co-sponsor Steve Chabot, the ranking Republican on the Small Business Committee. The bill was designed to "help connect veterans with all the small business resources available to them" and to require the U.S. Small Business Administration to create an outreach plan to assist "veterans, service-disabled veterans, reservists, and their spouses" to connect with relevant programs (press release, 13 November 2019). The House passed the bill by an overwhelming vote of 421 for and just 3 against. Despite the overwhelming bipartisan support for this legislation, it did not move out of committee in the Senate.

Representative Davids has remembered veterans in a variety of additional ways since entering Congress. She held a breakfast on Veteran's Day, November 11, 2019, in Overland Park to honor Third District veterans, stating in her invitation, "I'm excited to invite our district's Veterans to join my office for breakfast, conversation, and to learn more about how we can serve our nation's heroes" (press release, 6 November 2019). As Christmas approached, Davids invited residents of the Third District to participate in her "Holiday Cards for Heroes" program by depositing cards at her Overland Park or Kansas City office for forwarding to active service members.

Impeachment of the President and Beyond

As articles of impeachment were introduced against President Trump in the House on December 10, 2019, Representative Davids issued the following statement, which encapsulates the two articles of impeachment and offers her position on the charges:

> President Trump used the office of the Presidency to solicit foreign interference in our elections for his own personal, political benefit. He pressured Ukraine's President to investigate his political rival, while withholding millions in taxpayer-funded aide [*sic*] to Ukraine. And since this information came to light, President Trump has defied congressional subpoenas, withholding critical documents and testimony.
>
> After careful deliberation, I plan to vote for the articles of impeachment that have been brought forward against the President [press release, 10 December 2019].

Nonetheless, Davids made it clear that not impeachment but rather helping citizens of her district and her state is her primary purpose in Congress:

> It remains my top priority to deliver results for the people of Kansas. Just this morning we reached a bipartisan agreement on the USMCA that will bolster Kansas' economy and support our workers. Later this week, the House will vote on a historic piece of legislation to lower the cost of prescription drugs for Kansas families [press release, 10 December 2019].

Ultimately the Senate trial did not lead to removal of President Trump from office, with the final votes on conviction occurring on February 5, 2020. Article I on abuse of power failed by a 52 to 48 vote against removal; Article II on obstruction of Congress resulted in 47 voting for and 54 against.

As the second session of the 116th Congress continued beyond the President's impeachment and trial, Sharice Davids also continued to carry forward her commitment to her constituents in the Third District while continuing to work on behalf of the issues discussed above. She successfully gained reelection to Congress in 2020 and, as her first term approached its end, voted in support of a second impeachment of the President. Regardless of where individuals stand on various policy issues championed by Representative Davids, most probably could agree on how unfortunate and unjust it is that Native Americans had to wait so long to see the first Native American women elected to Congress.

References

Agoyo, Acee. "Native Women Make History with Seats in New Congress." *Indianz.com* 4 Jan. 2019. indianz.com/News/2019/01/04/native-women-make-history-congress.asp.

Davids, Sharice. Interview with Whitney Manney. *Starty Pants* Episode 12—"Whitney Manney Fashion Label" 12 Feb. 2018. www.youtube.com/watch?v=VTzDZplk1zY.

_____. *Linkedin* profile. linkedin.com/in/sharicedavids.

Lowry, Bryan, and Katy Bergen. "Sharice Davids Makes History: Kansas' 1st Gay Rep, 1st Native American Woman in Congress." *The Kansas City Star* 6 Nov. 2018. kansascity.com/news/politics-government/election/article221156115.html.

Manning, Sarah Sunshine. "Two Native American Women are Headed to Congress. This Is Why It Matters." *The Washington Post* 8 Nov. 2018. www.washingtonpost.com/outlook/2018/11/08/two-native-american-women-are-headed-congress-this-is-why-it-matters/?noredirect=on.

Moscatello, Caitlin. *See Jane Win: The Inspiring Story of the Women Changing American Politics.* New York: Dutton, 2019.

New York Times. The Women of the 116th Congress. Foreword by Roxane Gay. New York: Abrams Image, 2019.

Red Cloud Indian School. redcloudschool.org.

"Sharice Davids." *Ballotpedia.* ballotpedia.org/Sharice_Davids.

Steinhauer, Jennifer. *The Firsts: The Inside Story of the Women Reshaping Congress.* Chapel Hill: Algonquin Books of Chapel Hill, 2020.

Thunder Valley CDC. thundervalley.org.

Twelve Clans. 12-clans.com.

"U.S. Congresswoman Sharice Davids Representing the 3rd District of Kansas." Press Releases. Congressional website. davids.house.gov/media/press-releases.

14

Chelsey Luger
(b. 1987)

Chelsey Luger is a name perhaps not as widely known as the names of most people in this book, but it is a name that deserves to be much better known and surely will be. Chelsey Luger is very much a twenty-first-century woman who at the same time reflects much of the very best of traditional Native American values. A woman of considerable versatility, Luger is a reporter, columnist, fitness instructor, dietary expert, social commentator, and proponent of comprehensive wellness, with all of these efforts conducted within the framework of Native American history and culture.

Searching

Chelsey Luger was born on October 7, 1987, and grew up in North Dakota, the youngest of three daughters of an Ojibwe mother from the Turtle Mountain Reservation and a Lakota father from the Standing Rock Reservation. She was quite young when her parents divorced. However, she remained close to both parents and credits them with fostering crucial aspects of her life. In a podcast titled "Our Personal Wellness Stories," presented by her and Thosh Collins, she especially notes the effect of her mother on her own interest in education and her father for contributing to her "ceremonial upbringing" that helped her realize her traditional culture. Both parents achieved college degrees, with her mother earning both a master's degree and a doctorate. Education was important to the Luger family, and Chelsey would demonstrate her academic aptitude as well. She attended North Dakota public schools with many white students, and recalled living something of a split life, seemingly more white than Native American on the reservation, but definitely Native American in school. She excelled academically in high school and served as a cheerleader at hockey and basketball games. She was interested in sports and dance, especially tap and ballet. She refers to herself in the podcast as something of a tomboy. However, she found herself in plenty of altercations, both verbal and physical, as she had the proverbial "chip on her shoulder," perhaps the result of uncertainty regarding where she belonged culturally (Treuer 424).

Luger's strong academic record helped her secure enrollment at Dartmouth College, a highly regarded Ivy League institution in Hanover, New Hampshire. Founded in 1769, Dartmouth offers an extensive program in Native American Studies that, according to the college's website, "offers students the opportunity to pursue a program of study that will increase their understanding of the historical experiences, cultural traditions and innovations, and political aspirations of Indian peoples in the United States (including Alaska and Hawaii), and Canada." Students may choose a major or minor in Native American Studies; they also may pursue a "modified major" that combinßes Native American courses with courses from another program. Both Indigenous and non–Indigenous students are eligible to enter the NAS programs.

Given Dartmouth's active efforts to attract Native American students, Chelsey Luger at Dartmouth, as in her high school, found herself within a culturally diverse environment. David Treuer quotes her as stating that she was unable to identify her own niche, reacted with considerable anger to real or imagined slights, and mistakenly thought that she had no need to study her own culture. However, she admitted, "'eventually I learned there was all this stuff I never knew I needed to learn but I really needed to learn it.'" Subsequently, she immersed herself in Native American studies and did well academically (426). She graduated in 2010 in history and Native American studies, her academic foci including comparative histories of Indigenous peoples.

Life after Dartmouth was not especially smooth for Luger. She went to work in the District Attorney's office in Manhattan, focusing on sex crimes as a member of the Special Victims Unit. Far from home and her Native culture, she felt lost and began gaining weight, a not insignificant detail in light of the turn that her life would soon take (Treuer 426).

After considering but rejecting enrollment in law school, Luger entered Columbia University's School of Journalism, earning a master of science degree in 2013, with the intention of making a career in broadcast journalism. She quickly discovered that television broadcasting was not for her because she found little appetite on the part of network executives for subjects and approaches that coincided with her growing interests (Treuer 426). However, her journalism background remains valuable to Luger as she reports today on aspects of Indigenous culture that relate to her comprehensive approach to wellness. In addition, she worked as a personal trainer in New York, which also helped put her on the path to her current career.

Choices

The choices that Chelsey Luger had made so far, while worthwhile, did not lead her into a wholly satisfying arena. She had turned to physical fitness, but she realized that fitness, for her, needed to be about more than losing weight and looking better. She stopped drinking, noting that "'my history, my genetics, my ancestry, is not in line with that substance'" (Treuer 427). David Treuer writes that "she realized that her poor health and poor choices were related to her distance from her culture, religion, and ancestral self" (427). At this time, she met Anthony "Thosh" Collins, a photographer and wellness trainer working with the Native Wellness Institute. In an interview conducted by James Napoli for the *Dartmouth Alumni Magazine*, Luger recalls that Collins had contacted her when he was working on a photo shoot of Native people who were involved in fitness efforts. Collins is from the Salt River Pima-Maricopa community. His biographical sketch on the Native Wellness Institute website states that his photography career began when he was a student at The New School for the Arts High School in Scottsdale, Arizona. He then attended the San Francisco Art Institute and attempts in his photography "to document contemporary Native peoples and their many talents and the realities of Native people as they strive to help preserve their identities in today's world."

According to the Native Wellness Institute, an organization that includes both Chelsey Luger and Thosh Collins as trainers and which Collins serves as a member of its Board of Directors, the institute recognizes among Native peoples the prevalence of substance abuse, poverty, and other destructive conditions and behaviors that afflict them. The Native Wellness Institute, as stated on its website, helps individuals to identify the sources of these problems and provides "opportunities for growth and healing" by offering "training and technical assistance based in Native culture that promotes the well-being of individuals, families, communities and places of work." The institute functions within the "Native wellness movement" that originated in the 1980s.

The Native Wellness Institute website lists detailed goals and objectives that promote "physical, mental, emotional and spiritual health." Five major objectives are noted:

Healthy Relationships and Parenting
Youth Leadership and Development

Workplace Wellness/Staff Development
Strategic Planning, Program Development and Curriculum
    Development
Educational Wellness Conferences, Retreats and Training

It is clear that within this movement, wellness is much more than merely physical health, as important as that is. Wellness is a comprehensive state, understood within Native history and culture and incorporating people of all ages within the home, workplace, and the broader environment. The institute therefore is a contemporary and modern approach that makes extensive use of traditional practices within a historical framework while suggesting that one can, and should, strive to exist successfully within both the traditional culture and the twenty-first century.

Well for Culture

After their initial meeting in 2013, Chelsey Luger and Thosh Collins developed a friendship founded at least in part on shared values, including a growing passion for fostering wellness within an Indigenous context. They subsequently founded Well for Culture in 2014. The website for Well for Culture features a statement that seems to serve as the basic mission of the initiative: "Well for Culture … aims to reclaim and revitalize indigenous health and wellness." This attempt to encourage and facilitate physical wellness looks both backward and forward. It occurs within the cultural and historical framework of the Indigenous peoples of America but at the same time serves to help individuals live a healthier, happier, and more productive life in the twenty-first century.

This "indigenizing movement," according to the website, therefore requires implementing ancestors' "lifestyle teachings" while "incorporating new information to contribute to this ancient and ongoing chain of knowledge." Fitness is not solely about physical appearance or losing weight, and not something applicable to the few. "Strong indigenous nations are built by strong individuals," the Vision statement says. In addition, true wellness is holistic, including a balance among "mental, physical, spiritual, and emotional."

For most of the history of Indigenous peoples, this introduction to Well for Culture, points out, people had no alternative to being physically active, as so many basic activities, including the providing of food and even caring for children required physical skill and considerable physical action. Recreating a lifestyle from earlier centuries is not the point, and generally impossible anyway, but being physically active is vital, the website points out, for overall physical and emotional health. In addition to being physically active, Luger and Collins propose a different way of viewing food, a way that involves recreating as much as possible an "ancestral diet" and learning to respect food.

The website offers considerable information regarding ancestral food, defining it as natural and organic, essentially the way ancestors ate for millenniums. This approach to food also is seen as possessing a spiritual dimension as those adopting this diet will participate in establishing a stronger personal and collective connection to "Mother Earth."

After a brief overview of how colonization adversely impacted diet, specific details are offered on how to identify ancestral foods and harmful foods. Anyone who has attempted to alter his or her diet is likely to understand how overwhelming the effort can be and how easy it is to feel that the alteration is impossible. Luger and Collins obviously understand this well, as people coming to the website are cautioned to set reasonable goals to be achieved gradually. Tasty but unhealthy foods do not have to be abandoned totally and instantly, they point out, but instead reduced in frequency until, ideally, such foods are eliminated completely. A lengthy set of recipes is offered, with flexible directions to accommodate individuals' preferences for specific tastes and apparently in recognition that some ingredients may be difficult to locate.

As with food, physical exercise, within the Well for Culture philosophy, also looks back to Native culture. Obviously recognizing that modern gyms and gym equipment are both expensive and quite different from the patterns of exercise that Indigenous individuals would have followed, Well for Culture emphasizes "Earth Gym" and seven basic movements that require little if any equipment. The seven basic movement patterns—the squat, gait, twist, pull, lunge, push, and hip hinge—are illustrated with videos of Chelsey Luger and Thosh Collins performing them. The only piece of equipment used in these demonstrations is a weight. Presumably any number of objects could be substituted for the precise object that Luger and Collins use. Exercising is therefore treated as analogous to eating: choose the natural and organic methods rather than the artificial.

The definition of Earth Gym offered on the website is very broad, essentially involving any outdoor activity. The description of this approach emphasizes that in the past the only gym was the outdoors. While Luger and Collins state that indoor fitness centers and gyms are useful, the outdoors should be used as much as possible because doing so achieves, among other benefits, reduced stress, greater happiness, and improved spiritual and mental health. In addition, rocks, logs, and other outdoor objects pose special challenges since they are not manufactured with ease of use in mind but using them not only improves strength and health but also creativity.

Obvious activities that are open to everyone, as Chelsey Luger points out in an interview with James Napoli, are hiking and running. Adding to the comprehensive nature of what Well for Culture offers is the further reality that Earth Gym can also lead to enhanced understanding of "traditional indigenous ecology" as one learns more about the earth and the plant and animal life that inhabits it. At the same time, people are thus encouraged "to restore and/or preserve our earth in order to maintain harmony and ancestral teachings" (Well for Culture website). In fact, Earth Gym, as Luger states, is appropriate for all cultures (Napoli).

Along with physical movement and Native food, Well for Culture incorporates Indigenous languages into this approach to wellness. In doing so, Luger and Collins become part of a major movement within Native American communities to strengthen tribal languages by teaching them and encouraging their use. They created a list of terms used in physical fitness efforts and began encouraging the translating of the vocabulary into Indigenous languages. In the first of a promised series of online videos on the Well for Culture website, viewers are introduced to the "Seven Basic Movements in Indigenous Languages" (in Lakota, O'odham, Mohawk, Ojibwe), produced in partnership with the American Indian Cancer Foundation as an example of how to "indigenize movement."

Along with the considerable information and demonstrations on the Well for Culture website, Luger and Collins have conducted workshops for tribes, visited colleges, and partnered with Nike and Adidas to spread their wellness message. That message has extended to joint partnerships to train employees of companies. Despite their "hands on" appearances, the heart of their wellness efforts is embedded within the website, which led David Treuer to place Luger within the chapter "Digital Indians: 1990–2018" in his *The Heartbeat of Wounded Knee* (407–43). Treuer, an Ojibwe from Minnesota currently teaching at the University of Southern California, concludes the chapter with a general statement that is especially true of Chelsey Luger: "I can't help feeling we are using modernity in the best possible way: to work together and to heal what is broken."

The Journalist

Chelsey Luger, while devoting herself to helping people develop a comprehensive approach to wellness, has not abandoned her training in journalism. What she writes about, not surprisingly, connects to her commitment to wellness and Native culture. "It's World Breastfeeding Week—Here's My Story," available on the Well for Culture website, argues convincingly for breastfeeding as beneficial to both baby and mother, and obviously consistent with Indigenous practice. The subject is also personally important to her, as she describes her own experiences with her first child, Alo Akawe, with Thosh, who has gone from being a friend with shared issues and values to her life partner. She writes in this article about the health benefits to her child, including avoiding such common infant problems as ear infections and fevers while starting her daughter on a healthy trajectory. There also are benefits, she states, for herself, which include freedom from postpartum depression and less likelihood of developing cancer.

Luger is obviously excited with motherhood but also practical. She notes in the article that all mothers have their difficult moments, and parenthood typically involves emotional highs and lows, an important point that can reassure parents that occasionally feeling frustrated or anxious is normal. Luger states that her pregnancy went well but that she had to have an emergency C-section that then gave way to a positive experience with nursing.

After embedding in her article a video showing breastfeeding as more than simply feeding the infant, Luger discusses several important issues pertaining to breastfeeding. The first is that governmental and corporate interests are aligned against breastfeeding. She offers as an important example a proposal that Ecuador made at a United Nations World Health Assembly to limit false marketing of substitutes for breast milk. The Trump Administration, she states, threatened to withdraw military support for Ecuador if the country continued to push its resolution. The reason that Luger offers: declining profits for companies that produce baby formula.

Chelsey Luger then points out that some doctors are not fully aware of the latest research on breastfeeding and therefore are unaware of the full range of its advantages. She cites various advantages of breastfeeding such as its contributions to the prevention of childhood obesity and improved brain development, as well as avoiding digestive problems caused by some baby cereal substituted for the mother's milk. In addition, with clean, safe water in short supply in many regions of the world, breastfeeding can protect babies from being sickened and even killed by tainted water mixed with formula. The discussion points out the importance of mothers researching the subject of breastfeeding before automatically accepting a doctor's recommendation.

At the same time, Luger rejects any attempt to shame mothers who do use formula. Not passing judgment on others appears to be an important principle for her. Shame, of course, goes both ways, and she points out that there is much shaming of women who breastfeed their children in public, a practice partly the result of women's breasts being "hypersexualized" in the broader culture. She also calls for additional scientific studies of breastfeeding and refers to the observation by Dr. Katie Hinde of Arizona State University that more scientific research has been done on topics ranging from tomatoes to erectile dysfunction than on breastfeeding.

Chelsey Luger has since had a second child. In a recent piece, "Thank You, Ancestors, for Teaching Me That Nothing Can Break Us," published in *Well + Good*, she writes that when she feels "exhausted from parenting two little girls," she thinks of her ancestors. The article is an expression of gratitude to Native women who have preceded Luger and of their generosity, compassion, bravery, and love. She writes, "I will pour every ounce of your compassion, your love, and your strength into my future … my two little girls."

Another cultural tradition involving babies is the topic of an essay that discusses the use of cradleboards. In "The Ancient Baby Carrier Making a Comeback," published in *Yes! Magazine*, Chelsey Luger explores the growing use of cradleboards. She highlights two women who make cradleboards: Ava Marie Paul, who has been making them since 1974; and an artist named Wakeah Jhane, who has recently embarked on creating them after five years of studying the art. As Luger points out, cradleboards are not only often quite beautiful but also offer babies "practicality and health benefits." She quotes Paul: "'The cradleboard helps them have a straight back; there's a donut-shaped pillow inside so the baby has a nice round head; and they just feel so protected and safe snuggled in there—it replaces being in the mother's womb.'" In addition to carrying a baby in the cradleboard, one can lean the cradleboard against a piece of furniture or lay it flat so the baby is safe while the parent is occupied with something else.

The importance of healthy, nutritious food serves as the subject for a review that Chelsey Luger wrote for *Yes! Magazine*: "Colonization Destroyed Native Food Systems." The biographical note at the end describes her as "a journalist from the Turtle Mountain Band of Chippewa and Standing Rock Sioux tribe." The bio is interesting in two ways. First, it clearly states Luger's continuing and still important role as a journalist. Second, it ignores her position with Well for Culture. Nonetheless, the subject fits well the mission of Well for Culture.

The destruction of Native food systems, Luger argues, contributed significantly to the genocide committed by Euro-Americans against Native Americans, along with more commonly recognized tactics such as "European pathogens and American military aggression." That is the focus of historian Gideon A. Mailer and scientist Nicola E. Hale in their book *Decolonizing the Diet: Nutrition, Immunity, and the Warning from Early America*. The review is generally positive. Luger reports, for example, on the authors' research and conclusions concerning "the relationship between nutrition and immunity," noting that Europeans were able to recover from even the

Black Death because of a reasonably stable food system. Luger writes that among Indigenous peoples in North America a lack of traditional foods weakened their immune systems and made them more susceptible to new diseases such as smallpox and influenza.

Luger's closing statements align well with her detailed discussions about food on the Well for Culture website and her supportive but nondoctrinaire attitude: "Incorporating and revitalizing traditional foods is a worthy effort for those [Native American] communities. But Native people are still deprived of adequate nutrition, and their real need is to incorporate whatever foods give them that, whether from different parts of the world or from their own regions."

Additional examples of Chelsey Luger's journalism include, among others, a response to the use of Native American names for sports teams and portraits of "five Native American and First Nations women who are using their platforms in such profound ways that they are also, in a sense, making history." In recent years, there has been a strong rejection of the use of Native American names by non–Native organizations, especially by sports teams. Fortunately, many teams have reconsidered their use of such names and chosen replacements. Perhaps the most prominent team to resist, however, has been the Washington entry in the National Football League. The typical response by the organization was that the name was not intended to be insulting but rather to honor Native Americans. That response, of course, implies that the owner of the Washington club understands better than the people referred to by the name whether its use is appropriate. In this case, the word *Redskins* is especially insulting when used by non–Natives, and Chelsey Luger discusses this issue in her "The Word 'Redskins' and Natives: We've Earned the Right to Use It How We Want." Finally, the Washington team yielded, playing the 2020 season without any name other than "Washington" while beginning the process of choosing a new name for the team.

As Luger demonstrates, the word, in certain contexts, can be used without harm. "My dad calls us 'skins,'" she writes. She continues with a personal example of her father's use of the word:

[L]ast summer he hired an artist to repaint an antique sign—a family heirloom that once welcome[d] visitors to "The Diamond Z Ranch: RB Luger & Sons." On the sign was a faded outline of a man on a horse. My dad instructed the artist, "Don't make that jockey a white guy. Paint him brown. Make him a 'skin.'" He's proud of his heritage.

Other examples of appropriate use of Native American words she draws from the Turtle Mountain Chippewa Tribe and the Standing Rock Lakota Nation high schools: the Belcourt Braves and the Standing Rock Warriors.

So why can the same term be used appropriately and also inappropriately (even insultingly)? Chelsey Luger offers two major reasons that involve stereotyping and ownership. "Kids on the rez who use the Indian team names," she explains, "are not at risk of hurting themselves by stereotyping themselves. Off the rez, people actually believe the stereotypes." Further, she writes, that it is a matter of ownership. Those who are referred to by these terms are the people who should be deciding how and when to use them.

Luger raises similar objections to the world of fashion appropriating Native attire (actually, fake Native attire) in "Hey, Victoria's Secret: Cultural Appropriation Isn't Hot. It's Wrong," one of several essays that she has contributed to the "Global Voices" feature in the online magazine *truthdig*. She reports that in a Victoria's Secret show, "Models wore a hodgepodge of feathers, beads and prints that were supposedly inspired by 'indigenous African culture.'" Victoria's Secret had previously used imitation Native American attire, for which the company apologized. In this case, Luger notes that in addition to the issues of cultural ownership and stereotyping, the fashion industry is "hypersexualizing Native women, putting us further at risk of objectification and dehumanization in a world where we are already at higher risk of sexual assault and rape than any other ethnicity."

Other *truthdig* essays by Chelsey Luger include "Tackling Opioid Addiction in Indian Country" (which especially relates opioid use to unemployment), "What Do We Give Indigenous America?" (demanding acknowledgment of the price Indigenous Americans have paid in lives, land, and resources for the country that now exists), and "Was 2017 the Beginning of the End of Social Injustice in America?" (an examination of "social justice's biggest failures and successes of 2017"). The essay on opioid addiction was named by the magazine as one of "The Best *Truthdig* Originals of 2018."

In "5 Indigenous Women Asserting the Modern Matriarchy," which appeared in *Yes! Magazine*, Luger features five creative women leaders from a range of professional careers. As Luger correctly notes, "One of the least visible groups in historical narratives are Native American and First Nations women," which is the reality behind the reason for writing this book. Luger here steps forward to become part of the solution. She portrays Bethany Yellowtail (Crow and Northern Cheyenne), "CEO, founder, and designer at B. Yellowtail, a clothing line and artist collective out of Los Angeles"; Kim Tall Bear (Sisseton-Wahpeton Oyate/Cheyenne/Arapaho), a professor at the University of Alberta who "is at the forefront of the controversial and little-understood conversation surrounding Native American DNA and 'gene talk'"; Autumn Peltier (Anishinaabe), a teenager who "is on the front lines of environmental and social justice activism"; Kim

Smith (Diné), co-founder of the magazine *Indigenous Goddess Gang*, which "brings together a conglomeration of dynamic female indigenous voices who are refusing to remain marginalized in the press"; and Paulette Jordan (Coeur d'Alene), a candidate for governor of Idaho who, although ultimately unsuccessful, helped reclaim the "tradition of female leadership" that historically had existed in many tribal nations.

Luger's plea for Native Americans, especially Native women, to receive more attention also occurs in a piece that she wrote for *Well + Good* and that was published during Women's History Month (March) in 2020: "Women's History Month (and American History Itself) Rarely Includes Indigenous Women—and That's a Problem." Luger is especially critical of the little attention given in schools to Native Americans. She states, "Not only is this a detriment to Native people, who remain invisible or stereotyped in the eyes of most Americans, it is also a disservice to American society at large." She adds, "We claim to celebrate diversity in America, but if we ignore our indigenous voices of the past and present, do we?"

Another example of Chelsey Luger's journalism is an article about the Dakota Access Pipeline, "Native Americans at Standing Rock are Demanding 'Rezpect' in the Face of this Oil Pipeline," which was published in April 2016 as protests were peaking against building the pipeline. The pipeline, which extends from northwest North Dakota through South Dakota and Iowa to an oil terminal in Illinois, was opposed by various groups, including Native Americans. Native opposition centered around concerns about environmental damage to soil and water (including the Missouri River and the Cannonball River, the latter running alongside a number of towns in Standing Rock Reservation) if the pipeline leaked, as well as damage to historic and religious sites.

The Standing Rock Sioux sued the United States Army Corps of Engineers, seeking to stop construction of the pipeline, but the suit failed, with the court claiming that the tribe had not demonstrated any harm that would be avoided by an injunction. While tribal efforts continued, including appeals to the United Nations, grassroots protests were mushrooming. From throughout the United States, Indigenous individuals journeyed to North Dakota to protest at construction sites. A protest camp near the Missouri River within the Standing Rock Reservation attracted thousands of individuals during the spring and summer of 2016.

Chelsey Luger's article in *Fusion*, which is a Univision network that covers news through daily newscasts, documentaries, and investigative reporting published online, helped to bring Native American concerns over the Dakota Access Pipeline to a wider public. The title of her article includes the word *rezpect*, which blends *rez* and *respect*, and is drawn from a social media campaign titled *Rezpect Our Water* that features tribal children speaking against the pipeline. Luger focuses especially on potential damage to tribal water supplies by the pipeline. She argues that nothing less "than the health and wellbeing of tribal lands and reservation residents are at stake." She promises that "people of all ages from the Great Sioux Nation will continue to fight the pipeline, urging others to 'rezpect' their water," adding, "Consideration for future generations has always been a staple value in Sioux culture."

The effort to stop construction of the Dakota Access Pipeline seemingly failed, with the pipeline being completed in April 2017 and delivering its first load of oil the following month. However, legal efforts to shut down the pipeline continue, and as of April 2021 an environmental review was being conducted that might affect its fate. Regardless of the final disposition of the matter, the opposition movement demonstrated Native people's passion for protecting the environment and their sacred traditions, and their willingness to come together across tribal lines in defense of their Indigenous culture.

The major national issues of immigration and border security Luger brings to a sharp and very specific focus in "How the U.S.-Mexico Border Has Split the Tohono O'odham." She describes how the growing effort to prevent border crossings between Mexico and Arizona, more specifically between Mexico and the town of Sells, Arizona, has resulted in the Tohono O'odham being split into two parts as some members of the Tohono O'odham Nation live in Arizona, with Sells as the governing and economic center of the nation, while others live across the border in Mexico. Previously, members could cross back and forth for family, religious, and business reasons. Now, with a tight security fence barring that movement, not only is the Tohono O'odham Nation split but so are many of the nation's families.

The crossing of borders provides the starting point for "Traveling While Indigenous," which appears on Chelsey Luger's blog accessible through her personal website. She points out that borders were not part of Native Americans' earlier history, although specific tribes lived in certain territory. Now, of course, the boundaries between countries is considered sacrosanct, with crossing them allowed only under certain conditions and with specific restrictions, even as a tourist. Luger has crossed many borders, as she points out, far more than as a girl growing up in North Dakota she could have imagined crossing. Along with visiting Brazil, Canada, Costa Rica, England, Mexico, Morocco, and Spain, she has traveled (or had traveled as of 2016) through most states in the United States. She clearly relates her enjoyment of traveling and offers six reasons why. She affirms that she is grateful for the freedom to travel, finds that she can relate to Indigenous people in other countries, remains aware that she is, after all, a tourist and not an expert on that country, notes that given her physical appearance she often can blend in with Indigenous people in other countries (so long as she does not say anything), has the opportunity to share with others something of her own culture, and learns about others while recognizing, what she did not know growing up, that "much of the world is Native country."

In the aftermath of the George Floyd killing, and recognizing the pained and passionate response to it, especially in the Black community, Luger and Collins issued a strong statement on the Well for Culture website dated June 5, 2020: "Well for Culture Statement of Support for the Black Community: #Black Lives Matter." The statement recognizes the "validity and immensity" of Black people's pain regarding this specific incident but also as a result of "generations of violence and trauma." The statement affirms a shared relationship ("our Black relatives") and condemns police violence and inaction by those who see what is happening (and has been happening) but do nothing in response.

Reacting in this way to the killing of George Floyd is not only an obvious sign that Chelsey Luger remains a journalist as well as a leader in the Native wellness movement, but that her commitment to help others and her moral vision, while focused especially on Native Americans, extends to all.

Chelsey Luger, as an advocate for wellness within an Indigenous culture and as a journalist, has already accomplished much in her still young life. Much more lies ahead for her.

REFERENCES

Chelsey Luger. www.chelseyluger.com.

Estes, Nick. *Our History Is the Future: Standing Rock Versus the Dakota Access Pipeline, and the Long Tradition of Indigenous Resistance.* Brooklyn: Verso, 2019.

Luger, Chelsey. "The Ancient Baby Carrier Making a Comeback." *Yes! Magazine* 2 Jan. 2018. yesmagazine.org/happiness/the-ancient-baby-carrier-making-a-comeback-20170102.

_____. "Before You Try to Decolonize Your Diet, Read This." *Yes! Magazine* 24 Aug. 2018. yesmagazine.org/peace-justice/before-you-try-to-decolonize-your-diet-read-this-20180824.

_____. "5 Indigenous Women Asserting the Modern Matriarchy." *Yes! Magazine* 30 Mar. 2018. yesmagazine.org/peace-justice/5-indigenous-women-asserting-the-modern-matriarchy-20180330.

_____. "How the U.S.-Mexico Border Has Split the Tohono O'odham." *High Country News* 19 Mar. 2018. hcn.org/issues/50.5/tribal-affairs-how-the-u-s-mexico-border-has-split-the-tohono-oodham.

_____. "It's World Breastfeeding Week—Here's My Story." *Well for Culture* 7 Aug. 2019. wellforculture.com/blog/2019/8/7/breastfeeding.

_____. "Native Americans at Standing Rock Are Demanding 'Rezpect' in the Face of This Oil Pipeline." *Fusion* 29 Apr. 2016. fusion.tv/story/296563/Dakota-access-oil-pipeline-rezpect-native-americans/amp.

_____. "Thank You, Ancestors for Teaching Me That Nothing Can Break Us." *Well + Good* 19 Mar. 2021. wellandgood.com/ancestors-resilience-chelsey-luger.

_____. "Traveling While Indigenous." Blog. *Chelsey Luger Journalist + Wellness Advocate* 5 Aug. 2016. chelseyluger.com/new-blog/2016/8/4/traveling-while-indigenous.

_____. *truthdig* essays. *truthdig*, truthdig.com/author/chelseyluger.

_____. "Women's History Month (and American History Itself) Rarely Includes Indigenous Women—And That's a Problem." *Well + Good* 30 Mar. 2020. wellandgood.com/indigenous-womens-history.

_____. "The Word 'Redskins' and Natives: We've Earned the Right to Use It How We Want." *HuffPost* 24 Nov. 2014. huffpost.com/entry/the-word-redskins-and-nat_b_5876538.

Luger, Chelsey, and Thosh Collins. "Our Personal Wellness Stories." *Well for Culture* 2 Aug. 2019. wellforculture.com/podcast/2019/8/2/our-wellness-journeys-episode-03.

Napoli, James. "Living Well for Culture." Interview with Chelsey Luger. *Dartmouth Alumni Magazine* Jan.–Feb. 2016. dartmouthalumnimagazine.com/articles/living-well-culture.

Native American Studies Program. *Dartmouth College*. dartmouth.smartcatalogiq.com/en/current/orc/Departments-Programs-Undergraduate/Native-American-Studies-Program.

Native Wellness Institute. nativewellness.com.

Treuer, David. *The Heartbeat of Wounded Knee: Native America from 1890 to the Present*. New York: Riverhead Books, 2019.

Well for Culture. wellforculture.com.

Index

Numbers in **bold italics** indicate pages with illustrations